# THE COB NEPHEW

By Arthur Dinsdale

An autobiography of life in North East England, from 1924 up to the second millennium. More about the people I have met and the places I have been to as a marine engineer, than me. All the nice girls love a sailor it is said, so there's a love story for the ladies! A war time apprenticeship and two seasons whaling in the Antarctic for the lads. A lesson in living!

Published by Wynott Direct Publishing April 2012
66 Gypsy Lane, Marton, Middlesbrough TS7 8NG

**Wynott Direct Publishers**

Printed by MagsLaser South Bank, Middlesbrough

ISBN  978-0-9572454-0-2

# ACKNOWLEDGEMENTS

Grateful thanks to all the good people who contributed to my healthy and steadfast upbringing. A mother who survived many sad times and always brought hope. Thanks to my dear wife Dorothy who made me into a gentleman and cared for me for fifty nine years of happy marriage during the good times and the bad and never complained. A very sweet lady who I miss every day and will love always.

The teachers at the elementary Victoria Road school who gave me self-discipline and the desire to find things out for myself. Thanks to the operative men in the shipyard who taught me to work in steel to a thousand's part of an inch, yet manage great chunks of iron and steel weighing many tons to drive a ship thousands of miles in rough waters. Thanks to the Francis Frith Collection for permission to use the photograph Middlegate, Hartlepool 1955 where living behind the cobbler's shop I spent the first six happy years of my life. Thanks to Gilbert Fraser for permission to include in my book John Leask's account of the Loss of the Simbra. He was the only survivor.

I owe many thanks to my good friend and relative, nephew, Cliff Thornton, an authority on Captain Cook for his encouragement.

Finally many thanks to the District Nurses, Doctors and Nurses in The James Cook Hospital Oncology Department and later, and especially, Teesside Hospice who cared for my dear wife Dorothy for many months 2006 – 2007. Dorothy never complained, the nurses loved her as she loved them. She was so easy to live with.

It is my wish that some of the profit from this book will go to support The Teesside Hospice. I owe the Foundation and nurses so very much.

*Arthur Dinsdale   22nd May 2012*

# The Cobbler's Nephew Contents

# Introduction

I begin this story with my roots, born in Stockton-on-Tees into a family of Yorkshire folk going back centuries. Stockton is in Durham on the North bank of the river Tees and sadly I am not a Yorkshire tyke. My Viking ancestors though did not rely on such demarcation. They came from over the seas seeking good land to settle in and raise their kin.

The family name 'Dinsdale' indicates our origin; it is derived from 'Danesdahl' meaning 'place of the Danes'. This was the name the indigenous inhabitants gave their encampment as it mutated over the years into a village near Darlington by the river Tees. Another village with a similar name is 'Dunsdale' near Redcar in what would have once been the wide shallow estuary of the River Tees. In the ninth century another longboat of young people seeking land for the second sons came from Denmark. Seeing the earlier settlement we call 'Dunsdale', they sailed up river as far as possible then where the river narrowed and snaked its way inland they rowed the Viking longboat upriver until it grounded. The Vikings had come to settle in a green and fertile land. They would first build low walls of turf, turn the boat upside down to form a roof and call it home until a more permanent structure could be built. This is only supposition but it's what I would have done and I bear the name that evolved from their early encampment.

# CHAPTER 1
## A BROKEN HOME, LIVING WITH GRANNY

As a poor boy from a broken home, at five years old I fell in love with a little girl out of my league. Brought up at my granny's rented home behind the cobbler's shop, it may never have had such a great effect on my humble life. Only years later have I wondered what mysterious spirits were working their spell that day. Five years old I was making my way through the cobbler's shop on my way to the nearby beach. My mum's sister, dear Aunt Jenny caught hold of me as I was making my way past the sides of leather my Uncle Arthur cut pieces from to repair the townsfolk of Hartlepool's shoes. Those folk that could afford to have their shoes repaired because this was the great depression of the early nineteen thirties. "Come here Arthur", Aunt Jenny said, "let me smarten you up, we are going to Saint Mark's Church bazaar today." Normally everybody was glad to see the back of me, this was strange.

I spent most of my days on the 'fish' sands where the fishermen pulled their boats up on the beach to unload their catch. I lived with my mother's family, the Wright's, my granny spent her days in the big kitchen at the back of the premise or up in her bedroom that fronted onto Middlegate Street, peeping behind the net curtain at the folks passing by. She never went out and received very few visitors. Uncle Arthur cobbled away at his last, Aunt Jen served in the shop. Mrs Sivright, a Magistrate and Historian would call in for her shoes, sole and heeled, "thank you, that'll be three and six pence please." 'Wright's the Cobbler' had a steady business and sold leather belts, shoe laces, shoe polish and whitening for canvas tennis shoes, dog collars and all things that required this tough flexible material. Leather suitcase handles were repaired also. Leather was the only material suitable to sole a shoe and if they belonged to a busy outdoor person they wore through in a few weeks

Workmen hammered metal studs into the leather soles and the cobbler would fit a steel half circle to the edge of the heel, like a horse shoe, to extend the life of the leather heel. In 1930ish, a synthetic glue had been invented, this allowed rubber soles to be stuck onto the leather sole to extend its life. Fisherman's waterproof smocks and rubber thigh boots found a market. Uncle Arthur hung these high up outside the shop in July and August when the herring boats were coming into the Harbour to land their catch.

Aunt Jenny was well known in the Ancient Borough of Hartlepool, they had a shoe repair monopoly. We were going to mix with our customers at a Church bazaar. I meekly gave in to Aunt Jenny. A soapy wet flannel was wiped round my face then my sticky fingers, a clean pullover, socks and sandals. Hair parted and brushed, I submitted to this intrusion to please Aunt Jen. She was very sweet, she never raised her voice to me; no one did. I led a contented life among these docile adults. Let's get this bazaar thing over!

I only remember the Church hall was full of big old ladies with long dark skirts and big dark hats of brown, green, or navy blue as it was called, 'milling around.' At my eye level I didn't see much of their faces and hung onto Aunt Jenny's hand among a sea of big silky bottoms. Then the sea of bottoms cleared and I could see this posh lady, I judged by the amount of what looked like fruit or maybe birds in broad ribbon and netting on her extravagant dark straw hat. I couldn't make much of what was said but this pretty little girl four years old appeared and presented a bouquet to this lady. I was later told this lady had declared the bazaar open. It didn't look any different to me.

I fell in love with that pretty little girl with the chubby cheeks and golden curls. It was a strange feeling. I would have liked to have played with her as my cousin or even as a friend. I asked Aunt Jen what her name was. "Dorothy Fell", she said and she came from a very good family. Her father was the design engineer in the shipyard. One of the great mysteries in my life was evolving. I often saw her with her mum passing the shop. The feeling of love for her never left me but it was numbed by my station in life. I would never speak to her, it could cause embarrassment. I came from a broken home, although I didn't feel damaged by it. I didn't think I would have much of a future; she would never be my friend.

At nineteen years of age now an apprentice marine engineer I was still in love with her but we lived parallel lives. A stigma of parents separated in those days did not make the prospect of a relationship with a girl of good family very welcome. I saw her for the first time come in to the Borough Hall Saturday night dance. Dorothy Fell was stood near the stage where the Rhythmic Dance Band were playing those lovely melodies we danced to in those days. She was in the far corner of the dance hall. I wouldn't even think about asking her for a dance, she was out of my league and would probably refuse me. I was satisfied to dance with girls I was already acquainted with. I was

8

dancing with my cousin Lawson Wardell's fiancé Veronica; we called her Ronnie. Lawson was in the army fighting in Italy.

Our group of about six to eight boys and girls always occupied the centre of the walkway that surrounded the dance floor. Two or three of them were going steady. As Ronnie and I glided round the floor we chatted, then Ronnie asked me, did I know Dorothy Fell over there? I said, "I know who she is but I don't know her to speak to." "Well," confided Ronnie, "she would like a dance with you!" I was stunned for a minute but made no comment, my mind was in a slight state of shock. I was being asked for an introduction.

Dorothy Fell fancied me? I'd never had a girlfriend before, you know, to go steady with. I was a bit afraid of them I suppose, they were all right to dance with but I had been going around with my mates since we were kids. My school was all boys. I thought I will have to ask her for a dance and see what happens. She may decide she didn't fancy me anyway. When the band began playing the next dance a slow foxtrot I walked purposefully round the dance floor to satisfy the young lady's request. I made the formal question, "may I have this dance please?" I was pretending it was a casual pick up. She pretended it was too! I tried to play it cool, but we both knew different.

I knew she was not going to refuse. I was surprised to find she was very easy to talk to. We moved through the low rail onto the superb dance floor. This girl who I had secretly loved for most of my young life came into my arms and we moved across the floor as one. Her full golden hair brushed my face, our left hands were gently clasped together, my right hand was round her slender waist. I felt a bit weak somehow. We didn't have much to say, she wouldn't know I was madly in love with her. I hoped with all my heart she would find me suitable, after all it had been her command I was obeying. The slow waltz had been most appropriate for lovers, it wasn't going to last, now after a few precious minutes it ended. I escorted her back to the place where she had been stood waiting, perhaps for a boyfriend. Had I made a good impression? I needed to say something to contain this moment. I had no experience of chatting up a girl. Girls were just to dance with but I was reluctant to leave her. I suggested would she like to join our crowd over there?

"That would be nice", she said gently. I took her hand in mine and we walked round to the popular area where my friends and the girls chatted when not dancing. I began to realise Dorothy had been to the

Grammar School with some of the girls. Living in Middlesbrough for the past years I was accepted, but was not too familiar with this group. We young men on war work were in reserved occupation.

The Grammar School boys had been called up into the Armed Forces, I was glad I hadn't passed the eleven plus examination now. I wasn't bothered at the time because we couldn't have afforded the school uniform. Some of the girls, although only eighteen years old, were spoken for by these Grammar School boys and loyally kept faith with them. This suited me because I had little to offer a girl, so I thought! The next dance Dorothy accepted my request again and as no other gentleman intervened and Dorothy seemed agreeable we found ourselves becoming an item for the moment. I felt as though I had known her for years, well, I had in a way but things didn't usually go well for me. My expectations were not great; this girl would find a handsome young man with a wealthy family. Savour it while you can. The last waltz includes the privilege for the gentleman to ask if he may escort the lady home. Nearly all the couples go on the floor for the last waltz, but those unattached go for their coats and leave early. Dorothy and I were now alone. I suspected some young man would come along any minute to whisk her onto the dance floor. Hopefully, I suggested we do the last waltz. She smiled, probably thinking correctly, "what a jerk!" I was still a bit nervous to ask her but she moved comfortably into my arms, giving me a feeling of wonderment.

When the music ended we stood while the National Anthem, God Save the King was played. Now I plucked up courage to ask if I could walk her home. "That'll be nice", she said. As I took her cloakroom ticket I could hardly believe what was happening. I went to collect both our coats, I'd never done that before. Dorothy, as they all do, went into the cloakroom with the other girls. She seemed ages. What do they do in there? They came out smiling about something. What secrets they must have that we poor boys are unaware of.

I helped her on with her coat and we stepped outside into a beautiful moonlight night. The last Saturday in May 1943, there was only a rare chance of an air raid these days; Adolf was busy in Russia.

We left the Borough Hall and strolled across Middlegate street to the 14th century Town Wall. We leaned close to each other on the parapet for a while gazing at the shadowy silhouette of the Pilot Pier. The sea was lapping quietly onto my fish sands beach. Neither of us spoke, it wasn't necessary. er perfume and nearness fascinated me. I

Ancient Water Gate - Sandwell Chare Hartlepool 1908

*14th Century Town Wall, Water Gate, Sandwell Chare 1908*

suspect we both felt that this could be the beginning of a love that would probably last a lifetime. It did occur to me, but I had nothing to offer the girl. I wouldn't push it, I was afraid to start something that would end in embarrassment. We strolled round the promenade. I knew where she lived, in Rowell Street. My pal, Alan Martin, lived there. I had seen her going into their house when I called for him. We reached the door of her house. I just said goodnight then, and left her.

I made no attempt to kiss her or anything. As I walked away, I turned my head and over my shoulder called, "will you be there next week?" "Yes!" she replied in what I took to be a welcome voice. I hurried away, back to Aunt Jenny feeling a bit more confident.

The following week we met each other with eyes that glowed with joy. We danced the night away and I walked her home again. This time when I left her at her door, I bravely said, "should I call for you at your house next week and we can go to the dance together?" "Yes", she said, "that will be nice". When I did call I was invited in to meet her Mum, a lovely gentle lady. Dorothy's Dad had died when she was only fifteen. Someone in the Spirit World was working a miracle. Dorothy

11

had given up further education because of their reduced income and had a job in the Co-operative bakery Office. She didn't seem to mind my low expectations as an apprentice marine engineer. I needed a family, they needed an anchor man. We were good for each other. After four years of war time courtship working long hours in the shipyard with Home Guard Duties and evening classes for engineering, life was very full and hectic

I needed some money to marry her. The post war wages in the shipyard even with overtime left little money to save at the end of the week. I had to save up to buy a pair of shoes. I applied to 'Salvesen Whaling Company' for a job as an engineer to sail for months to the Antarctic in a whale catcher vessel. It was a rough life and even in moderate seas there was danger of icebergs in fog. The pay was only £7:00 per week, working seven days a week at sea on two watches, twelve till four o clock. We were eight thousand miles from home for a six months whaling season, with a month to sail down there and a month to return home. The crew took the risk of a poor season with the Company. I was fortunate in being with a good Captain/Gunner.

He had us out hunting for the whale when other boats were seeking shelter from the big seas that existed in the lower latitudes. I paid off after nine months away with a cheque for eight hundred pounds. It was a year's good salary in those days, but earned in full.

In 1945 Britain was bankrupt. Sterling was unacceptable abroad to buy food abroad. The British people were rationed for a further eight years for meat, sugar, butter and other materials bought from abroad. To feed a devastated Europe the British Government restored the whaling industry. The ships were built here on Teesside from British steel in the Sterling area. The whaling business lasted for seventeen years until it became uneconomical to continue.

I worked the first season from September 1947 until May 1948. When the season ended the whaling men returned from the Antarctic to pay off in the, then, great Port of Liverpool. This gave us the start in life we needed. We were married on June 16th 1948. In August I got orders from the Whaling Company to work by the Whale Factory ship, 'Southern Harvester', in dock at South Shields. We managed to see each other at weekends. In September I was ordered to join a Transport vessel, 'S.S. Polar Chief', lying at Bidston Dock on the river Mersey, to return to the South Atlantic for another nine months. Then returning from the rough life aboard a little whale catcher we were able to settle down and make a home. This story is a social history of eighty five years of very ordinary people of the 20th Century. Enough has been written of footballers and minor celebrities and their foolish ways. What will people in the 25th Century think about us?

# CHAPTER 2
# THE VIKING LEGACY.
# AN APOCRYPHAL STORY

North East England where iron, coal, ships and men merged to produce vast wealth. The money didn't stay in this area. Now in the year 2008 billions of Pounds has disappeared! Where has it gone? Money doesn't vanish from banks, it is moved. Where was it moved to? Prime Minister Gordon Brown might know. The rivers of the East coast of Britain have spawned a breed of men who altered the lives of millions of people all over the world. By the banks of the river Tyne George Stevenson produced the early railway. The first passenger train ran from Darlington to Stockton-on-Tees. Over many years great industries evolved. The banks of the rivers enabled great ships to be built. Coal was mined nearby in Durham and transported by the early railway to both rivers. It was exported by ships to London and Europe. Alum was extracted along the Yorkshire Coast; it was needed for dyeing cloth. The North East was like Aladdin's cave to men who could exploit it.

Armstrong on the banks of the river Tyne created an armaments factory selling big guns and shells all over the world. A pity really, but if he hadn't done so someone else would probably have. Better to be first then?

At Stockton on Tees a Chemist John Walker in 1827 found by accident it is supposed, a chemical paste hardened on a stick struck against a hard surface flared into flame. He applied this knowledge to produce the friction match. The tinder box was made obsolete! A later development on the Tyne was the Steam Turbine invented by Charles Parsons. A man from the Tyneside area, Joseph Swan was one of many men demonstrating an electric light bulb with a carbon filament.

This production of the North East's wealth was not wholly an accident. The North East location provided the cold wet days that gave men the incentive to do practical things to improve the life of their families and themselves.

Captain James Cook born a few miles from the river Tees was of the same breed but a different type of man with a desire to know what existed over the horizon. He altered the map of the known world. Not everybody is pleased with some of the changes resulting from his work. This pool of talent extended North and South along the East coast where materials like timber, coal and iron ore were found to be exploited. It is called 'progress', it seems to arise in different ages from the prehistoric cave man to the Ancient Greeks and Romans to where we are today. Each of these civilisations faded away. We must learn from history to be ready to accept some downturn in our standards. With rising global population and distribution of the world's decreasing benefits it is difficult for the leaders of the world to deal with this impending chaos. Lives are too short to create the urgency to surmount this mountainous task.

The Ancient Romans had occupied Britain for four hundred years but trouble in Rome caused the Roman legions to return to their native land. The Romano British who had embraced the benefits the Legions: fine villas for the British tribal chiefs, an organised way of life, a higher civilization for the many tribes who obeyed the Roman rules. In the vacuum of authority created by the Roman departure chaos would exist for a while as militant tribes sought to take advantage now available to dominate the weaker tribes. Some tribes may have joined forces to establish defensive areas. Nothing much is known of this period. The indigenous British had left, recording events to the Romans. Christianity arrived and seems to have put down roots with monasteries.

The monks earned the respect of the people by treating the sick and putting some organization into their lives by teaching, but the ancient British without a strong master let the Roman infrastructure decay. The network of roads became overgrown. Roman forts were stripped of the stone by the monks to build their monasteries. The Romans had built great fortresses; the foundations of one can be seen in the under croft of York Minster. What else would the monks do with the Roman stone? The populace wouldn't be interested in work unless there was something in it for them. By what we read the monks spent many hours praying and writing so there wasn't much innovation going on once they had established their life cycle. Let's face it! Most people have to have a good reason to do hard work, it's enough trouble to keep warm and well fed. Progress can be very slow in conditions like this. In Africa, a continent rich in minerals and oil, the Europeans still have charities to care for the devastating famine and troubled people, not helped by the wars of rival tribal leaders. The solution must come from the indigenous people themselves.

I suspect something like this was at work here around 800 AD. A few men from Denmark and Norway arrived in their long boats. Originally it was probably more by accident, being unable to beat against a strong Easterly wind, unable to return home. Some sailor Captain, curious as to what lay over the horizon thought, we have enough rations for a few days, let her go! Some of these sailors were second sons who would not inherit the farm. Denmark was a small country; arable land was in short supply and who would want to work for his older brother? Not everybody!

The boats were a unique design of the age. Built long and narrow to slip through the water, high and sharp at both ends, the stem post extended and generally carved with a dragon's head or some other motif probably to give their identification to other craft at sea. This practice of identity at sea later and in peace time of course, was a courtesy exchanged by passing ships and lasted until the twentieth century. It took the form of "what ship, where from and where about" if within hailing or signal lamp distance. This would be noted in the ship's log with a map reference so that an overdue ship's last recorded position may be identified if need be. Today with satellite navigation the owners know to a few metres where the ships are; curiosity only would require the signal. This courtesy probably arose as these early Vikings improved their navigation skills and extended their voyages. The long boat's design being sharp at each end gave grounding on a beach in rough surf less chance of the sea pushing the boat broadside on. It also made it much easier to go astern. The crew only had to sit facing the other way to row out of a narrow beach entrance.

The Danes landed on beaches along the Yorkshire coast. The Norwegian Vikings landed further North in Northumbria. They were all of the same breed; builders of fine ships, sailors and workers in metals.

This inherited talent eventually resulted in the North East of England producing the products already mentioned and the fabrication of the Sydney Harbour Bridge in 1932 by Dorman and Long Company

Ltd. of Middlesbrough. It was shipped to Australia to be erected from the South to the North shore of the Harbour.

In 1947, at twenty three years of age, I had the good fortune to sail with the descendants of those early Norwegian Viking sailors on a ship built on the river Tees. I got on well with them. They nicknamed me 'Danskegutt'. In Norwegian it means 'Danish boy'. When I was told my nickname I asked them why they chose to call me 'Danish'. The answer surprised me. "You speak Norwegian with a Danish accent and your name 'Dinsdale' is derived from 'Danesdahl' meaning, 'place of the Danes'!" After a thousand years the Yorkshire/Teesside dialect echoed my Danish roots.

I was an engineer on this small but powerful whale catcher ship. All the commands were in Norwegian, the syntax was the same as in English, I picked up a working knowledge but I had no grammar book to help me.

There is a village called 'Dinsdale' near Darlington by the river Tees, about as far up river as it would be possible to row a longboat. A few early Danish Vikings must have made camp there. My Norwegian Danish accent is possibly due to the mixture of my Yorkshire Teesside accent. The Danes have a more guttural voice. I'm not an expert in such matters but I found the Norwegian voice is noticeably thinner.

After a formal dinner at a Yorkshire hotel near the coastal town of Whitby I was asked to respond to the toast to the visitors. I told this apocryphal story to an audience of tough Yorkshire businessmen of mixed ages of their first early Danish ancestors. They'd had a good meal and a few drinks so were easy to please. I had cobbled this story together and refined it a couple of times. They were in the mood for a good story. I know it to be apocryphal because I made it up myself!

## AN APOCHROPHAL STORY
*How the first Vikings came to North East England*

In a quiet little Village in Demark Eric Bloodaxe and the lads were going for a night out in Sweden where the girls were tall, blond and comely. About thirty of the lads gathered by the jetty and stowed their provisions in Eric's longboat, enough for a few days just in case they were longer away than expected. Well you never know, they thought, we might get lucky! Harald cast off and jumped in as the craft swung away from the jetty. The oars were run out and they rowed away from the coast until they caught the light breeze coming from the lee shore. The big square sail was set and the longboat headed North East. Within an hour the breeze dropped and a thick fog came down. With no star to navigate by they pressed on trusting to their bit of string and piece of lodestone compass. After a few hours they suspected they were lost, the sea was oily calm. The fog persisted. Eric decided to turn back, he asked Olaf to go to the bow as lookout. A rota was setup, one hour on look-out then a turn on the oar. They rowed for many hours. A few lines dropped over the side with the hooks baited with bits of bacon caught a few fine fish. They always carried bread and dry rations in case the weather caused them to take shelter on some remote beach. A day went past, sailors don't worry about time. I know they do now but in those days they didn't! The grey day passed into evening. Olaf, again his turn as look-out in the bow; straining to see anything through the sinister fog called for quiet! The sound of surf breaking on a shore was heard, Eric ordered the men to row slow ahead. The leadsman took soundings with his lead line, knots in the line every elbow length gave the depth of water. Well something like that, I did say this was an apochrophal story!

A few rocks gave way to a sandy beach. The bow raised slightly as the vessel gently grounded. Wherever it was they were weary and would make camp until the fog lifted. They pulled the boat further up onto the beach and hoyed a rope with an anchor dug deep onto the beach above the high water mark. Nothing was ever left to chance. There was no lifeboat service to call on in those days. Safety was instinctive as it is with any men who put to sea. It was in my day!

Below the high decorated stem post of the bow was a big sea chest, built to fit the shape of the bow and sealed with bitumen. It may have been glue from boiled animal hoofs. It was essential they were waterproof. These longboats would be very wet in heavy weather. The boat would need constant bailing to remove the ingress of the sea coming over the side.

Another similar chest aft would together act as buoyancy tanks to keep the vessel afloat should a high sea breach the low sides and swamp the boat.

The for'rard chest served as a look out post. The after chest was a platform for the steersman to pull on his large steering oar. The rudder had not been invented yet.

This steering oar was larger than the conventional oar and was hung from the top side rail. With a handle through the long shaft of the steering oar the steersman was able to twist the blade in the sea to keep on course to a few degrees when sailing to a star or a land bearing course. When rowing an extra pull on the starboard side steered the boat to the port side. Port left, starboard right facing front. It's no good calling the front the sharp end because if you remember both ends are sharp.

In these chests were stored dry foodstuffs, tinder to make fire, sealskin over jackets for protection in heavy weather. Ropes and ships tackle. Swords if required to fend off the ever present pirates and raiders from other European areas.

Now they had landed security needed to be seen to. Eric sent a party of the lads to check for potential enemies along the beach. High cliffs secured the surrounding area, when all was safe the lads disembarked, glad to stretch their legs. Eric and a couple of the lads went inland through a ravine in the cliffs to kill a couple of wild boar that roamed all over Europe. That's the reason for his name Bloodaxe he was the butcher.

You probably thought it was because of all the stories of raping and pillaging that's been written, not so! I will deal with that offensive story later.

The other lads gathered drift wood and made a great camp fire. Eric and the foraging party returned with a couple of wild pigs. They were swiftly prepared and roasted.

The young sailors lay around the sand dunes feasting and drinking. They carried a spirit on the boat called 'aquavite', water of life, just for emergencies, you understand? They had a few drinks to loosen up the voice. A couple of the boys told a saga or two. They sang a few homely songs that sailors have always sang about Barnacle Bill, Maggie Maggie May and other well-known sea shanties and sagas of pretty girls, where to find them, and what you would do when you did find them. This was the thing that was missing. It was soon put right.

On the top of the high cliff out of sight in the fog was a monastery. The nuns heard the merriment going on down there. The smell of roast pork wafted up to entice them. St. Hilda wouldn't have approved but the young nuns were sure those fine young men would enjoy their company. They made their way down to the beach, all young folk like a party. The lads were delighted to see them and immediately invited them to join in the feast. Sailors are always very hospitable regardless of creed or colour. There was no impropriety, well, the girls made no complaint, a bit of slap and tickle perhaps. The tall blond fair skinned sailors excited the girls. Religion was not all pious and forbidden pleasures in those days. It wouldn't have got started if it had been!

They made up into couples trying to find ways to overcome the language difficulties, it was not always necessary to use words. Signs and facial expressions conveyed all that was required and soon giggles and laughs gave way to cuddles, kisses, murmurs and sighs. Some couples drifted away into the sand dunes to seek privacy and snuggle down for the few hours of darkness. When dawn came the embers of the fire were built up and they shared breakfast. Harald took out the oats and in a big cauldron made the porridge sweetened with honey. It revived the party but the lads were ready to sail now. A few final cuddles and promises to see them again, whenever! The fog was clearing, the rising sun warmed their young bodies. Eric made a firm promise that they would return again, as sailors always do to the girls they leave behind them.

It's good for the gene pool and the population count. In a way I suppose it was the start of the Europe Union.

Unbeknown to the Vikings the monks had witnessed this merriment and jealously wrote in their manuscripts, these Vikings are coming over in their longboats with swords raping and pillaging the countryside. It's human nature to tell fibs to suit your readers. This would be a good cover story for the girls too, the few who later found themselves pregnant. Maybe they told the monks that's how it happened, he forced me? The blame lies with mother nature; I'll bet it happened before the Viking arrived too? The victor always writes the history, the monks were builders in stone, strong men who would be well able to defend themselves. What would the Vikings want to fight for? It is usual to resent the incomer, disputes would occur until the monks found these Vikings had something to offer. The Vikings could provide fish from the sea, they made fine swords and ornaments, exchanges would be made, harmony replaced suspicion, during the period the Vikings were coming to these shores both parties thrived. The monasteries became vast wealthy estates alongside the Viking settlements. The truth is that Henry the Eighth was responsible for the ruins we see today. His wars with France were expensive, he needed a divorce and the Pope wouldn't give him one! Henry decided to take over, he sent his men out to demolish the monasteries, they possibly would have assaulted the nuns too, they were rough old days for girls.

History this time would be written to please King Henry and who would get the blame? It was already written in the chronicles, the poor old Vikings I suppose!

The moral of this apochrophal story is, 'never believe all you read in the newspapers'! This brought roars of approval from the Yorkshire businessmen and I was pleased to have entertained such a tough lot of tough Viking descendants!

# CHAPTER 3
# THE EARLY YEARS 1924 – 1955. DEPRESSION
*My early years brought up in*
*the Ancient Borough of Hartlepool 1924–1955*

In 1924 my mother brought me, only six months old, to her family home in Hartlepool living with my Granny and Aunt Jenny behind the cobbler's shop. My Grandfather Alex had started the family business, my Uncle Arthur was now the cobbler. Life was very different from today. Traffic was still dominated in the provinces by the horse and cart. Bus services had been set up in 1918 by ex-service men in some places. Early in my life I was taken on a church outing in a charabanc. A charabanc was a bus designed like a motor car with rows of long seats across the vehicle. Each row with a brass handle opening a small door entered from a narrow platform on each side that ran from the front mudguard to the rear mudguard called a running board. I can't remember much of the ride because I was too small to see over the side of the vehicle to see much. We were taken to a large grassy meadow not far from town and I was sat among buttercups, daisies and pretty yellow cowslips. I must have been two or three years old, my hair was cut like a girl with a fringe cut just above the eyebrows and my hair hanging straight down in a round ball over my ears. I wore a smock, a white dress over short white trousers with a matching white floppy cotton sun hat! As far as I can remember I didn't know anyone there but an older girl gave me a brown paper bag with something to eat in it and a drink of homemade lemonade in a white enamel mug. I gathered a few cowslips but the pretty yellow flowers soon drooped in my hand. I wasn't very impressed with the whole thing.

Back in the town I saw everyday life going on around me. Everything was done with horses. The local breweries delivered beer in big wooden barrels from the four wheeled flat cart pulled by two magnificent shire horses, the barrels were rolled down into the cellar of the pub on a couple of wooden joists connected together with thin steel bars shaped to clear the belly of the barrel. This ensured it did not run off as it was lowered down with a rope. Some of the shire horses were being replaced by steam lorries. I remember they had the boiler in the cab next to the driver, his assistant would put a bit of coal in the furnace when required. A big chain from the engine shaft drove the wheels with their solid tyres. These steam lorries didn't seem to last many years. It must have been very hot in the cab in summer.

The diesel engine came along and the assistant wouldn't be required. Things that had stood for centuries were changing. Horse manure would be in short supply.

My mother having left my father with me a baby returned to her family home so the first six years of my life were spent behind the cobbler's shop at my maternal grandmother's house in the Ancient Borough of Hartlepool. This headland, going back in history to Anglo-Saxon times is built for the most part on an outcrop of sandy limestone. It rises out from the North Sea forming a peninsular with one of its beaches facing south on the east coast, locally known as the "fish sands". This beach was a delightful suntrap and still is, sheltered behind the 25 foot high 8 foot thick 14th century old town wall.

It is alleged by mischievous neighbouring towns that during the Napoleonic War the fishermen having captured a ship wrecked monkey, washed ashore on ships' timbers and unable to understand its chattering decided it was a French spy and executed it by hanging on this very beach. Thus the folk of Hartlepool were known as 'Monkey Hangers' in the villages of Durham!

This mischievous story cannot be true since Hartlepool fishermen would know what a Frenchman looked like. Several Whitby fishermen died of wounds received in the Battle of Trafalgar as testified by tombstones in the church grounds high above the town. The fishermen of Hartlepool would be very familiar with Whitby and many would have fought with their countrymen. A battery of cannon was set up on Hartlepool's Heugh, a local name for the high cliff facing the sea, to repulse an expected French invasion in 1805. The invasion didn't happen but an invasion scare did occur in the 1914 war.

The Heugh battery was maintained later with two breach loading six inch guns and another six inch gun mounted at the Lighthouse battery for 109 years. They first came into action during the German Fleet's bombardment on16th December 1914 at five minutes past eight in the morning. At the time my mother was only a few days from her 19th birthday. She was on her way to work going on the walkway along the top of the old town wall to the ferry. These ferry boats carried the people of Hartlepool over the shipping channel to the little village of Middleton. They were large flat bottomed rowing boats manned by old fishermen. With shells whistling overhead and exploding in the town my Mum ran back home to find people evacuating their homes expecting a German invasion. She didn't say but I expect they joined the evacuation. What a dreadful experience for families expecting an invasion. Being near Christmas most families carried their Christmas cakes with them.

My wife Dorothy, nee Fell, told me her mother lived at No 1 Rowell St. near the Heugh gun battery who was firing their six inch guns in reply to the German battleships. German shells were screaming overhead to explode in the town.

Her Mum had torn up bed sheets to bandage the injured and swears a priest who she tended to was a German spy! In a town like Hartlepool everybody knew everybody else and he was a stranger. It's a good job there wasn't a monkey about at the time, they might have both been hanged!

One hundred and nineteen people were killed and many wounded in the 35 minute bombardment. The Hartlepool gun batteries did serious damage to one of the three German battleships and the raid was not repeated, the batteries were finally dismounted in approximately 1960. They are now being established as an historic site.

The ancient Borough has a rich history of an early Christian monastery with the 11th century St Hilda's Abbey church holding relics of the past thousand years.

The 14th century sandstone town wall remains in part along the south facing beach with what was the "pilot's pier" creating a harbour which until the second great war sheltered the few remaining fishing cobles of the fishermen, at one time numbered up to fifty or more. A cut in the pier was designed to enable fishing cobles to enter and float onto a slipway at high tide where the boats were pulled into a repair shed to be overhauled. It is still there today unused. The beach, only a couple of hundred yards from my granny's house, was my playground from the time I could walk. I would go with the older kids during the long school holidays, learning to play shops using seaweed and stones from the seashore as "goods".

The pedestrian route from Ancient Hartlepool to West Hartlepool then was to cross the harbour channel by the ferry paying one penny to the old fishermen who manned the ferry boats, when men were going to work using two sets of pulling oars. If the ferryman was alone, a passenger would sit and take a pair of oars. I think most Hartlepudlians could use a pair of oars. The custom built ferry boats had a broad foot platform at each end of the boat to allow the many men travelling across in those days to walk from the ferry steps into and out of the boat. Workmen went each weekday to the shipyards, about forty or more sat on the seats running along each side of the boat with often many more standing like penguins each side of the oarsman in the middle of the craft.

It appeared to me as a kid to be grossly overloaded, it was probably the reason the men stood so rigidly together! Two or three ferry loads went back and forth morning and evening each day. I was fortunate to see this busy time because after the 1929 economic crash there was no work for the shipyards and the ferry business suffered with them. There were still some people using this route on a fine day but the trolley buses going round the road would be more comfortable and easier to carry shopping made in the bigger shops of the newer West Hartlepool. My mother had used this ferry route to walk through the little Middleton village three miles or so to work in Hill Carter's, a ladies dress shop in West Hartlepool.

Around about the 1850's, Ralf Ward Jackson, a solicitor working for a Durham colliery, had raised a company to build a railway branch line to Hartlepool with the intention of shipping coal from there. One of the early railways already existed from the coal fields to the River Tees and coal was shipped from there to London and other various ports. The Ancient Port of Hartlepool was not large enough to satisfy Mr Jackson. The shipping companies were charging him more per ton than the River Tees companies were being charged. He formed a shipping company to move his coal. He raised another company to build Docks to load his ships next to the village of Middleton. Workers came from far and wide to live in the area. Mr Jackson formed more companies to build houses and schools for the men's families. He had a word with the Bishop about building a church for the new community. When the Bishop gave him the choice of the Vicar he chose a young man he thought malleable. However problems arose with the young Vicar. He declared the Church of England schools would not admit the very many Roman Catholic children of his workmen. Mr Jackson did not agree but was unable to get rid of the troublesome priest. I can imagine the Bishop smirking away, he'd got his church built, now it was game over!

Mr Jackson was not a man to be frustrated by a couple of priests. He sent men to brick up the doors of the church! When the materials arrived the priest went to the docks and invited a few of the men with a few of the ladies who frequent dock areas to a drinking party in the church. He bought crates of beer and they partied long and hard. Jackson and the Vicar finally found a way to accommodate their problem. It was probably to build a school for the Roman Catholic children. He seemed to be able to raise capital from wealthy Hartlepool shareholders with little trouble. He built a fine meeting hall, The Athenaeum in a fine wide High Street for the workers evening classes. Sadly for this fine entrepreneur at an annual Company shareholder's meeting a shareholder named Mr Chapman exposed the Chairman's method of using shady accountancy to raise Bank capital. Mr Chapman had made an account and got up in the meeting and gave the game away. Ralf Ward Jackson was ruined! A broken man he died penniless poor chap but he left a fine new town as his monument.

The people of old Hartlepool despised the new town, "West Dockers" as they called them. West Dockers in return called the old side folk "Cod Heads"!

Middleton village was gradually demolished as the old houses became unoccupied. The area now in 2006 is an industrial estate. The West Dockers won, amalgamated with West Hartlepool, the Ancient Borough of Hartlepool with its 13th Century Charter is now just part of a much larger conurbation and to my mind sadly called the Headland.

# CHAPTER 4
## MY IDYLLIC CHILDHOOD, TOTAL FREEDOM

Back to my beloved old Hartlepool and the little harbour that nestles behind the ancient town wall to give shelter from the cold North winds. Before the introduction of engines as many as fifty fishing cobles, boats about eighteen feet long, worked from the harbour with a square sail as their ancestors the Vikings had done a thousand years before, long before the town wall was built in the fourteenth century.

The beach, only a couple of hundred yards from my granny's house, was my playground from the time that I could walk, going with the older kids during the long school holidays, learning to play shops using seaweed and stones from the sea shore ground up into different colours as "goods". Going to the "fish sands" I would pass from Granny's kitchen into the through passage that went from the kitchen all the way to the front door. I passed the side of the "best room" for want of a better word for it. One of the rare times I ever used this best room was the morning I was married. I had my breakfast there with my eighty six year old granny. I didn't realise the significance of that special breakfast at the time. Regretfully I didn't see much of my dear old granny after that day.

The house had a small upstairs landing which led to the two front bedrooms. Downstairs next to the stairway was the door to the cellar which was never used. I only saw the door open once. The cellar had rough wooden stairs and was half full of building rubble.

The passage continued as I went down two steps into the cobbler's shop past the shop counter with shoes lined up awaiting collection. The double front doors of the building opened into Middlegate St. One door was left open on fine days and had a well worn highly polished brass sneck. Returning home from my adventure on the beach I came and passed through the cobbler's shop where Uncle Arthur would be stood at his bench on which was laid the tools of his trade. Working away with a sharp knife he used to cut the leather to fit the sole of the shoe. Then with a hammer and a mouthful of nails, picking the nails from his mouth, he would tap them in around the new sole. Slices of leather and dust laid all over the floor, bench and shelves in the shop.

The eighteen inch thick walls of Granny's rented property were built from the limestone rocks worn and rounded from the beach, held together with limestone mortar and plaster.

There was no bathroom in the house nor drain in the kitchen. Waste water had to be disposed of to a drain in the yard. Piped water had been put in a corner of the kitchen before my time with a tap about eighteen inches from the floor. A galvanized bucket stood under the tap to collect any drips. The elaborate town water pump with its cast iron green painted tracery and ball topped finial still stands, minus the handle, on a concrete base in the remains of the High Street below the Abbey Church of St. Hilda. This Abbey Church of the early monastery, circa 11th Century, with square tower supported by six flying buttresses two on each of the three sides, stands in a large grassy, walled cemetery. The knave of the church has been added to in length sometime in its long history. Many historic artefacts, model ships and heraldic plaques are contained in the body of the church. A member of the De Brus family is laid to rest in the chancel.

*Wright's the Cobbler's Shop, on the right, this side of the man on ladder. Mum's shop is on the left by the handcart.*

Many of the houses had a well at the back of the house that had supplied the family with water for past centuries.

The Wright family lived in the kitchen with its earth floor covered with a few paving slabs and 'hookey mats'. These were made from old clothes cut into thin strips prodded to loop through coarse hessian material to make a thick pile worked up in a wooden frame. Several of these were made with the same frame and made the floor warm and comfortable to walk on. I was bathed in a galvanised tin bath put in front of the fire, with hot water from the copper kettle. The back bedroom, my room, was accessed from its own staircase behind a door in the kitchen, the first three stairs turned through ninety degrees then up a narrow stairwell to a small square landing and the bedroom door.

In the ancient kitchen a square table covered with a dark green chenille cloth stood in front of a long window of small square panes which opened with a sliding frame.

This was never opened probably because being the original window, when put there in the early 1700's, it was secured with many coats of paint. The room had originally had a hearth fire six feet across with a retaining wall at each side and a two foot square chimney above. Fuel would be burned in some sort of fire irons but I can only speculate from the modifications that had been made probably in the nineteenth century with a cast iron oven fitted at a convenient height on a brick base. A small fire basket level with the oven heated the oven when hot coals were pushed with a poker underneath.

Granny sat for hours on an upright kitchen chair, by the window next to the table with the kitchen fire on her left, on the other side of the fire by the curtained off set pot was a black bentwood rocking chair, with well used cushions and a crocheted woollen shawl thrown over it. She never sat in this rocker. I suppose it was my late Grandad Alex Wright's chair. Aunt Jenny used to sit in it sometimes. I often had a good rock in it, or sat gazing into the fire as puffs of gas emitted from a piece of coal and caught fire, and glowing ashes dropped through the grate behind the brass fender causing red hot coals to slip down behind the bars that contained the source of our little comfort.

A table of similar dimensions to the former with a bare wooden top working surface, about four foot six inches square, stood at the other side of the kitchen in front of a kitchen dresser, a rough set of six shelves about nine inches wide that stood against the whitewashed roughly plastered wall. Willow pattern plates stood at the back of one of these shelves with jugs, bowls and other kitchen items.

A local lady magistrate and historian, Miss Sivright, having her shoes repaired one day, had asked Aunt Jenny if she could have a look around the building and told her from the design of the windows and the through passage the property had been built in the early 1700's.

*The shoe shop Mum opened in 1924-5. I would be in my pram somewhere. On fine days I was strapped in and parked in the shop door way enjoying the passing folk and trolley buses.*

The property was demolished in about 1956 in the Council's slum clearance scheme.

My mum had rented the empty shop across the street from where her brother, the cobbler, my Uncle Arthur, was living with his wife in the spacious accommodation above their shop.

Mum got a joiner to fit shelves on the walls of the shop to hold boxes of shoes and had a counter with a drawer for the money made for the shop. Next she went to Leng's the wholesaler of Stockton where the family had an account to buy the leather for repairing the shoes. Good quality shoes were ordered and mum was in business! This was late 1924-25. Women didn't have the vote until 1928. My wealthy play-boy father could have claimed the business so my mother had put the business in her brother Arthur's name. There would obviously be a quid pro quo!

As a baby I must have been a bit of a problem. Aunt Jenny served customers in the cobblers shop and wouldn't want a baby to look after. I didn't do much crawling before I learned to walk. Jessie my practical

Mum strapped me into my pram until I was about one year old. On fine days she would put me at the shop doorway. The passers-by amused me. I probably amused them too. There was always something to see, trolley buses and horse and carts passing by. I must have been a happy baby, I was easy to please. I still am!

My pram in those days was an all weather big thing on four wheels with a folding black canvas hood. A black canvas cover fitted over the bedding with a six inch flap that fastened to the hood to shelter the infant me and restricted my view. The pram was deep with a storage department below the mattress. Often when an item was required from this vault the mattress was pulled up with the bedding and I was squashed into the top of the carriage as one of three padded boards was lifted out together with the item. I don't remember what, probably a rug to keep me warm or some nappies. During the day we lived behind the new shoe shop. I had a high chair, again strapped in, with a tray in front of me. I remember the pleasure I would have from turning my bowl of creamed rice over and with joyful ah's spreading it with both hands over the tray. My mum never scolded me, she took it all in her stride and seemed to enjoy it too! Otherwise I was no bother, I had a good childhood. I can remember my first steps in my granny's kitchen pulling myself up onto a low dilapidated chaise lounge by the back door and doing a side step along it. I probably let go then and fell down onto a well-padded bottom. The family cat shared my days and I received her affection with her purring. People seem to think it unusual to remember as far back as that but when I meditate on the past I see the scene in my mind and with concentration can recall many things.

By the time I was a toddler the older kids took me in tow. It would be a financial arrangement. My mum would give the kids a few pence to look after me. I don't remember seeing much of my mum at this time but she would see that I was well fed. She enjoyed food herself but she would be working until nine and ten o' clock at night across the street in her shoe shop. When I became a toddler I spent more time at my Granny's.

Granny Wright and Aunt Jenny had fish and chips every night Monday to Saturday and me too! Later Aunt Jenny would put me to bed. It's only now that I realise how much she did for me. My bedroom was above the kitchen and had its own staircase from behind a door in the kitchen. Three stairs turned ninety degrees into a narrow stairwell that led up to a small square landing to the bedroom door.

At three and four years old, I didn't have a teddy or anything to go to bed with, but in the absence of electricity going to bed with a candle was comforting. Later I had a night light, a short dumpy candle in a cardboard ring placed on a saucer. These burned for several hours and gave a warm glow in the big whitewashed walled bedroom. I lay listening to the burbling voices of the adults below until I drifted off to sleep. The mattress was filled with feathers and often felt damp. Aunt Jenny put a hot water bottle in my bed. It was only left in with me when I was older. There was a washstand in the bedroom with a big bowl and jug. I never saw it used.

In the kitchen a large copper kettle stood half on the hob, the other half of its bottom exposed to the fire. The hob was a shelf level with the open fire in the kitchen. The kettle was kept filled to supply constant hot water. Aunt Jenny would wash my hands and face in the kitchen from a bowl using carbolic soap and a flannel. I liked the smell of the carbolic soap, probably a bit antiseptic.

Almost a daily routine was a run to the beach, a couple of hundred yards away. Leaving my Granny's shop, I would say "hello" to my Uncle Arthur who was generally working at his cobbler's 'last', a metal post that held a metal foot the size chosen to suit the shoe. The customer's shoe which was being repaired was held in place, with his foot, using a loop of rope over the instep of the shoe leaving the sole and heel firm to be worked on. At other times he might be stitching a replacement sole onto a shoe. He didn't stitch many, for it seemed difficult to do with the pedal operated machine. He was a father figure to me and showed me how to sharpen and use a knife to cut leather by pulling the leather at an angle past the blade.

To get to the street I stepped through the green front double-doors. leading from the shop. Only one side of the door was kept open unless the weather was very bad. I then stepped down onto the stone flagged pavement and turned right outside the shop to run up Middlegate St. as far as the three story post office built in the Scottish style with a rounded corner, then turn right into "Pinder's Chare" (it was officially named Vollum Chare after a former Mayor of Hartlepool but it got the name Pinder's from the draper's shop on the corner). This chare which led through to the High Street., was demolished in the late 1950's slum clearance by a Labour Council. The ancient High Street. that had existed for centuries was obliterated leaving only a narrow road to the Parish Pump. I then would run across the ancient wide cobbled way, past the row of shops on the south side of the High St, (now semi-detached houses with back gardens), to a narrow street laid with sets (stone blocks about 6" x 4") called Sandwell Chare.

This chare, a local name for a wide passage way or a narrow road, gave access to the beach through a gothic arched opening in the Town wall which was protected by 'V' shaped battlements on the seaward side designed to repulse 14th century Scottish raiders invading from the sea.

In the Spring high tides, the sea came through this arch in the wall and at times threatened the nearby houses. The arch is still there but the area ground level has been raised about six feet from the demolition rubble and steps made to go through the arch. A wide breach in the wall had been made many years previously to access horse and carts to transport the fish landed on the beach. This part of the wall was restored when the demolition of the fishermen's Croft took place in the late 1950's. The demolition of the fisherman's Croft enabled the builders to level the land raising it along the wall in the area of the arch with steps thus eliminating the flooding.

This idyllic childhood existence ended when at the age of six, I was dragged screaming by my mum to the little Prissick Church School. I remember that very well over eighty years later. It was the best yelling performance of my life! I must have been a little horror but my mum just ignored my dissent and calmly pulled me along. I have no memory of her ever smacking me, but she never gave in to me. On the way up Middlegate St, the local baker 'Geordie Markum' whose bakery was opposite the Borough hall, tried to console me but heartbroken I only wanted to go on the sands. What else was there in life for a six year old? The school occupied a plot of land east of St Hilda's Church cemetery. This plot is now a tiny grassed island surrounded by road.

My first lesson in this small two roomed school was to sit at a table and unpick a piece of coarse cloth. This may have been to stuff a toy with. I don't remember the teacher saying why, and at the time didn't care. I was probably, correction, I was definitely uncooperative. Come to think of it, I was probably being punished, I didn't misbehave but I wasn't used to being restricted. School wasn't much of a challenge after my 'beach' education and a lot less fun!

Miss Walker a formidable tall woman was the headmistress but it was Miss Hunter, the teacher who taught the class I was in. She was a pretty woman who wore gold rimless pince-nez spectacles perched

31

*The cobbler's shop, a sketch by the author*

*The loss of the W/Catcher Simbra 1947, Painting by the Author, donated to Middlesbrough Museums. All perished except for John Leask (See pages 158-162).*

precariously on her nose. She was obviously going to tame this wild little individual. We were each given a slate and a stylus to write with. I lost some item of issue, I can't remember what it was. This is still a mystery but it has only occurred to me now that another kid must have nicked it? I do remember I got a rap over the knuckles with a ruler for losing it. I yelled and was very confused. I'd never been smacked before! This was the first of many injustices in my life which I still find confusing. Why do people want to control me?

In winter a great coal fire threw heat into the classroom surrounded by an enormous metal fire guard with a brass rail along the top. Small bottles of malted milk, each with a cardboard lid and a press out middle to put in a drinking straw, were warmed by this fire for our break.

I distinctly remember Betty Cox, the coalman's pretty daughter. She wore bright red knickers and short skirts which must have excited me at six years of age because I was dared to run into the girls' toilet which I boldly did and made Betty bend over and display the pretty red knickers to the lads crowded round the toilet door! Betty seemed to think it was fun too! I didn't get a smack for that!

Granny Wright , nee Scott, had married Alexander Wright who had with his cousins including James Barrie, later Sir James, author of Peter Pan, been left a legacy of sixty pounds each by a solicitor uncle on the Barrie side of the family. I don't think I have any of James Barrie's talent for children's stories, but my Granny's father, Thomas Lawson Scott, was a wood carver, an artist! I do have the ability to draw and paint a picture. Not art but illustrations useful often when no photographs are available. Alex and his brother Peter, had opened two shoe shops with Peter in charge while Alex operated a two man cobbler's shop and lived with Margaret Ann, my Granny, behind the shop. When No14 Middlegate Street was demolished in the late 1950's, the site was covered by a bus station. Now in 2006 the bus station has been replaced by gardens and a town square with trees and a toilet block.

About thirty yards west of the cobblers shop, beyond Northgate, a square led off to cottages in Sunnyside. Another street from the square led further west to the inner Harbour fish quay. An entrance to the north side of the Harbour was on the left along Northgate, it may still be there. The trolley buses with solid tyres came down the bank of Middlegate St from Durham Street and stopped outside Granny's shop before turning into Northgate. It was a busy corner, people passing from the shops waiting to catch the trolley bus and others dismounting from the buses to return home.

Mum told an amusing story of Granny when they were young. Grandad, Alex and Granny went to the theatre every Monday evening. This particular evening during an interval in the live performance a white screen was lowered to the stage and the first silent movie was shown. It must have been an extravaganza with a cast of 'thousands'. When the parents returned home the family asked "what was the show like?" In her broad Geordie dialect their mother said "it was all reet, but where are arll those folks ganna stay the neet in Hartlepool?" She evidently thought the action was taking place outside the cinema and reflected onto the screen inside. Not such a daft idea because a camera obscura could do just that. The Geordie dialect is directly descended from the Norwegian language. Granny would say, "arrs gannen yem", translated "I'm going home". Later working with Norwegians I found that this was pure Norwegian! This is another legacy of the Norwegian Viking ancestors.

On Saturday evenings the Salvation Army bandsmen and some of their ladies, all in uniform, would assemble at the junction of Middlegate, Northgate and Sunnyside, the adjoining square with a narrow road leading to the fish quay. They formed a circle and held an open air service, the mellow tone of the brass instruments playing gentle hymns. The words and music created an air of peace and tranquillity over a wide area.

At the end of the service pennies were thrown onto the cobbled surface in the middle of their circle, to be picked up before the leader mounted the flag in his holster. They then formed fours and generally playing a triumphant "Onward Christian Soldiers" the leader carrying the flag flying aloft they marched up the bank of Middlegate Street to the Salvation Army headquarters beyond. Two of their ladies would make a collection of coins from passers-by with little dark blue cloth pouches mounted on wooden handles as they returned to their headquarters in Lumley Street.

A friend of Granny's lived in a cottage down Sunnyside. I would be asked to visit her and take the kitchen waste greens for her hens. It was probably a social thing. These old girls had no family and liked to see the kids. Mrs Barker's husband was killed in the Boer war and his photograph in full dress uniform stood on the mantelpiece in a silver frame. A china dog kept guard at each end of the long mantelpiece with its brass rail and tasselled drape.

Another friend of Granny's, Dorothy Lilly, as a kid I called her

Dossie, also kept hens at the back of her house. I was occasionally sent to take greens for her hens. I thought it was a good idea to keep hens and Dossie would give me a few grains of corn to feed them. Food was abundant in this way, fish was cheap and generally plentiful except in bad weather when the boats couldn't get out. There were no private freezers of course but an ice house was built in the harbour. I was taken inside it once. It had a few frozen sides of beef hanging there. Mainly it was used provided the fishing boats and fish quay with ice to preserve the fish for a few days. Years later during the war Uncle Arthur kept a dozen or so hens at number eleven Middlegate in his cellar which had a window at the back of the property. This was the shoe shop Mum had created. I don't know why my Mum didn't do that during the war but there was probably a shortage of chicks by then. We knew nothing about keeping livestock either.

At five years old, on Sunday mornings, at about eleven o clock, I was given a jug and sent over.to the corner of Northgate to the Golden Lion Pub to see Mrs Ibbetson, the landlady. I was told to ask for "a pint of beer for Mrs Wright's table please." The pub, never very busy in the depression of the 1930s, was always empty at that time of the morning. As I walked in to the bar, the smell of the hops fascinated me. I gazed in wonder at the spittoons on the floor, freshly filled with sawdust. I don't think I realised what they were for but there was a lot of chewing tobacco at the time and this may have been the reason for them. It seemed a tranquil place where men could sit and relax after a hard day's work. There wasn't much of that though. The shipyards in the depression had no orders. Few men were employed and would have been glad of any work. They couldn't afford to buy beer but congregated at street corners in their dishevelled clothes, cloth caps and white 'mufflers', a scarf, it wouldn't be silk either! These 'mufflers', as they were called, replaced ties since the shirt in those days had loose collars held with a stud at the back of the shirt neck. The 'working man' wore the shirt without the starched collar, which required regular expensive laundry.

If a works foreman required a few men for a casual job, he would know where to find them – on certain street corners. There was a 'market' for men who would present themselves at the shipyard gate on the off chance that they would be selected for a few days work. If the weather was fine they would also congregate on the corner of the street near the Labour Exchange finding succour in adversity from eachother's company.

This situation existed up to 1939 when I started my apprenticeship. It ended when the shipyard geared up for war and thankfully did not return afterwards.

Some of these unemployed men, if they could get hold of an old bike, would go a few miles north of Hartlepool to the village of Blackhall to gather sea coal from the beaches. Here seams of coal were exposed under the sea bed. This coal breaks away in heavy seas and is washed up as fine black gravel on the beach at every tide. In places it was two or more inches thick. The coal was easy to rake up and put into sacks. A couple of hundredweight bags were slung across the bike and trundled home, the bags laid across the cross-bar. The men would then straddle the back wheel, free-wheeling when they could on the down-bank inclines home. A couple of bags would provide a few days of heat and fuel to cook for their families. Any extra that could be gathered was sold cheap to help other unfortunate people.

When a storm broke away an abundance of sea coal, the better off people took advantage of the opportunity to buy it. This 'black-market' income helped the unemployed through the hard times. Sea coal burnt very hot and bright. Being fine it was useful to 'bank up' a fire for the night. After the war the council forbade the taking of coal from the beach and sold the gathering rights to contractors. This seemed a mean trick for a Labour Council, denying poor men a few bags of coal.

Other men would go fishing. They didn't have any fancy fishing rods, but used a hand line with two or three hooks fastened onto it above a 'sinker' made of lead. The 'sinker' was often made from an old bit of lead pipe, if any could be found, otherwise a stone with a hole in it would do! To cast out, the sinker was twirled around the head with about three feet of line in the hand and let fly over the sea. It required experience to catch fish, for you had to know when the fish would be inshore. Before the War, August was a time of plenty when the sprats came in. Sprats were similar to a long sardine and came in thick shoals close up to the beach. The mackerel chased them and they too could be seen jumping out of the water close to the beach. So close in fact that young lads could wade in and throw mackerel onto the beach to be taken home for tea! In the 1920s and 1930s, at this time of the year, the sea was thick with fish as they annually migrated slowly down the coast.

On Sundays in the summer people would parade en family along the extensive promenade in their best clothes. Aunt Jenny used to take me to the Abbey Church of Saint Hilda. I didn't like being dressed up and having to sit in church but I did it to please her. We then would have a bit of a promenade along the sea front saying, "nice day", to the mums and dads passing by with their offspring. I did have a feeling that I was different in not having a dad at home. I had mixed feelings about it. I would have resented having a nasty dad, so I accepted my situation.

Everybody needed to have shoes repaired in those days. 'Wright's the Cobblers' had a monopoly! When I was five years old my Aunt Jen, as I called her, got me smartened up one Saturday, probably a Bank Holiday because the shop was closed. She took me to St Marks Methodist Church bazaar. All I can remember of it was the pretty little girl with golden curls presenting the 'lady opener' with a bouquet. The little girl was four years old. Aunt Jen told me her name was Dorothy Fell whose father was the chief draughtsman and design engineer at the Richardson Westgarth's Shipyard.

I was captivated by Dorothy Fell and would look out for her on the Sunday parades. Through the years I caught glimpses of her but our eyes never met. On one occasion she came into the shop with her mother to collect some shoes. I was stood behind the counter and admired her lovely copper golden hair. She had a rosy round face with a small pert mouth. I would have loved to have been her cousin or just even her friend, but had no idea then where this was going to lead.

Fourteen years later and then living in Middlesbrough I used to cycle to Hartlepool, or travel by bus in bad weather, to stay with Aunt Jen at weekends, when I was free of Home Guard duties. This was to attend the Saturday night dance at the Borough Hall. Although it was war time, young folk enjoyed these dances. They were very social events, but a young person had to learn to dance to qualify for the privilege of being able to ask any unattached girl whom he fancied to dance. Foxtrots, quicksteps and waltzes were the basic dances. To liven things up, every now and then the Band would play an old fashioned dance or two. The Paul Jones dance was where males and females formed two large circles, men on the outside ladies on the inner circle, changing  partners progressively with phases of the music until they returned to the partner they had been dancing with at the outset. Not popular with a chap going steady with his girl.

Now going back to my younger days. Across the road opposite to the cobblers shop, my granny's half-sister Lily Wardell had lived behind a fresh fish shop for a few years before they moved to a big house on the sea front No.1 Albion Terrace about 1930. They still had the shop, but now lived in style. Granny Wright's father Thomas Lawson Scott had died before granny had married Alexander Barrie Wright in Newcastle. They came to live in Hartlepool sometime in the late 1880's. My maternal great-grandmother, now a widow, had married again to a Mr Johnson. They had a baby daughter and named her Lily. When Lily was eleven years old her mother also died and Lily came from Newcastle to live with her older married half-sister, my granny, in Hartlepool. This was before there were any social services. Families had to be more responsible and look after each other.

Lily Johnson became one of the Wright family and eventually married a Mr George Wardell. They had a family of five daughters, Norah, Lily, Elsie, Margery and Winnie and three sons. Of the sons, Harry worked on the fish quay or at the kipper house during the herring season in July and August. Arthur Wardell went to sea, before the mast as it was called, and very soon passed his exams and became one of the youngest sea Captains. He was a very nice young man but died at a young age, probably from being a heavy smoker. Lawson, my age, was called up early in the war. He was in the army and fought in Italy. After the war he owned a grocery business in South Bank, a few miles east of Middlesbrough. His wife Veronica, always known as 'Ronnie', had a post office in Thornaby for some years. They retired to Great Ayton but with my own work and family problems I lost touch with them altogether.

My Uncle George & Aunt Lily Wardell had a lovely little cottage in the charming village of Elwick a few miles North of Hartlepool. This led to my first ride in a motor car when I was five years old! I was returning from my daily sortie on the fish sands, as I approached granny's shop Aunt Lily Wardell was getting into their recently purchased car. She called me over, "come on son, we're going to Elwick, get in!" Aunt Jenny heard this and came to the shop door. She took me inside to clean me up before I was allowed to climb up onto the running board and plonk myself down alongside Harry Wardell who was driving. This new mode of transport was fascinating to me. As the gears were changed by Harry the car jerked forwards and we were off along Northgate travelling the five miles or so to Elwick. On reaching our destination I don't think we stayed long, but the car ride was memorable!

Uncle George was a good business man and was 'well up' in the fish business. He was a buyer with an office on the fish quay and also had one of the many herring smoke houses, producing kippers, on the edge of the town. It was a pongy fishy area but not too near the town. Hartlepool then was a big fishing port and July and August were the busiest times of the year in the 1930's. Up to a hundred boats "herring fishing drifters" mainly Scottish, some Dutch, North East boats of Lowestoft and other ports arrived.

Uncle Arthur did a bit of business selling white rubber thigh boots and yellow waterproof smocks to the fishermen. He had the boots hanging outside the shop front above the window.

When I was thirteen he arranged for me to have a trip to sea with the skipper of the herring drifter 'Fisher Queen' who called in the shop now and then. I had a couple of trips and Uncle Arthur always gave me a 'bass', a shopping bag made from woven strips of palm leaves, common in those pre-plastic days. This was to bring back a few pounds of herring. Uncle Arthur would fry the fish in dripping, with oatmeal, in a big black round iron pan on the fire for our breakfast. They were delicious! No wonder I've lived so long!

The herring drifter 'Fisher Queen' was a wooden boat about seventy feet long with a small two cylinder steam engine about three feet high and a simple coal fired boiler. We left the fish quay, steamed around to the coaling quay, pulled up under a wooden coaling chute and about a ton of coal cascaded amidships between the scuppers and the coaming. The engine man lifted a round iron manhole in the deck and shovelled the coal into the bunker hold. That done, we sailed out of the Victoria Dock into the channel past the Middleton ferry, fish sands and the "pilot pier" to the sea. I was thrilled as 'Fisher Queen' rose and fell with the sea and poked my head into the engine room to see the engineman shovelling coal into the small boiler furnace. The little engine silent except for a few puffs of steam now and then, it's small bright steel crankshaft turning round rapidly flashing from the various shiny parts as they moved up and down and round and round. This was to influence me greatly in my life although I didn't realise it at the time.

I soon accepted the primitive conditions on these fishing boats. The toilet was a small wooden barrel with a rope handle, catch a bit of sea water in the barrel over the ships side, then sit on it hanging onto the gun'nel, the side of the ship, on the open stern rising and falling with the waves, with my trousers round the ankles, do it, stand up, staggering about a bit as the deck heaved, pull up my trousers, and chuck it!

We sailed out for about nine hours at about eight knots as far as I could judge, then stop. 'Fisher Queen' now drifting, wallowed in the swell, then set up a steady roll. I felt a bit queasy for a while. Action on deck took my mind off the rolling.

The lads would then cast the net. The net, ten feet deep with green glass floats attached to the top and lead weights at the bottom, was flung over a long wooden roller fastened to the bulwark. It ran out for what seemed to me hundreds of yards with yellow buoys at intervals to show other boats the position of the net.

A small gaff sail at the stern now kept 'Fisher Queen' head up to the wind, this reduced the rolling a little, but not much! I much preferred the steaming motion.

The net was hauled in by hand, one man at each side of the wooden roller, the herrings shaken from the net onto the deck. With wooden shovels the fish were then put down into the hold. This operation was repeated until the catch was suitable to return to the fish quay in good time to satisfy the buyers

After watching this operation I became very tired. It was long past my bed time and I slept on the floor of the wheelhouse. The crew slept in bunks in the for'd peak. That's the sharp end of the boat! It was dark and very smelly, I didn't sleep there. I awoke to find we were approaching the coast, and with the sea air I felt reasonably refreshed. I watched as the coast appeared, then was able to pick out landmarks, the lighthouse and piers. We steamed between the port and starboard buoys that indicated the dredged channel into the harbour. I was looking forward to my breakfast with Uncle Arthur.

Fisher Queen came 'bow up' to the fish quay and made fast. It was about nine am.

To arrive late meant a poor price for our fish if other boats had arrived with good catches. When the buyers didn't want more herrings for retail the fish would be sold at a lower price to be salted down in barrels for export to Russia and other parts of the world. Wooden boxes were on the quay. Two men in the ship's hold shovelled the herrings into a willow basket. This was hauled up with a rope round the winch drum over a pulley on the ship's derrick until it was level with the quay. Another rope swung it over to the quay as the winch lowered it near a box when the contents were poured from basket to box. Each box when full held a measure known as a kran. Give or take a few fish I suppose?

When there was a glut of herrings and there were no buyers one or two boats, who had come in late, had to return to sea to dump their catch. It didn't happen often, as most went for curing, smoked as kippers or bloaters but in the thirties tons of fish were also salted down into big barrels and sold abroad. Salting the herrings was done by Scottish 'fisher-lassies' who came down from Scotland as the herring fleet moved slowly down the coast following the shoals of herring.

The 'lassies' lodged with local families. If the fish did not require salting, there was no work. They didn't waste their valuable time and had to earn a living. They knitted fancy cable Scottish pullovers for sale. Even as they walked around the town in small groups they would knit as they walked along generally in twos and threes. They carried the wool in a linen bag slung over their shoulder. They were happy girls, laughing and chatting in the Scottish brogue, well liked by the townsfolk. They lodged with the same families year after year.

In preparation for salting, the herrings were tipped into long wooden troughs about ten feet long. Four or five girls, wearing green waterproof aprons, would work at each side of the trough taking their knives from their apron front pocket to gut the fish. They worked at great speed. There were fish scales everywhere! The fish were then tightly packed into barrels with a shovel of salt on each layer until the barrel was full.

Uncle George, cigar in mouth, brown suit and trilby, gold chain across his waistcoat, although a busy man always had time for me and was very kind. His youngest son Lawson, he and I were some kind of cousins I suppose. As I have said, his mother and my Granny were half-sisters. In our infancy, Lawson and I were brought up together. With busy parents a girl was paid to take us out in a double pushchair. Later we were both put into sailor suits. Mum never could persuade me to wear the sailor hat. A few times only maybe under protest!

In winter until I was four years old I had to wear soft leather gaiters from just above the knee to ankle, with lots of round buttons down the side. A button hook was required to fasten them around the leg from ankle to thigh. I hated them! They took ages to put on and made my legs sore, the short trousers were still draughty and the tops of my legs were cold in winter.

The Wardell family prospered with the abundance of fish and had moved from living above the shop premises into a big three story house on the sea front.No.1 Albion Terrace overlooking the Tees Bay. This house had two large basement rooms, not really cellars. The front room had a window half above ground level, this was the kitchen with a large fire and range. The second room was a dark laundry. Lawson and I played in the big attic rooms where originally servants would have lived. He had many expensive toys, guardsmen soldiers four or five inches high, an old rocking horse, probably second hand and well worn which had served some family well. He had a toy "lantern slide", a more modern toy, a cinematograph which used a few feet of celluloid film wrapped around a spool to show moving pictures by cranking a handle for a few seconds of action.

Cinema was just coming to town, this was 1929. At the 'Palladium Cinema' in Northgate we saw Tom Mix silent cowboy films on Saturday mornings. The noise of the kids shouting things like "look out! he's behind you" was deafening! The manager would walk down the isle shouting "quiet" which was futile and only added to the noise! Tom nearly always ended up unconscious and locked in a barn which the 'baddies' had set on fire! We had to go the following week and there was Tom always with a white stetson hat, 'up and at 'em again'! We never knew how he escaped! The "baddies" always wore black stetson hats!

Uncle George's business included a Bedford lorry. I was allowed to go with the driver Richard Thomas (married to George's daughter Norah) to take a load of herrings in boxes to 'Fortunes' the fish merchants in Whitby, on the cliff under the Abbey. This was early in the season when the herring boats were not going as far down the coast as Whitby.

In 1937 it was a long journey to Whitby, over the Transporter Bridge, through Guisborough and along the moor road. We had to stop after climbing about a hundred feet snaking up Burke Brow to allow the engine to cool down. Richard, 'Dickie', would have to take the sparkplugs out of the engine and clean them. We would then negotiate " jolly sailors", so called because of the Pub near-by, a steep bank which had an 'S' bend at that time. Nowadays the bank is much reduced. Once across the moors it was then downbank nearly all the way into Whitby! On our return, the five miles pull back up didn't bother the Bedford now that we were offloaded. We delivered herrings to Nobles and Fortunes fish merchants. They had kipper houses where they smoked the herrings under oak chipping fires and are still there today in 2006 sending kippers all over the world.

We were given a ham tea with salad and cherry tomatoes, bread and butter and big mugs of tea. Nice friendly people. I was a lucky lad to associate with so many nice people. I didn't know it but my father had a 48 ton yacht named 'Penn Donna' in Whitby harbour at about this time. I was told by a Captain who went to sea with him that they sailed over to France with his friends aboard. Dad wasn't a family man!

Hartlepool had its own Pilot Boat, called, the 'cutter'. It was run as an association by the pilots. The boat was quite a substantial craft, with a funnel painted light brown with a black band at the top, coal fired boiler and steam engine of course! It was designed to go out into the bay for long periods to meet ships arriving at the port. At high tide the cutter would go alongside the ship and a pilot would climb up a rope ladder to guide "her" into the harbour. The channel being rather narrow, it was under the almost permanent attention of a 'bucket dredger' which clanked like a broken church bell all day, every day in the harbour! Well it seemed like nearly every day.

Mum had a school friend Marjory Raine, who had married a river-pilot and a day out was arranged on the Pilot Cutter. We walked along the 'old pier' where the Pilot Cutter was always berthed when not at sea. We climbed down the side of the pier onto the vessel and sitting around the stern we were soon out in the bay to wait for the cargo ships coming up the coast. There was a party atmosphere with family of other pilots aboard. Fish were caught and taken to the galley to be cooked. Coming alongside a 'Frenchman', it could have been any nationality as the pilot clambered up the ladder. Mum called up in her schoolgirl French for some bread, a crewman appeared and threw a loaf down which together with mugs of strong hot tea regaled the company nicely. The business of the day over, we returned to the pier in good spirits, a happy day!

We often went to Middlesbrough to visit Mum's younger sister Lily who married Richard Metcalf. They had moved into a new house built about 1928 in Devonshire Road, Linthorpe. Sometimes we went by bus to the Transporter Bridge. This bridge was built in 1911 and is still running today. It is not a conventional bridge with a roadway. A tower of steel girders at each side of the river carries a horizontal track from which a trolley is pulled back and forth across the river by a steel wire rope which wraps around a large electrically driven drum. Suspended from the trolley by wire ropes is a platform capable of taking several vehicles depending on their size.

I enjoyed the 'Transporter' route but at other times we went around the road via Billingham, - don't ask me why! These were the early days of long distance buses which were put on the road in Teesside by an ex-army sapper, after the 1914-18 war, called Mr Blumer. Hence we had 'Blumer's Buses'. The route was quite an adventure, for when we reached Billingham Bottoms, which regularly flooded, going up the bank into the village, the passengers would all have to get out to enable the bus to reach the top! The engine generally boiled over and steam would erupt from the radiator. The bus would have to stop and wait until the engine had cooled, water would be added to the radiator, and off we went again!

My mum told me that before they had buses, ferry boats plied between Stockton and Middlesbrough, along the river Tees, and went to Hartlepool. Mr William Lillie in his "History of Middlesbrough" gives a good account of these early years.

# CHAPTER 5
## HARTLEPOOL CARNIVAL WEEK

The first week in August the town went into holiday mode. Carnival was a great celebration; the main streets were decorated with bunting by the Council. The families of small terraced houses hung flags from their windows with bunting to their neighbour across the street.

In the nineteen-thirties it was generally 'Murphys' or 'Hoadleys' Fairground Shows that arrived, early on the Sunday morning having travelled overnight by road from their last venue. Unlike the circus that travelled by train. It wouldn't be too far to travel because most of the fairground rides were packed on to trailers and towed by the giant steam tractor engines that would be hard pushed to exceed twelve miles an hour. The men who designed these rides were masters of their craft. Each part marked or numbered and loaded onto the trailer to be erected quickly and safely. They arrived with their families in their expensive motor caravans. The caravan was mounted on big lorry frames behind the engine and driving cab. The glass windows were decorated with tasteful designs etched into the glass. Glimpses in the windows showed expensive items adorning the furniture. Opulent is the word I need. By early evening the fairground was in full swing. The rides were now more modern. The latest was the bumper cars and racers, the bumper cars had a seat for two with a car steering wheel and ran on a thin steel plate deck, a pole at the back of the car had a trolley that ran across a steel wire mesh covering the area of the deck, this conducted the electricity to the foot pedal in the car that controlled sufficient speed to make bumping another car safe. The racing motorbikes were shaped and painted with wheels and engine to look like a small motorbike with a saddle and handle bars to hang on to that went round at speed over the undulating track mounted on the circular amusement ride for a period of a few minutes. An attendant would move around the customers as the ride was in progress collecting the sixpence or whatever the price was at the time. The atmosphere was exciting, another new stall that arrived was 'The Clocks'. It consisted of a long board about fifteen feet by four feet painted black with twenty numbered ten inch clock faces in two rows of ten. People bought a ticket with a clock number. When twenty tickets had been sold the chap in charge switched the clocks on and they raced round for a minute or so and when he switched them off the clock nearest twelve o'clock won a prize. It was a fascinating way to lose money!

Street parties were organised by the mums for the kids. Trestle tables set up in the middle of the narrow streets, laden with jam sandwiches, buttered scones and home-made cakes where money was available pennies had been saved every week to buy little prizes, a bar of chocolate for the winner of the egg and spoon race, and a sherbet-sucker for second prize. A brown paper bag was given to each child containing a paper hat a few monkey nuts and perhaps a small toy for each of them. I once got an apple in mine, they were not common as far as I knew in those days! Mothers with flowered wrap around aprons covering their ample bodies bringing kitchen chairs from the house directed the kids where to sit, with the known naughty ones handy for a threatened slap round the ear. That's all it took the threat! Then with big teapots they poured strong condensed milk sweetened tea into the mug each child had brought with them. When the meal was over all was cleared away and an impromptu stage set up. Some of the kids would do their party piece, a piece of poetry or a sweet little song. My favourite was a piece of poetry recited by the girls called 'Big Steamers'. It was about the big steam ships that carried people all over the world.

In the nineteen-twenties it was the 'Wild Beast Show', as it was called, that came to town and set up in the High Street. 'Murphy's roundabouts' came to town every year. With a 'roll a penny' stall, a Boxing booth, four wheeled trailer cages with lions and other poor beasts. One year they had a couple of elephants housed in a big tent. Giant swing boats were operated by a steam engine. Electricity from generators on top of the giant wheeled traction engines driven by leather belts from the steam engine shaft supplied rows of lights round a ride called 'The Peacocks roundabout', these were carriages to seat two with the peacocks head rising from the front of the carriage and the back carved and spread out forming the gaily painted tail rising up above our heads rising and falling as they moved slowly round to the tinny music. A gaily painted roundabout named 'The Chairoplanes' had individual chairs suspended by chains from the roundabout canopy that flew out as it spun round to a caleopy in the centre of the ride playing more tinny music.

At this time the best houses were electric but the not so well off still were lit by gas, oil lamps or candles to read with. That was us! The firelight would do to sit and talk to friends. Imagine the excitement seeing all these coloured electric lights! A four wheeled trailer had an organ played stilted music with mobile figures pirouetting and miming with small model drums and instruments, highly polished brasses on everything. I became tempted to make my fortune on the roll a penny stall. I was given a few pence at a time to play with and soon learnt the odds were against me and gave it up, I taught my son the same lesson on gambling on a visit to Blackpool.

I was very fascinated by the steaming fancy line painted monsters, the traction engines with wheels twice my height, snorting steam, huffing and puffing as the flywheel spun round; the leather drive belt to the generator slapping in rhythm to the crank of the engine. So much so that when the show left town passing Granny's shop, at three years old I followed it for about a mile to the railway station and was caught up there by my caring breathless Aunt Jenny! I was well satisfied with myself! I'd seen them safely out of town! After the High Street had been demolished in the name of slum clearance in 1938 the show's venue was moved to the Town Moor which being grassland soon became a quagmire in rain.

On the last Saturday of Carnival a parade took place. The parade assembled at the old Barracks near marine Drive and came along Durham Street and down Middlegate. It made a circular tour of the ancient Borough, to disperse where it had started, at the well-constructed Barracks, probably built like the Gun Batteries to repel Napoleon.

We waited a long time, to a youngster, on the pavement for the procession to appear. First we heard the brass band in the distance, as the music got louder kiddies faces would appear from between the adult's legs looking anxiously up the road, then Councillor Tommy Pailor the organiser, came into view, stepping proudly out, alone in the middle of the road followed at a respectful distance usually by the Blackhall Colliery Brass Band. Councillor Pailor had during the German bombardment of Hartlepool in December 1914 been active in organising the removal of civilian casualties. He made a good job of organising the carnival parades too! I would watch agog the chap with the big base drum "boom! boom! boom!" And two chaps with the highly polished big base euphoniums, playing a throaty "umpa! umpa!"

Then arrived the King and Queen of Carnival, theatrical crowns sat jauntily on their majestic white wigs, faces made up with powder, lipstick and wimples. In appropriate royal dress, sitting on elaborate line painted decorated plywood thrones fixed at the back of an equally polished and decorated flat four wheeled cart drawn by two magnificent shire horses, their hooves waxed and well groomed, their harnesses with brasses polished to perfection. In later years this flat cart carrying the thrones was replaced by a motor lorry equally polished up but the horses were sadly missed.

On the float the Court Jester and female attendants in medieval dress lounged about throwing coloured streamers into the crowd, some streamers trailed along the road adding colour to the scene. The townsfolk entered into the spirit of things, everyone cheering and waving. Then came the floats entered by local business people, some by individual street parties interspersed by other folks in fancy dress, bicycles decorated with coloured paper were pushed proudly along by their owners.

Individual costumes, some quite scary to a doubtful youngster ran from side to side of the road, half naked bodies with sea weed or straw skirts painted as mermen or native savages waving wooden spears. Old ladies were screaming and laughing enjoying the attention given to them.

Being a small town it created a wonderful atmosphere of pleasure among the locals and encouraged friendship where there may have once been doubt and suspicion.

This era was renowned for Kid's Jazz Bands. The kids in bright coloured taffeta uniforms playing kazoos, a small trumpet with a paper disc that vibrated to create a trumpet noise when blown with a tune given with a throaty buzz. The band was led by young high stepping teenage girl Majorette in short flared skirts. Each step exposing firm white thighs and tight rounded knickers. At thirteen years of age the sight of these girls with firm bare thighs awakened my first hormones. It puzzled me but I ignored it. They were showing off with their fancy parading. It was fun!

These Majorettes twirled their silver maces overhead and occasionally flung them high in the air! They never failed to catch them in the twirling rhythm established by the marching tunes of the kazoos. As I have said little tin trumpets with tissue paper giving the player blowing a buzzing tune tremolo sound. Following the older Majorette was a minor Majorette imitating the steps of the senior Majorette. Next, two well-built juniors carrying the banner poles in a socket on a leather belt. The banner elaborately created with a gold fringe and the name of the band spelt out often in gold letters on the banner, with the Street or area denoting the band's origin. The banner poles were supported fore and aft with silk like ropes held at the shoulder by four outriders, self-conscious high stepping youngsters.

The Jazz bands were very popular with the public. The kids enjoyed the discipline and were obviously very proud as they strutted their stuff! Smartly obeying the orders to mark time or advance as the procession was held up for one reason or another. Signals were given by whistle from one of the proud ex-army dads who had trained them. They came from pit villages and towns far and wide, their banners proudly displayed names such as Wood Street, a Hartlepool band, and pit villages like Horden and Easington . As many as four or five bands would arrive by coach to swell the parade. Each band had one or two anxious mothers who would walk alongside an embarrassed daughter. Mum carried a shopping bag of "first aid" a bottle of water, a flannel to cool a fevered brow, hand towel and such like. One or two dads discreetly encouraged young sons to "chin up" as they marched along. It was a fairly long route round the town. This would be quite an ordeal for many young chaps.

One float mounted on the flat of a lorry, which was entered for many years by the Collins family had the wives heavily made up pantomime style, dressed in their summer finery, lounging in deck chairs with potted plants and drinks on tables, while the men in pinnies, kitchen aprons, were doing the washing, possing at the tub, ironing and hanging out fancy knickers and undies! This in Hartlepool the home of "Andy Capp" the little waster who with his put on wife Flo, featured in a newspaper cartoon by Reg. Smythe at the time. This tableau created roars of laughter and banter from the crowds lining the street .This was the 1930's when the reality was very bleak with so many men unemployed and it showed with the sunken cheeks of men who had only had menial jobs before the depression came and were more affected than most.

Uncle Alex was unemployed for three years and the 'means test committee' decided that as his mother had a business he was not eligible for 'dole' she had to keep him!

So the business had to keep Uncle Arthur the cobbler, Granny, Uncle Alex, Aunt Jenny and me! Five of us! Jessie, my Mum made a useful contribution with the shoe shop! We lived a lot on fish, it was cheap during July and August when the herrings were in. Sunday was roast beef and cold beef sandwiches for tea. Uncle Alex took me over the ferry to Richardson and Westgarths shipyard in Middleton. The remains of the ferry can still be seen at the west end of the town wall. From the Middleton landing stage we walked to see what was probably the last ship launched at Richardsons Westgarth's shipyard.

I was five years old then in1929. He had been a turner, a skilled machinist working to thousandths part of an inch in the shipyard. Later in about 1934 he got work at Reyrolls Electrical factory at Hebburn upon Tyne. Only then was he able to marry at fifty a very sweet lady. They got a council house in Hebburn and as a skilled man they became mildly prosperous. His wife was another Aunt Jenny for me and very kind, she made presents of her home made wonderful toffee. When Uncle Alex died she gave me a sum of money he had left for me I think it was about one hundred and fifty pounds. Alexander Wright a kind and upright gentleman died at eighty years old, his Jenny a few years later.

Uncle Arthur, the cobbler, had been in 'Harry Tate's Navy' during the 1914 war. This was Admiral H.Tate's Royal Navy Coastal Defence, armed trawlers, mine sweepers and anti-submarine defence.

They were in constant active service. He rarely spoke of it. He was a do-er and had a set of roof ladders with three sections which extended by pulleys and ropes to reach the roof of his property. He knocked a hole in a brick wall to put in a window and another for a door. For our pleasure he created a holiday living hut. There were no caravans in those days. It was very substantially built of tongue and groove half boards with framed windows. The whole thing mounted on four twelve inch iron wheels, which kept it off the ground if not very portable. When this was on site he built two small bedrooms onto the hut which made it very comfortable for the family.

This holiday "bungalow" was situated at Crimden Dene, a deep cleft where a wide shallow river, generally dried up in summer, ran through to the beach. This Dene is about five miles north of Hartlepool. We could go there by bus but it was just as quick to walk the five miles along the beach from the north side of the headland carrying our food supplies. There were only a few huts in the early days, oil lamps for light, primus stove to cook with, but a 'pot belly' stove on cold days, which then took the place of the primus. The wooded dene was wild so we tidied it up for fuel! There was plenty of dead wood which we carried to the hut to feed the pot belly of the stove. Water was carried from a spring on the south side of the dene in white enamel buckets, with lids! The water bubbled out of the side of a grassy bank. We had made a chute from a tin can to enable the water to run into the buckets. It tasted beautiful, brilliantly clear, soft and sweet. The river was dried up unless heavy rain had fallen, then most of it ran into the sand when it reached the beach. It was ideal territory for safe adventure expeditions and with my cousin Arthur, Uncle Arthur's adopted boy four years younger than me and Martin, a nephew of Aunt Lily, we had many happy sunny days, strangely enough I don't remember it ever raining.

Hartlepool then in 1936 had a thriving croft of fishermen's cottages. Cambridge buildings looking onto the pilot's pier was a three story tenement building along the town wall. Most of these properties were occupied by families of fishermen conveniently near their boats the cobles. These boats were double ended, 'sharp at both ends' unlike the Whitby cobles which had a transom stern. Double ended boats are better for a beach landing, an oncoming wave could not easily push the boat broadside on to the beach where it might be swamped. They were at this time in the 1930s being motorised. When the older kids were at school I was a loner on the 'fish sands', poking my nose into what was going on. I would watch the men drill a hole through the stern post of a coble to pass the propellor shaft through. The engines were generally second hand lorry engines complete with gear box, they were mounted on wooden blocks near the stern. These vessels had been sailed with a square sail hanging from a spar suspended from the mast up to this time. Almost the same rig as their ancient ancestor's Viking ships. The square sail was pulled up the mast on the wooden spar with the clew, a bottom corner, fastened at the bow, the other held at the tiller. They sailed well, the spar could be pulled across the beam to sail fairly close to the wind but they were easy to manage by one man to tack near upwind. The boats were not without long heavy oars to manoeuvre in harbour. These oars were fitted with a pin and thole a metal ring, to keep them secure if it was needed to let go of the oar to handle a line. They were well balanced so that man power was not wasted on the weight of the oar pulling the boat when lack of wind made the coble becalmed.

I saw how the fishermen moved their boats from the beach to the water on wooden pit props of which there was a plentiful supply in those days. Hartlepool imported ship loads of pit props for the Durham coal mines. Often ships would come into port listing after passing through a storm on their way over from Norway. The deck cargo of props sagged over the side of the vessel leaving a trail of props astern in the sea. The props were about eight feet long and four to six inches diameter. They would wash ashore for days after the ships arrival.

The cobles were got in and out of the water by being pushed to slide over the line of props laid a couple of feet apart on the sand. If this was done at high tide there would be ample time to repair or repaint the cobles hull before the tide returned. To the kids on the beach it was a bit of fun and everyone was happy to lend a hand. Later when living in Middlesbrough, every school holiday I stayed at Grandma's. With my friends we would hire a boat for a few pence from Mr Bond who had six boats moored along the town wall, near to where the ferry crossed over by the lifeboat station.

With the hard economic times of the thirties Mr Bond had little business hiring his boats. We kids were probably his only customers if we could put together threepence or so we could have a boat as long as we cared to use it.

We would row for hours round the little harbour and over to Landscar rocks near Seaton Carew, these rocks were only visible at low tide, we were warned to keep a weather eye out! We learned to handle a boat here from the age of eleven, at times sculling from the stern which was easier than rowing and done standing facing aft, pushing the oar with the body and twisting the blade left and right to act on the keel as a lever. As a child there was a lot to interest me around grandma's shop. Often if the trolley bus driver coming down Middlegate Street was careless in turning the corner wide, one or sometimes both trolleys would come off the overhead wires.

The conductor often a bit annoyed would pull a long bamboo pole from under the bus. This pole had a hook on the end. With this he hooked it onto the trolley and set the little wheel onto the wire. It wasn't always so easy since having come off the wire in the first place it wouldn't stay on in that same place. The conductor would then have to keep the trolley on the wire with his pole until the driver was able to move the bus a few feet further along to a section of wire in easy reach of the trolley.

Photographs of Granny as a young woman, a Scott, show her with a strong face, a firm mouth, high cheek bones, dark hair and brown eyes, slim with a straight back in a skirt down to the floor. My memory of her when I was five was of a grey haired old lady slightly stooped, still with the long black skirt and the face strong but well wrinkled. The chin square, the mouth firm aged sixty five. She was born in1863, christened Margaret Ann Scott the daughter of Thomas Lawson Scott, a wood carver. She died aged eighty seven in 1950. Meggie as her contemporaries called her, was an ardent snuff addict and had a black oblong snuff box, it was probably made of bone or paper maché. From a very early age I was invited to 'have a pinch' and was shown the art of taking a pinch by putting a little between finger and thumb putting it on the knuckle of the other hand, sniffing to both sides of the nose with the resulting explosion of a sneeze! She suffered from bronchitis badly in the winter, maybe taking the snuff helped to relieve her condition. I don't remember her ever sneezing or having a cold but her chesty cough in winter seemed to never end.    The house was very damp in any but summer conditions, the walls being built with pieces of lime / sandstone from the beach worn round by the sea, held together with lime mortar to a thickness of eighteen inches. A heavy sustained downfall of rain, wind driven against a wall, would soak through and run down the wall in the room in droplets.

Granny said the property had been a tavern called 'The White Hart' the name being visible under the repainted shop front when they had first occupied the property. After some research by my friend Cliff Thornton, it appears the property had extended through to the Main

Hotel in the High Street. The Middlegate Street property being for the carriages horses and staff.

There was a carriage way next to the property which had led to the back of Granny's property. The property had been separated from the carriage way by a six foot high brick wall at the back of No 14. The yard area was paved with building bricks set round a drain where rain and kitchen waste water ran away.

Across the yard at the back of Granny's property was a brick built flush toilet next to a coal house to hold a few bags of coal. Adjacent property had signs of gable ends of once connected roofing indicating smaller dwellings maybe stables and cottages had existed round the yard. The house had not had running water originally. The town pump in the High Street was not too far away. A water tap had in more recent times been fitted in the corner of the kitchen. It was two feet from the floor and a galvanised bucket was under it to catch any drips. The obsolete town pump still stands there today. A magnificent tower of cast iron tracery painted dark green minus the handle, topped with a ball pinnacle. It stands in the centre of what was once a wide, part cobbled historic high street below the Abbey Church of St Hilda. .

Now after centuries, thanks to social engineering vandalism, all that remains is a minor road, gardens of a rockery nature and car park. This is now to be further modified to create a Town Square. Not another improvement! It has been planted with mature trees and shrubs that will require expensive maintenance and do little to bring money into the town.

Granny's kitchen with its earth floor and a few concrete paving stones later filled around the one time open hearth with some concrete. Linoleum covered most of the floor and 'hookey mats', made from cast off clothes cut into strips and prodded through sheets of sacking stretched on a wooden frame. The strips were formed into loops which were cut with scissors to create a "pile" and gave some insulation to the feet.

The original "open" hearth was about six feet wide A thin steel rail was still there in the ceiling where cooking was done hanging from chains above the hearth fire. It had been brought into the 19th century with the cast iron oven next to the fire basket which was about a foot wide with the oven raised on brickwork. There was a space for the ash to fall behind a polished brass shield we called a fender; this was removed each morning to shovel out the ash. The two foot square chimney allowed most of the warm air to escape, only the radiant heat came into the kitchen which with the eighteen inch walls must have been enough because I never felt cold. Winters were not so bad then perhaps, I don't remember it ever snowing or freezing in those days!

On the right of the small fire a shelf level with the red hot coals often carried a black enamel pan of stew but at all other times the ubiquitous copper kettle which maintained an unlimited stream of boiling water. At the back of the fire was a deep shelf where a shovel or two of coal was kept, this to be dragged forward as required. When it was available sea coal was supplemented here. To the right of the kettle was the brick housing of the set pot, hanging by its flanged top this pot was a metal dome dropped into the "brick box". It could heat five gallons of water filled with buckets from the tap and heated with hot coals from the fire, previously built up for the extra need, thrown into an opening under the 'pot'.

There was no drain tap; the hot water had to be bailed out with a ladle. A wooden lid normally covered the set pot, and firewood was stored on top there when not in use.

Except on Mondays, washday, the whole set pot and things stored above it was covered by a curtain hanging from a brass rail fastened under the mantle shelf.

On washday Aunt Jenny and Grandma started early, hot coals were shovelled under the set pot already filled with water. A small wooden table put out in the yard to scrub the collars and other soiled things. The poss tub! In earlier times this was a wooden barrel cut down to a convenient height but an improved model in galvanised steel with small corrugations to assist in the agitation was purchased. Soap flakes (yellow bar soap sliced thin with a knife) was added to the hot water then the soiled clothes were 'possed' with a wooden dolly, an agitator made of a wooden round post with slots and holes drilled into the bigger diameter bottom part. This instrument had a handle bar at the top, waist height to lift turn and thrust up and down onto the clothes in the tub thus to agitate the water and slosh the clothes in the lathered hot water. Handkerchiefs and white things were boiled; a 'blue bag' was put in with the white clothes. Don't ask why! It's supposed to make them whiter.

Uncle Alex disappeared after breakfast most days, but very early on Mondays! Being unemployed and "kept" for three years sadly he must have been humiliated. He had an allotment three miles away with a hut to keep his garden tools in. I went with him once or twice, it was about three miles away on the edge of the town called West View. He grew the usual veg. and a few flowers. Uncle Alex was a gentle man in every sense of the word very quiet but always seemed cheerful. In the shipyard he had operated a lathe turning steel parts to make the steam engines. I presume this by the size of the callipers he had used to measure various diameters to very accurate limits. He passed them on to me when her retired. I used to watch him shave with a 'cut throat' razor generally humming to himself the music from 'The Merry Widow' "Deliah O, Deliah"! He was a member of a Working Mens Club. A misnomer since they were nearly all unemployed. On Christmas morning he would take me to the club, not far from Middlegate when the children of members were given a treat. This was a brown paper bag with some monkey nuts, peanuts in the shells, a few boiled sweets and an apple and orange. Maybe a penny bar of chocolate if funds allowed!

By early Monday afternoon wash day was over and all dried. Dinner was a stew, the left over Sunday roast meat with added vegetables. I was glad to see order restored and the kitchen put straight. I was often given 'dripping' spread on bread with a good sprinkle of salt, this was the fat which dripped from the beef, it was delicious !

The high mantle shelf, over the fireplace, about six inches wide ran the full width of the six foot ancient hearth and was covered with a six inch drape of green velvet like cloth, with small tassels along the overhanging edge.

A hexagonal mahogany framed mirror hung above the middle of the shelf, to the right of which, the tea caddie, a tin box of black enamel with Chinese figures in medallions on each side. A pot vase held wooden spills, used to light the single gas mantle from the fire. This was the only source of light except for the fire.

Granny would read the newspaper laid open on the square table with its chenille cloth, her mouth moving as she quietly read each word, she told me her parents paid sixpence a week for her schooling, her father Thomas Lawson Scott, the wood carver a good craftsman and artist I like to think, but granny never talked about him. She did sing a nice little song she had learnt as a child. I remember it still.

"Won't you come over to my house, won't you come over and play, I've got a dolly a play thing or two, won't you come over the way, I'll give you sweeties and candy, I'll put your hair in a curl, won't you come over to my house, and pretend that you're my little girl". That simple melody goes back to about 1870 when my granny was a little girl and life was innocent from childhood to old age. You'd be suspected of being a paedophile if you sang that to a child today!

Back to the mantle shelf, there was a little brown teapot, never used for making tea. Aunt Jennie would take a few pence from it on a Saturday night when the cobbler's shop closed, usually about nine o' clock, to take me across the road to Billy Robinsons' fruit and sweet shop. We would gaze at the abundant display of sweets and decide what to buy this week! One or two widows made boiled sweets and toffee apples in their kitchens and sold them on a table or shelf in their kitchen windows. Health and Safety had not been invented then, yet I never heard of anyone being unwell from food poisoning! Mothers trained their daughters to manage a household however poor they were, perhaps all the more reason to make the pittance go further.

Next door to Granny's shop and joined to the property by a room over the ancient carriage way was a bit of a pretentious building, ornamental timbered, it had been the public library. This library was moved to a much bigger building far along Northgate paid for from a bequest by a wealthy Scottish Mr Carnegie who made his money in steel in America and left it to provide libraries to many British towns. The old library was of later vintage to No 14 and adjacent to the General Post Office and Sorting Office separated by a Chare (a passage about six feet wide leading to the High Street). The Library was taken over by Mr Pinder for a Draper's shop and later by Mr Robson as a chemist shop. That too was demolished by a crazy council who seemed determined to destroy the Ancient Borough of Hartlepool.

Just fancy in 1938 they destroyed the ancient High Street to put gardens in its place. Why gardens when there was a Town Moor, wonderful promenade and beaches with a view over the glorious Tees bay? This destroyed the ancient town, the folk of the demolished properties were all re-housed miles away which then destroyed the small shops, pubs etc, The town needed houses and people, planning gone mad!

Aunt Jenny was one of six children, not unusual in those days, three boys, Willie, Arthur and Alexander, and three girls, Jennie, Jessie and Lily.

Jessie, my Mum married my father when she was 21 years old. I worked out many years later she was pregnant with my eldest brother, it was common enough in those days but they seem to have always married. My father Fred had been called up into the Royal Navy. Jessie visited him in Chatham, he was on battleships and took photographs of the several big ships at Scapa Floe when he was there during the first Great war in the Royal Navy as an engine room artificer, a marine engineer.

Mum said he had worked in a hatters and hosiery shop, however he was very capable mechanically and obviously intelligent being able to print his own photographs and maintain his motorcycles, not easy in those days. Jessie and Fred had a happy courtship, they used to go to the countryside on Fred's Indian motor bike, not many about in those days. Mum told me he played the cello whilst she played the piano. He told me one day as we sat reminiscing, she didn't play very well. He was still annoyed with her! She must have had other good points because Jessie to his surprise had fallen pregnant but as I said it wasn't unusual in those days either!

It was obvious she still thought a lot about him, probably still loved him but wasn't prepared to continue living with his parents while he wanted to live the life of a playboy. With me only a few weeks old we went to live with her mother, my Granny Wright. Many years later in his last years when we were reconciled, he told me that he was on duty aboard ship, I think he said it was the battleship 'HMS Orion' when a boiler furnace, crown, came down! This very dangerous damage happens if the water in the boiler becomes lower than the circular furnace which went through the boiler, the heat then softens the steel furnace and the pressure of steam inside the boiler forces the top of the furnace to buckle down onto the fire. "They blamed me!" he said in his tired old voice. It suggests that the duty engineer failed to check the boiler water sight glasses, a routine each watch. The gauge can give a false reading. Not like him to neglect his duty at that time but he would be responsible.

His father, my Grandfather George Simon, he didn't like the Simon! He was in Australia when the war started in 1914, he had sold his milk round and left his wife to look after their general shop in West Hartlepool. They must have been pretty well off, because young Fred had expensive things like a quarter plate camera, and an Indian motor cycle which were wealthy toys in those days!

Things didn't go well for Granddad in Australia, he had bought cattle to put on the land and as the story goes, flash floods came and he lost everything! He took to the bush. He told me he used to light his pipe with a magnifying glass and the sun. He couldn't have smoked at night then! He probably had a camp fire!

He would be doing odd jobs as a horse doctor or any work that would feed himself and buy the tobacco for his pipe. With little hope of getting back to the UK in 1914 at the outbreak of the First World War he joined the 10th Australian Light Horse regiment. To qualify for the regiment a man had to mount a horse without a saddle and go over several jumps. No problem for my Grandad Dinsdale. He had worked in stables since he was ten years old.

The Regiment was shipped to Egypt and then in 1915 to create a second front landed at Gallipoli to invade Turkey. He was wounded with shrapnel near a kidney on night patrol by a Turkish shell splinter. He was taken back to Australia and recovered from his wound. Although discharged, he joined up again and fought on the western front in France until the end of the war. He then asked to be discharged in the UK. That was one way to get a passage home!

I have a letter he wrote to my Mum in March 1918. In copying ink pencil he describes the lack of sleep in the trenches when the guns were firing and how pleased he was that his son was in the Royal Navy where he would have a place to sleep at night.

His letter shows great affection for Jessie his daughter in law. I don't think he would have approved of his son's ill treatment of her. How difficult it must have been to communicate with his wife Ada when he was in Australia. It took a ship six weeks to steam to the UK and ships didn't leave every day. It may have been possible to send a telegram by then, but very costly.

This was my grandfather George Simon Dinsdale. I saw him regularly when I was old enough to go alone to visit the family on a Saturday. I pedalled on my fairy bike from our house 68 Granville Road to Stockton, about eight miles?

George was a good man with horses and had started work in a livery stable at the age of ten, when he decided he'd had enough of school, he must have been a good scholar because by the age of seventeen he was put in charge of the, entire, the name given to a stallion. His duties were to take the stallion round to the various big houses and other stables to, serve, the mares. This would entail keeping a book entering the dates of the serve and collecting the fee, a responsible job for a young man.

After the war he got a job with Ashmore, Benson and Pease a famous Company of Stockton in those days, his job was Ostler, to look after the carriage horses for the director's stable's.

In December 1914 after the bombardment by German battleships when 500 houses were damaged by the shelling, Granny Dinsdale sold the shop in Derwent Street, West Hartlepool. She moved inland to Stockton and bought a nice house with a garden No 11, Austin Avenue, Hartburn , a suburb of Stockton.

In 1916 Granddad George as I have said although wounded and discharged from Gallipoli and sent back to Australia, recuperated and joined up again. At this time he would be with the Aussies in France, communication would be easier. He may have had leave to visit her, there are photographs of the family with the men in uniform. Jessie lived with her mother in law at Austin Avenue, Eric, the eldest son is shown in a photograph of the four generations. Eric is about two years old with his Great Grandfather and namesake, Francis Eric, who had been a groom and coach driver at Theakston Hall. Also in the photograph is Grandfather George, and Father Fred. After the 1914 – 1918 war, motor vehicles were becoming more popular, now the directors of Ashmore Benson & Pease decided to invest in one, probably more economic than the horses. They asked Grandad if he knew anyone who could help them and Grandad said, yes my son knows about motors, Fred had had motor bikes since he was about seventeen and was now returned home from the Royal Navy.

The Directors asked Fred to go to the Midlands car factory, purchase the car and drive it back on roads that had not changed much since the stagecoach days. Since no one knew how to start the thing, or drive it, Fred my father was offered the job of chauffeur. He taught granddad to drive, and this was the beginning of the business, including a taxi service for a while, then car repairs and eventually the distributorship for Rover cars. He had the franchise for South Durham and North Yorkshire. This business was developed from houses in Yarm Lane, Stockton. They were big houses and the family moved from Austin Avenue to live there when one became vacant. The house next door was eventually used for the business, selling Rudge Whitworth motor cycles as well as Rover cars.

In the early days, before petrol pumps Fred had a shed, to store two gallon cans of 'Pratts petrol', he had put the shed by a beck in what was probably council land. The council objected and said it was obstructing the path or something like that so my Mum told me. Fred then put timbers into the beck and moved the shed back over the beck to comply with the order! My mother told me in the early years of motor cars people would sometimes call at the house late at night to buy petrol, I assume when they lived near the shed in Austin Avenue. They most likely had a few cans of 'Pratts petrol' in the back garden for just such an occasion. Fred and Jessie had lived en family with his mother and father until I was born. The business was thriving, Jessie wanted a home of her own but Fred was becoming a play boy. Jessie took me a baby and left, to return to live at Hartlepool at the Wright family home. There was a legal separation, Jessie was granted £1:10 shillings for herself and 10 shillings for me. £2 per week was a good sum in 1926, it was a tradesman's wage.

It wasn't long before Jessie who had an eye for business found the means to help her family, as indeed she had helped Fred before the kids arrived.

Alexander Wright had died tragically by his own hand about 1924 as a result of his brother Peter embezzling the accounts of the shoe shops, leaving his wife to run off to Australia with some woman. I'm not so sure about this, it's more probable a result of the breakdown of my mum's marriage. Jessie had been the apple of her father's eye; it wouldn't help in any case. The shame of this probably accounted for Granny very rarely leaving the house. Uncle Arthur who had been in the Royal navy until 1918 now worked in the shop repairing shoes and supported his mother, my Granny. He was married and lived across the road in Middlegate St. above an empty shop.

Jessie now rented the shop and had a local joiner fit it out with shelves and a counter. She then went to 'Leng's where they had an account for the business to buy leather to repair the shoes. 'Leng's' was a wholesaler of Stockton, she ordered a stock of good quality Portland shoes for her shoe shop. The business thrived but had to be in her brother's name because the law at that time gave wives no rights and Fred could have claimed the lot. This was in 1925, women, did not have the vote until 1928.

Problems eventually arose when I was about six years old, Arthur's wife Lily, a good person, very kind to me but not well versed in business, got into the habit of taking money from Jessie's till, just to buy a few things as she would say. This would upset Jessie's book keeping, I imagine she would have had an arrangement with Arthur for her to take a wage for running the business, but the business was in Arthur's name. There was little she could do but she decided she would not put up with accounts she had no way of controlling. I wasn't aware of any argument about this Uncle Arthur was obviously unable to persuade his wife to leave the shop business till alone. The outcome was Mam and I left Hartlepool very near Christmas 1930 to stay with her sister Lily and her husband Uncle Richard Metcalf in Middlesbrough. I remember it as an unhappy time. We couldn't stay there long, within a couple of weeks Mum had found two rooms with a good family called Johnson.

# CHAPTER 6
# MOVING TO MIDDLESBROUGH, HOMELESS!
*Moving to Middlesbrough, living in two rented rooms and*
*An introduction to the mystery of the Spirit world.*

I didn't know why we had moved from Hartlepool, I wasn't told, so didn't realise the serious homeless situation we were in. Mum had taken refuge with Aunt Lilly until she could find somewhere else to live.

Uncle Richard had been training to be an architect At nineteen he was called up into the army. He was badly wounded in France during the 1914 war and had his right arm amputated from the shoulder and other serious wounds but slowly recovered. His mother and father had been taken over to France to see him in hospital, it was that bad. Eventually he was able to work and finally became Head of Pensions in Newcastle. He had a peculiar problem with meals, and would only use his own personal knife, fork and spoons to the extent that my Aunt had to take them out with her if they were to visit friends or relations. He didn't mind me watching him shave and he showed me how he was able to fix things to the washbasin to overcome the disability of only having one arm. It wasn't desirable for us to stay too long with Aunt Lily and Uncle Richard. "Tricky Dickie" as you might say! I don't think he liked little boys, probably due to his serious wartime injuries. It must have been difficult to adjust his whole life from what he had expected to do. They were recently married and wouldn't want us living with them. Somehow mum found a married couple who wanted to let two rooms in Granville Road and we lived there for many months until an opportunity to rent a house came along.

Up to the age of fourteen I occasionally went with mum to Mrs Scrafton's little Spiritual church. It was in a room above a shop in Southfield Lane off Linthorpe Road, Middlesbrough. I was asked to give the hymn books out. The service consisted of a couple of the good old hymns, What a friend we have in Jesus, Rock of ages, and the like. After an opening hymn there would be a lesson from the New Testament and then another hymn. Mrs Scraften, a plump 'motherly type', would give an uplifting address then pray for a few minutes, then just standing quietly, eyes closed, hands clasped as she meditated and then gave three or four "messages" that the recipient seemed to understand and accept. It was uncanny. There was nothing "funny" going on, the room was fully lit, Mrs Scrafton just spoke quietly in her own voice. There was a remarkable message my mum received early in our living in Middlesbrough. Mrs Scrafton could not have known anything at all about us. During her meditation, eyes closed, hands clasped together she said, "I've got a gentleman here and I can smell gas. Does anyone know a gentleman who had anything to do with gas"? Now coal gas had a definite smell no mistaking it. My mum raised her hand, my grandfather her Da' as she called him had gassed himself during the family problems with his brother's embezzlement and mum's separation. Well said Mrs Scrafton, "he's showing me a golden key and you've got to take it". As we walked home mum said she didn't know what it meant. It was a mystery. Two weeks later a friendly neighbour Mrs Wade at number 68 had said to my mum, "Jessie! We are buying a house". Her husband was a Customs Officer never to be unemployed. She said "If you take this key for 68 to the housing agent he will let you carry on paying the rent for the house when we move". The key wasn't golden but it was bronze!

Mum was able to afford the rent of £1 per week. A married school friend and her husband, Jim Pilcher, who lived in Middlesbrough, helped her to move, carrying our bits and bobs the short distance from 58 to 68. We had a large kitchen table Mum had designed with cupboards she had paid a joiner to make. Good storage to suit our circumstances. The houses in Granville Road are in the form of a long terrace with small front gardens about fifteen feet by twenty. A panelled front door with a second door half panelled the top half of decorated glass, opened on to a short passage with two doors to the two rooms downstairs. The staircase led up to the back bedroom which was passed through to a bathroom. From the small landing three stairs led up to the other two bedrooms, the front bedroom having two flat windows above the downstairs bay window. They were warm houses. However the outside toilet was down a narrow yard some twenty feet from the back door. It froze up every winter despite mum's efforts with a small oil lamp and attempts at insulation. We had many hard frosts in the 1930's and 1940's. Mum used to swill and scrub this yard with copious buckets of water and a stiff broom regularly until her later years. She was a hard worker. Windows were cleaned with hot water and a splash of vinegar. The windows were of the 'sash' type. The top frame could be pulled down and the bottom frame could be pushed up. Counter weights in the outer frames with ropes attached to the window frames were intended to make this easy but several of the ropes were rotten. The agent was loath to have them repaired and the many coats of paint over the years caused the windows to jamb. Despite this it was home and mum was fairly content.

Jessie now had her own place and with money she had earned as wages from the shoe shop she set about furnishing it. I shared her pleasure with each piece. We bought a little sideboard, a three piece suite and a wind up gramophone. We went to Woolworths and bought records at sixpence each. Gracie Fields was a favourite. The most important item was of course the piano, which was second hand, as were most of the things. It was a happy home for me until I was twenty three and left to go to sea.

When mum had to give her home up at sixty seven years of age I arranged a buyer of household goods to come in. This woman went around the house with me and priced everything. The whole of the effects raise only twelve pounds ten shillings! Her son and another chap carried everything out to their lorry. It was a very sad day.

The beginning had been a wonderful time! A whole house with three bedrooms was a vast improvement to the two rooms we had rented from the Johnston family where mum would ask me to play quietly so as not to disturb Mr Johnston.

Mr Johnson was a recruiting Sergeant in the Army. He was well built, fair with a ginger moustache and round rosy face, a pleasant man but rather intimidating. We had rented the front room and the back bedroom. Mum would have had to share the kitchen stove with Mrs Johnston. What a crime to have to live like that after having five children to a man because he wouldn't provide my mum with a home of her own.

One night in the early hours of the morning when I was seven years old,1931, there was a slight earthquake! I woke to feel the room vibrating and things rattling on the chest of drawers. It was quite scary for a few seconds.

During this time my mum hadn't been feeling too well, the doctor had been and called it the 'change of life' and collected his fee one Guinea (£1/1/- ) That was half my mum's weekly income! A day or two later mum collapsed heavily from a dining chair to the floor whilst we were having a meal. I screamed and Mrs Johnston came running in. She was a very nice person with two daughters, Eileen and the youngest, four year old, Dorothy. Mum became good friends with their eldest daughter and later when we were living at no 68, Eileen at nineteen would bring her boyfriend along and Mum would play the piano and amuse them for an hour or so. It was very sad when Eileen died shortly afterwards, I don't know what of. In those days a lot of young people died of mysterious diseases. As there was no telephone in any of the houses when mum collapsed someone must have gone out to call an ambulance. This took mum first to the Carter Bequest Hospital, where the doctors discovered that she had typhoid fever, a contagious disease contracted from open drains. Mum later said that she had passed a smelly drain where men were digging up the road. This put the medical top brass in a tizzy! Carter Bequest Hospital had to be fumigated! It was the first case of typhoid for fourteen years and mum was moved to West Lane Hospital which was then a fever hospital.

Aunt Jenny was told of my predicament, I don't know how, maybe by telegraph. She came over to Middlesbrough and took me to stay again at Hartlepool. I'm glad they didn't take me to Aunt Lily's house. Uncle Richard was a bit highly strung. He once lifted me up by the hair when I supposedly misbehaved at the table. I can't remember what I had done but my Uncle Alex wouldn't have done that. He would have teased me and made me laugh. I don't remember going to school at Hartlepool on this occasion, it would be near the summer holidays. After some weeks when my mum had recovered and was convalescing Aunt Jenny took me by bus to visit her but I was only allowed to see her from standing in the hospital grounds and through a closed window. I remember it was a very high window but mum looked very happy now she was recovered and later told me how good the nurses had been to her. One nurse became a close friend and visited us when we had moved into No 68.

I had probably missed a few weeks of school in Middlesbrough while my mum was ill. I was enrolled at Victoria Road Infants School. According to Chief Librarian Wm. Lillie's History of Middlesbrough these were the first two schools built by the Middlesbrough Council in 1862. At that time this area of Middlesbrough would have been a very busy building site of open fields being covered with rows of terraced houses. Granville Road houses on each side of the road had two poplar trees in the small front garden. This was not a good idea for such small gardens. When we arrived many of the houses, owned by landlords, had the trees removed but privately owned houses were reluctant to do this until the trees became a nuisance. The road surface was not made up either. Slag from the steel works was cheap and plentiful and broken into inch diameter lumps which were packed tight with fine slag dust to make an unsatisfactory surface. The housewives complained that crossing the road ruined their shoes. It didn't do bicycle tyres any good either! I am not sure but it was near to 1938 before a tar macadam surface was put down on top of the slag. That was nearly eighty years after the houses were built.

I had enrolled in the infant school in Middlesbrough in January 1931 at six years old. I don't remember being there long before being moved to the integral Junior school. I had learned to read in the short time I had been at the little Prissick infant school in Hartlepool. They used small cards with a letter of the alphabet on each then once you came to recognise the sound of each letter it was fairly easy to spell out the word, "CAT, MAN, DOG"! I can't understand why for the last years of the twentieth century education freaks thought they knew better and kids were expected to recognise the whole word! The experts who decided this should be prosecuted for sabotage!

Victoria Road School was only two streets away from our house in Granville Road. I was able to run there to the playground for lining up to march into our classes at nine o clock. Skip home for my dinner at noon, run back to start lessons again at one o clock and run home after school at four! That's how I remember it, I ran everywhere!

I didn't pass the eleven plus examination to go to the local grammar school, Middlesbrough High School or the Technical Hugh Bell School. I felt badly about it at the time. I think some of the boys with dads had been given extra tuition. Thinking about it now it was probably fortunate I wasn't so clever as not all the grammar school boys did well. Some ended up as managers of a multiple store having to keep the accountants happy by doing 10% more business than the previous year, and some gave me the impression that after the High School education they didn't need to do any more.

After failing the eleven plus at the Elementary school we were taught that you never give up learning! We were told we had to find the information required to do the job in hand. I did a lot of reading, history books I loved. Comics were very enjoyable although limited to a certain extent by lack of pocket money. I probably bought two a week. 'Chips' was an early one with a story of two broken down toff tramps on the front cover. They got into all sorts of scrapes but always came up smiling. Other comics for older boys were the 'Adventure', the name of which says it all, and 'Hotspur' with a story every week about a football star. I think they were educational in that they connected the script with the illustrations and demanded interpretation.

Education never stops! This belief carried me through a variety of occupations. I had an interesting apprenticeship building magnificent marine triple expansion steam engines and being in charge of them at sea. How about that Fred Dibner? Then, I worked with the mighty marine diesel engine. The Doxford two stroke engine silent except for a slight whisper of the pistons, designed and built in Sunderland.

When I married and left the sea I found myself in a new world of technology I was offered the opportunity to train in automatic instrumentation for the Chemical Industry. Always in a 'hands on' position where often I had to sort out the problem the designer had hoped he had coped with but didn't work in practice. I don't think a grammar school would have inspired me to have the concentration necessary in this field. When I in turn had an apprentice to train in the practical side of instrumentation I would give him a few days then if he wasn't being curious ask him why if he wants to learn he wasn't asking any questions. Use the words "why, how, and what if"?

The Grammar Schools taught classics and languages. I would have liked to study them but I wasn't ready for such things. At sea I had time and inclination to study languages. With a Norwegian crew I had plenty of unqualified help. When I signed on to a Greek oil tanker I learnt the alphabet and a few useful words from my fellow officers most of whom spoke excellent English. So much so that a few years later I took formal lessons in Greek from Mrs. Lula McNicholas a Greek lady in Middlesbrough who had married a British soldier in Alexandria and was qualified to teach, Greek, English and French. It made holidays much more interesting being able to speak a little of the language.

The last few years at the elementary school I was now a bigger fish in a smaller pool if that makes sense. I had gone up in the class. It was some consolation and after failing the eleven plus I soon recovered my self-esteem. Of course there are always some who are not versatile, dull people, there always will be, but today it is sad to see intelligent young men filling shelves in the supermarkets. There isn't room to make them all managers.

In the school sports of June 1939 I won the hundred yards race and apart from not being able to afford the vest and running shorts I was looking forward to racing for the school in the town sports. Alas, with the imminent war all large meetings of people were declared unsafe. It was a good job I was used to disappointments.

Mum liked people and people liked her. A school friend, Rose had married Jim Picher, he had flown in the pre RAF "Flying Corps" I think he was a pilot. He certainly flew! He worked in the unemployment office and in his spare time had got a few of the unemployed chaps who could play a musical instrument together and formed a band. They played at small dances in church halls. This would supplement their unemployment benefit. I don't suppose it would have to be declared since it wasn't a regular source of income.

Jessie, that's what they affectionately called her, would have Rose and Jim around to our house, number 68, to have supper and a musical evening. Jim so it seemed could play any instrument, the acoustic guitar, then he got the latest thing the "slide" guitar when Hawaiian music was all the rage. He had a go with the banjo and played the piano accordion. They sometimes came with one or two other members of their little band to practice one or two numbers for the dances. They were good friends for many years. Rose went blind in later life and Jessie would take her out for the day. This gave Jim a bit of support until Jim's job moved them to Northallerton. We did go to see them once or twice but when the war came along we gradually lost touch.

One thing I do regret is not being able to play an instrument although I could knock a tune out on a penny whistle and the mouth organ. I'm only eighty five now so there's time yet! Mum gave me some tuition on the piano and I learnt to read music. I practiced the scales but when it came to reading for both hands I couldn't take it in at that time. It didn't seem important enough in my life to make such an effort. Starting work at fourteen I came home tired. Then as an apprentice there were important lessons three evenings a week at night school for engineering.

Mum and I often went to the Empire Theatre in Middlesbrough where live weekly variety shows were on stage. Marie Lloyd was top of the bill one week. She was supposed to be a star and dressed in magnificent gowns and a big hat. She sang the popular songs of the day or maybe they were beginning to be yesterday's songs when we went to see her. I wasn't that impressed but there was always a good comedian or other acts to suit all tastes.

We must have been living at Hartlepool when my mum brought me over to Middlesbrough to see a stage showing of Peter Pan at the very impressive Opera House. The book was written by my Grandfather's cousin Sir James Barrie. My Grandfather's mother was the sister of James Barrie's father. Barrie was now mixing with Royalty and would have nothing to do with his relations. Sadly he had no children of his own but seemed to like kids and was very charitable. Well it gave him a knighthood. He helped Captain Scott of the Antarctic's son and left his copyright to Great Ormand Street Hospital for children. What a pity he couldn't help little me.

At four or five years old I enjoyed the Peter Pan live show. I remember it very well. We were in the Upper Circle seats looking down on to the stage which gave reality to Peter Pan, Wendy and the children flying when they went to Never Never land. They were in harnesses of course but the effect was convincing. The fairy Tinkerbell flitted about, on a wire I suppose, illuminated

*Margaret Ann Wright, (nee Scott). At the 'Holiday Hut!' Crimdon Dene in 1937*

with a spot light, again an incredible illusion. I do remember the crocodile who's presence was brought alive with the ticking of the clock it had swallowed. The Pirate Captain Hook did not feature much to me but I do remember he didn't frighten me!

We travelled from Hartlepool by Blumer's Bus to Port Clarence and then over the Transporter Bridge and caught a tram from the Middlesbrough side of the Transporter to the town centre.

The Opera House was a magnificent building and closed in June 1930. It had a large stalls area, a circle, an upper circle and a third circle. When I was older I used to pay eight pence to go up in the 'gods' as we called it when it opened as 'The Gaumont Palace' cinema. This was in the thirties and the forties. The building was eventually demolished when television made it uneconomical to run. A magnificent theatre and a great loss to Middlesbrough.

# CHAPTER 7
## SCHOOLDAYS TO 1938 MY FIRST JOB

Victoria Road Elementary School, A temp Telegraph boy, leaving school, my first real job as a lab boy at Middlesbrough Borough Analysts.

On a winter's evening in our early years living at number sixty eight Granville Road, when we arrived home after dark, we had no electric light in the house. I generally had a small battery torch to see our way into the house and mum would light the gas mantle. The gas light was suspended from the ceiling with a slim brass pipe. The gas tap was at the top and was opened by turning a lever, pulling on two fine chains at each end. It was rather tricky to do because a match had to be struck and put near to the gas mantle to start the gas burning. If you touched the delicate impregnated cotton mantle with the match, it would disintegrate and a new one had to be fitted. The landlord wouldn't pay for electricity to be put in the house but mum with her careful house keeping managed to pay for it.

We did once or twice spend an evening at The Winter Gardens in the town. I can't remember much about it but we sat at tables and could have refreshments. There was some entertainment but it can't have been memorable. The cinema would see it off as nothing lasts for ever.

From a previous visit to see Mrs Scrafton, I had forgotten about her mentioning seeing my name in gold letters. However when I was sixty four years old I was installed in the Chair of King Solomon at my lodge. I wished my mum could know the honour that had been bestowed on me. When the ceremony ended I was accompanied into the dining room by the Director of Ceremonies. and was sat in the Master's chair at the top table. I turned to the honours board where all the names of the past masters were inscribed. There fifty years after Mrs Scrafton had foreseen it, my name was inscribed in gold letters! "Arthur Dinsdale, Master 1988". It's funny but I hadn't actually thought of it being on the board. I had reason to believe that mum's spirit was there and she was well pleased.

Dorothy too had a similar experience. Whilst I was whaling in the Antarctic and communication was practically nil, mum invited her to stay with her for a couple of weekends. Dorothy was living with her mother who had recently married again. Dorothy's mum was a kindly trusting woman and had made a big mistake in this second marriage. Dorothy's father had died six years before and this 'gentleman' who had worked with her husband and was considered a friend had changed his ways. He had said, "you sell your house Sally and we'll buy a new car. I'll sell my house and buy a more modern house". But the car was driven by him and the more modern house was in his name only. Now his personality changed. His wife had died three years earlier; now he had his 24/7 housekeeper. He neglected to remember her birthday and showed no consideration for her. She had given up a good lifestyle playing bowls every week with her friends. He had no interests like that at all. Dorothy's mum wasn't happy so Dorothy would not be happy either.

Dorothy often worked late in the Hartlepool Bakery Office and subsequently could take other afternoons off early. She took the bus from Hartlepool to Middlesbrough one Friday to stay with my mum. I think she would confide in my mum her anxiety with no word from me to either of them. Dorothy's diary for 1948 shows she was writing to me nearly every night but only a few letters arrived at South Georgia Island. There were only two or three ships calling during the whaling season and sending a cable was very expensive. Mum said, "let's go to Mrs Scrafton's little Spiritual Church". After her meditation Mrs Scraften with her eyes closed said "I've got a gentleman here and he's doing this" raising her left arm and passing her right hand with the fingers pointing down the left forearm, "and I don't know what it

70

means. Does anyone know a gentleman who did this?" Dorothy raised her hand in acknowledgement.

Dorothy's father was the design engineer in the shipyard. He was brought up in his father's pub The Duke of York in Grindleton, West Yorkshire and went to Clitheroe Grammar School where he won prizes for latin and other subjects. He studied engineering at college and came to work at Hartlepool where his grandfather Ben Wright had an engineering boiler maintenance business. He became the design engineer and chief draughtsman in the shipyard. His health was poor and he had operations, considered serious at the time and was given seven years to live. He was stoic and never complained but their savings were all spent on his operations.

Now as to why Dorothy put her hand up as knowing this action with the hands. When her father came home from work he would take his good jacket off and put on an old smoking jacket. He was a heavy smoker of Gold Flake cigarettes. He removed the handkerchief from his left sleeve and stuffed it with his fingers into the sleeve of the other jacket to replace it on his person. Mrs Scrafton, passed his message to Dorothy, "he just wants to say that you must not worry, everything will be all right" We were to be married when I returned from the whaling season in May 1948.

In 1941 Dorothy's father died. He had a very good obituary in the local paper stating what a well respected man he had been in the community and the Parish Church. I am pretty sure there is a spirit world but it is a mystery we can never know. Some animals have what we call a sixth sense, cats particularly. In my newspaper today a cat in a nursing home goes to sit with old people hours before they die. It has even gone to a patient who died before the doctors thought she would die. What can you make of that? I am an animal lover in spite of the fact I was on a whale catcher killing whales but Man has to be fed and it must be done in a professional manner even with some risk to the ship and crew. An injured whale can jump out of the sea like a salmon and land on deck to sink the ship.

I had mixed with one or two kids from school who lived near Granville Road and I attended the Parish church, St. Aiden's with them. We did the 'Stations of the Cross' with the young vicar. I joined the cub scouts at the church, which was a wooden structure then on a prime piece of land fronting onto the main road, Linthorpe Road. We met in the church hall. It wasn't very inspiring after my days with the

71

fishermen on the sands at Hartlepool but it was all that was going on.
The scout camp came along, but it cost seven shillings and sixpence. I knew Mum was short of money, and had other priorities, so I dropped out. Hartlepool was a better venue for adventure.

I wasn't academic at school, fairly good at art, but there was no route from a secondary school to a job in art. I may have found the way with parents who were able to guide my education, but it didn't seem to be so important in those days. I always had a feeling that I didn't belong in this environment . I expected to learn a trade. In 1937 my mum had put my name down to be a marine engineer in the shipyard. My mum wouldn't know that some apprenticeships were passed down from father to son or even from uncles in the family. Human nature again, even plants do it.

In the 1930's kids would ask "What does your father do?" Most of their dads were on the dole. It was always a source of embarrassment that I had a father but I didn't have one! They wouldn't believe me if I told them what he did, driving around in posh cars and riding to the hunt. They would think I was telling lies!

I wasn't deprived but something was lacking. However it was better than living in a household of rows and violence. I attended Victoria Road Senior School, built in 1862. Mr Johnston was the headmaster. I wasn't even average, about twenty third for academic things like arithmetic, but I enjoyed history and even english. I didn't find the apostrophe a problem as some people do today, how could we do without it?

Mr Jackson was the young art teacher. He was a well built chap and seemed more human than the other teachers when we saw him coming to school on his racing bike. He explained perspective and demonstrated it on the blackboard. He demonstrated shading and how it is used to give depth to a drawing. I discovered I had a hand and eye co-ordination and when we were told to illustrate some scene I was getting good marks, eight or nine out of ten. I don't think he ever gave ten but I was satisfied with nine.

The teachers were all characters, strict but kind. At Christmas each teacher was able to hand out many freebies gleaned from food companies. We all went home with a bag full, a model glider made from balsa wood, which was propelled into the air with an elastic band, model houses to cut out and stick together. These items all had advertising logos printed on them, I remember 'Shredded Wheat' was one!

'Pop Hornsby', the english teacher, was plump with a rosy face to match, blue eyes and a pink bald head with a ring of thin snow white hair from ear to ear. Cigarette ash dusted his grey three piece suit which reeked of tobacco smoke. He was the one who gave me the stick, for nothing! It was a shock and really hurt! Fingers black and blue across the palm of the hand. Punished for not concentrating I think. I was a bit of a dreamer? Selective in what I wanted to learn I would say! I was in the wrong place at the wrong time, I liked Pop and my feelings were hurt more than anything, I had to have the stick because my pals were up for it! Or Pop was having a bad day at the races! I was probably carrying on with the boy behind me. It made me pay attention anyway! I was punished with the stick only once and I soon got over it. Some of the lads got the stick nearly every week!

Pop took us through 'The Merchant of Venice', the boys taking it in turns to read out the lines, and poetry too. I can still remember the odd line," I will arise and go now, and go to Inisfree, and a small cottage build there, of clay and wattles made". Another favourite was "my name is Ozymandious King of Kings, look on my works ye mighty and despair!" We were expected to remember the lines. In our last weeks at school at the age of fourteen, Pop decided to prepare us for the real world and he said " no more English, boys, I'm going to teach you about engines!" He relished this lesson and he got my best attention. He taught us about the steam engine with eccentric sheaves that operated the valves and moving parts , then the internal combustion engines, two stroke and four stroke , the diesel engine, the suction, induction ,compression and exhaust. That was interesting! Reciprocating engines! I'd forgiven him!

Mr Makereth, the maths teacher, didn't need to use the stick. He had a sergeant major's waxed moustache and voice! He could bark! This induced immediate attention and respect, though he seemed to have a kindly twinkle in his eye! He walked with a bit of a limp, the result of a 1914-18 war wound we suspected.

It took six months before I found a job. It was decided I should stay at school in the mean time, I had a temporary job as a telegraph boy for a couple of weeks, before Christmas 1938, It was beginning to dawn on me that there was no such thing as a level playing field and I was looking up hill !

Permanent Telegraph boys with their uniforms and pill box hats held on with a chinstrap, received the 'best' telegrams to take out to the posh areas of town where they would be sure of a few pence tip, in easy reach of the office, and with a well maintained bike. The poor temps, had no uniform, just the broad leather belt with the pouch for the telegrams and a bike which seemed to have a mind of its own. These bikes were very heavy machines, painted yellow, with a plate below the crossbar bearing the GPO number. They were hard work to pedal. They'd be good for going to take sea coal from the beach!

This temporary job could have resulted in my being kept on as a regular boy but I think what scuppered me was the night I was given telegrams for three different places around Middlesbrough. The final house was in an unfinished road that no one had heard of! In my determination to succeed I eventually found this address, but it never dawned on me to take the telegram back at the first sign of trouble. It was raining and dark and to my horror the house was only half built!

When eventually I got back to the office the boss was waiting to go home. "Where've you been" he grumbled, not impressed with my story. I have never learned the lesson; all through my life I was taught to do my best. Mum used to say "keep your nose to the grindstone and you'll get on!" It only seems to pay if you work for yourself. I found out the hard way that any credit made is generally usurped by others but I could never change, always keen to please.

I think my wage for that two weeks was eight shillings and a few pence which was good to have because inflation was reducing the value of the allowance from my father .

I went back to school for a while and then got a proper job!

Mr Johnston the headmaster called me into his office and told me there was a job as a lab boy in the Borough Analysts 'Pattinson and Stead' in Queens Square, Middlesbrough. The job of lab boy entailed setting up equipment for different analysis procedures taking instruction from a well worn little red note book. The wage was eight shillings a week. It was well within my capability but being all glass equipment there was risk of breakage when assembling the different glass condensing tubes, flasks and beakers etc. They were all expensive items. When the analysis was over we had to dismantle everything, clean it and put it safely away. I was fascinated by the balance scales in glass cases that were used to measure fine powders in grams with great accuracy.

The boss, Alfred Scholes, had a habit of coming down to the lab with pipe in mouth, a test tube in one hand and a beaker in the other shouting "water boy!" Whichever one of us was in the lab, for there were two lab boys, we had to run to the 150 gallon distilled water barrel and open the tap for him to put some water into the test tube!

He was a fierce looking character in an expensive brown tweed suit with a heavy gold chain across his waistcoat, a Victorian type of man with a strong head of tweed looking hair, big moustache to match and a Roman nose. I found out later that he had been a distinguished Freemason whose name is in on the same Erimus Lodge honours board as mine .There wasn't much future in this job. Lab boys grew up to take samples from iron ore boats in the docks. I'd been to the docks and seen the job. There was iron ore dust everywhere and the ships were unloaded at all hours,- I didn't fancy it a bit!

At the age of thirteen my mother had put my name down for an apprenticeship at Smiths Dock's shipyard at South Bank. I didn't have much expectation of being selected, as jobs were handed down from father to son. This is natural in a way but hard on the youngest son of a playboy father. However, the First Sea Lord of the Admiralty came to the rescue! The shipyards were going to be busy. I got a letter from Smiths Dock, "would Arthur come and help us build ships for the war effort?" or words to that effect, dated the 13th September 1939. This was ten days after war was declared. I was flattered! I handed my notice in at the Borough Analysts. They didn't want me to leave. This was a first! However their war work was no match to building ships! I think it was a Wednesday when I presented myself at Smiths Docks along with about twenty other young hopefuls. This time not having a father didn't bother me!

My father must have tried to be paternal towards me in my early years but not very successfully. For my fifth birthday he had a model speed boat made for me, in wood with an electric motor. It was about 18 inches long. However he didn't present it to me and he never saw me sail it. It consoles me to think that he must have designed it and thought of me. When I was four years old Mum had taken me by bus to Stockton to a jetty on Boathouse Lane, by the river near to Victoria Bridge. They had arranged for him to take me out in one of his outboard speed boats. He entered races in these speedboats and had a carpenter build them on the business premises. He won thirteen silver cups that were proudly on display in a cabinet in his office. It is odd that my parents could arrange things like this ride in a speedboat of all things, yet were unable to get together again.

I was plonked in the side of the boat. It was very shallow with no seat. He set off up and down the river at full speed. Those boats could do 30 miles an hour in those days. I was scared stiff, hanging on to the side of the boat as it bounced about, yelling my head off! He didn't seem to notice, perhaps because of the roar of the outboard engine and the slapping of the hull on the water! Was he trying to tell me something? It didn't put me off going to sea later in life! I think I must have disappointed him, maybe that's why he lost interest in me? He didn't have much idea about getting along with youngsters.

I'm sure Jessie always hoped they would be together again, especially in her later years. She always said he would send for her at the end. He had done so on one occasion when he was arrested by the police, drunk and disorderly, in Thornaby and mum had gone to the police station and bailed him out! Years later my mother had tried to get her £2 weekly allowance from my father raised. It was the maximum allowed by Law. Mum had written to Mr Simon MP to ask him if the maximum allowance for wives could be raised since over the years inflation had risen a great deal. Mr Simon put a bill through parliament and it was raised. That's the kind of woman my Mam was! She got things done !

One Wednesday, mum paid a chap to take her to Glaisdale, on the North Yorkshire Moors ,where father had a country house. I went with her in the car because I'd never been further than Saltburn and a car ride was a novelty. When we got there we were about three hundred yards from the terrace of houses, if indeed it was his house? I took a photograph using an old box brownie camera. I had been given the camera by a sympathetic cousin of my mother's.

The following Saturday I cycled over to the business premises in Stockton to see my Grandad. As I walked in, one of my brothers, who had been brought up by our father's parents along with my other brothers and sister, saw me. Without speaking he went smartly into the office where the great Fred surveyed his pile. I don't think I'd taken my cycle clips off my trousers when the great man strode out and in his domineering voice said to me "what the hell was I doing at Glaisdale?" Before I could reply, as if it was any of his business, he told me to "bugger off", which says a lot about the man and his character. What a bully! He must have been using binoculars to see me. I was nowhere near his property! I was on a moor road three hundred yards or more away. I got on my bike and returned home feeling very depressed. It appeared so final! I don't think I saw my Grandad again until I was twenty one when I went to see them. Granny Dinsdale gave me a cup of tea and father, who made an appearance, gave me a white five pound note for my twenty first birthday. What a strange man? I missed the shilling pocket money Grandad had given me every week when I cycled over to see him but more than that I'd lost my only Grandad for a few years.

During the war grandad once took me in a car to a paddock where he kept large white goats for milk and I suppose meat, but I wasn't given any to take home. The war rations were very hard for two people without means to supplement their food supply. Some people caught rabbits I suppose, but we couldn't even grow a carrot!

When I was sixteen, my ten shilling a week allowance from my father had been cut off. That was typical of the man. Now I had to support myself only earning twelve and sixpence a week in the shipyard. An apprentice did not get the wage of an errand lad in those days, you were supposed to be imposing on the Firm by learning a trade, but they made sure you earned your coppers! I was sixteen when we got our first wireless radio set! When I was fourteen mum had said we could afford to buy a wireless set or an electric vacuum cleaner. It was becoming difficult for her to take the 'hookey' mats out into the yard to beat them over the line to clean them. Hookey mats were made on a frame with strips of old clothes pushed through the hessian sacking stretched onto the frame. Later "up market" mats were made using different coloured balls of wool, pushed through the hession into loops in patterns drawn on the hessian material. The loops were then fixed with glue on the back of the mat, and the loops cut to, make a pile.

Coal fires made a lot of dust and dirt! Mats required frequent cleaning. With the old adage "what you never have you never miss" I decided mum was more important than a wireless set. Two years later Lily Redman, nee Wardell, a cousin to my mum and Lily's husband Fred, called at our house one afternoon and gave us their old wireless set. There was nothing wrong with it! They said it was because they had bought themselves a new one. It was a nice way to disguise their charity. This Fred was a freemason, as was my father also named Fred but the latter had no charity for his own family, poor rich man! I once met a chap who told me what a "grand chap" my father was. He told me he had seen him put a five pound note on the bar and say "drinks all round." This was when five pound notes were white and more than a weeks wage for the working man. I thought to myself, "tell me about this chap as I don't seem to recognize him." There was an antenna (aerial) in the house from the previous tenant and when the wireless was plugged in and switched on Churchill's voice was making his famous 1940 speech, "we will fight them on the beaches, in the streets, and in the hills, we will never surrender!" That gave us all hope!

We certainly lived in interesting times. The Chinese wish "interesting" times on their enemies, I've had my full share! The old wireless radio served us for many years. At last I was able to set the time for our erratic alarm clock that often was twenty minutes out one way or the other in a day. I had taken the back off it and tried cleaning the works but I could see that the spindles were worn in the brass frame. Mum wouldn't or couldn't afford to buy a new one. She probably thought that as long as it told the time accuracy wasn't that important. I was always worried that I would be late for work and had previously relied on the works buzzer. This was not always easy with an adverse wind. The wireless never replaced Mum's music on the piano. Without prejudice I thought she played very well. Obviously she had had plenty of practice by then! Fred should have given her more time! He missed the best years of her life the silly man. In my later years I felt sorry for him, he sowed the seeds of a miserable old age.

# CHAPTER 8
# 1939 WORLD WAR 2 THE SHIPYARD

A War Time Apprenticeship. September 3rd 1939. Growing up quickly, coping with the black out, bombing, and rationing

I was in Albert Park, Middlesbrough when the sirens sounded that first day of the war. The date was Sunday 3rd. September 1939. A group of us all about the same age, fifteen year olds, had made friends and met regularly in the park on the big green opposite the tennis courts.

We were from all areas of Middlesbrough. Three of us came from the West Lane area, the others came from Grove Hill. About seven of us in total, sometimes more, both boys and girls. We had passed many happy hours that summer doing nothing in particular. Chatting, gossiping, larking about! None of us had any money. But on that 3rd September Sunday morning the wail of the air raid siren at eleven o clock stopped us in our tracks. We stood like rabbits in front of a stoat, expecting bombs to drop at any minute as we had seen of Poland on the news reels at the cinema. "What shall we do?" was voiced by one of the boys. .There was no sound of aeroplanes, it was such a beautiful sunny day. It seemed unreal. One of the girls said quietly "we'd better go home" There was no panic, and we all agreed that we had better go home, our parents would be worried for us. Casually as we had done many times before, we wandered away in the direction of our homes, saying "bye!" to one, turning, to repeat it to another, until our voices faded in the distance. I have never seen any of those fleeting friends again since that day. Nothing war-like happened for weeks, but I never ventured into the park again.

I lost my Middlesbrough friends but I still managed to maintain my Hartlepool friends of long standing. A very good friend was Alan Martin. We were friends from being five years old until he was called up into the army at eighteen. His mother was a lovely person and the family were very kind to me. I was impressed with their family life. It was something I recognised as missing in my life, in my brothers and my sister too I suppose.

Alan's father Joe was a lovely man and a rugby football referee. He would take Alan and me to a rugby match he was to referee at the 'Friarage' field in Hartlepool. This area had been part of the pre-16th Century monastery that Henry the Eighth dismantled near the site of the now dismantled gun battery. At fifteen years old, I was very upset to hear by word of mouth from a third party that Alan's father had died. When I eventually called at Alan's home they made my condolences easy for me. With the friendship of the Martin family I was privileged to see Cliff Harrison a famous international, playing for Hartlepool Rovers in a few games of rugby. When the Rovers won "the Cup" I was only about five. I witnessed their homecoming, brass band playing "we are the Rovers" to the well known hymn tune Crimond. The band lead the team who were waving from the open top of a bus coming down Middlegate Street to the throng of people lining the pavement.

Alan's older brother had gone to college, became a teacher and later a headmaster. He had two sisters, Margaret who married well and Mary who caused a bit of gossip with an innocent flirting with a handsome church curate. Only Aunt Jenny could say "they are just good friends." She would have said that about the most torrid affair. She was a gentle kindly person who never raised her voice.

Another perk from my friend Alan was a little job we once did for a relation of his Martin family. This relation, the Proud family, had a bakery business and they provided the catering for the 'Floral Ball' Alan asked me if I wanted to give him a hand to take the cakes from the shop in Northgate to the Borough Hall where the dance was to take place. We were only kids of fourteen or so. I would do anything legal with Alan. We went along to the shop early in the evening. The cakes were laid on wooden trays on a custom built bicycle. The bicycle had three wheels, two at the front with a wooden box between them about a cubic yard in size! The machine was too heavy for us to pedal so, one of us either side, we had to push it the half mile or so to the Hall. I remember when we got inside, pausing for breath, the place was beautifully decorated. Hartlepool is very proud of its Borough Hall. It has a wide balcony around three sides of the arena with coloured lights along the lower edge. People not dancing could sit there and watch with refreshments from the bar at the rear of the balcony. The reward for this little job was a sixpence, I think, but we didn't get a cake! Later at seventeen we were together one weekend, and I had no money; Alan gave me a ten shilling note. What a wonderful thing to do! He did it so naturally it left me without embarrassment. I didn't offer to pay it back, I doubt if I could at the time. However I have repeated his generosity myself since, with other young people in the same fix as I was, which I feel settles my account.

Alan was called up into the army at eighteen, and after the war went to University and got a BSc.degree. He eventually married his Hartlepool sweetheart, the second one I knew of, and they settled in Hong Kong, he as a teacher. He played the piano well. Before he was called up he played the piano for me in their front room in Rowell Street and introduced me to classical music when he played Chopin and other lovely pieces.

Sadly I lost touch with Alan and his family. The difficulty of communication, my living in Middlesbrough, no telephones in the house and our going different ways led to a gradual parting. I owe him and his happy family a great deal of thanks for showing me the value of a cultured family lifestyle. They will know somehow that they were a good influence on me.

I saw Alan only once many years later in 1946 following the war. I came across him as I walked along the promenade to Dorothy's house near the 'new' pier, a breakwater that protects the beaches from the heavy North East seas. He was with an ex-girlfriend and we spoke with difficulty of our current affairs.

He was out of the army and then about to go to University, a move above my level. He was one of very few pre-war school leavers to go to University but the Government of the day made it possible for people discharged from the forces to do so too. He looked older for the smile with the eyes and mouth and his dimples were no longer there. He had grey streaks in his still young hair. Our lives had changed but the childhood we shared would be remembered by us both. It was the only thing we had in common now.

Alan would remember the summer of 1939, just before the war. With another friend Syd Wall making a threesome of us, we met at the Martin's house, changed into our swimming trunks and ran down Rowell Street, the one hundred yards to the beach. What made this so memorable was that high tide was at six o'clock in the morning and this was the time we had chosen to swim! We were in the sea for about five minutes, came out, dropped our wet trunks and ran up and down the beach in the buff to get our circulation going. I thought my willie was ruined, it had shrunk so much! We used the towels we had taken with us to dry our cold, stiff bodies and put on coats lent to us by Alan's mother. We finished off by dashing up the cast iron stairs from the lower promenade sixty feet up to street level, then on to Alan's home at No.16 Rowell St. feeling fit and ready for anything.

We never expected that one month later we would be at war. This would be the last time I saw Alan until the war ended. I regret very much losing a very good friend.

In Middlesbrough from about eight or nine years old I used to go to the nearby Gaumont Cinema on the corner of Southfield Road and Linthorpe Road. This had been the rather grand Opera House. This was where my father had 'befriended' a young barmaid who became his mistress until she died of a brain tumour at forty years of age. I went to the side door of the cinema and paid my eight pence to climb up the many flights of stairs to the seats in the upper circle. There were three circles, this was the top one and the cheapest, 'The Gods' we called it. I went there nearly every week, alone, and saw many great films. My favourite actor was Spencer Tracy. He was like a father figure to me, and always took the part of a kind man whose philosophy set a good example to the younger guys.

When I got older I ventured further afield and went to other cinemas in the town, always on my own except when there was a film my mum wanted to see. Mum liked musicals with Nelson Eddy and Jeanette MacDonald. She would buy sheet music and play it on the piano. We would sing the lyrics of another great favourite, Ivor Novello. I think mum had a crush on him as so many young women did in the 1920's. She gave one of my brothers the middle name Ivor; it wasn't a family name. We sang duets to his lovely romantic, rather sad songs of lovers yearning to be together again. "We'll gather lilacs in the Spring again, and walk together down a country lane". I have his music on CD to remind me of happy days. The young folks of today don't seem to have lyrics of love and romance. It went out with the Beatles in the sixties.

I made friends with others who like me were in reserved occupations, war work. We got together and we enjoyed a restricted social life.

Cinemas were closed for a time, then allowed to reopen when the bombing was re-evaluated. Dance halls had to close at ten pm. This was later relaxed when the enemy was finding out that he'd bitten off more than he could chew.

The 'blackout' was the first problem of the war. Mum had to buy blackout material to line the curtains. Sticky brown paper tape was stuck across the glass of the windows supposedly to prevent injury from splinters. To go out at night when there was no moon it was possible to bump into a low kerb or other obstacle, but people became accustomed to these conditions.

Barrage balloons protected important industrial sites. When we got geared up to defend against attack from enemy planes,. a field near Brambles Farm, Middlesbrough was planted with about fifty 'rocket' guns. Each rocket gun had two rails that elevated through 90 degrees mounted on a platform that turned through 360 degrees. A metal rocket with an explosive head was slid onto each rail. They were all coordinated to fire at once and make a "box" of anti- aircraft bursts covering a large area of the sky. It was a very hostile environment for any aircraft. By this time enemy activity seemed to be restricted to laying mines in the River Tees Bay. When a Royal navy vessel sailed from Smith's Dock's she hit a mine in Tees Bay. This happened twice. We lost a Corvette and another time a Frigate to mines laid at the river mouth by enemy planes.

One evening riding home from a two until ten shift during an air raid there were no planes or any other activity to be seen. As I cycled along I wondered what the red flashes and tinkling noises were. Then I realised it was shrapnel landing nearby from gunfire, a long way off, that I couldn't hear. I was wearing my steel helmet but I pedalled for a shop door way and took cover for a few minutes until the shower was over.

It cheered my greatly to see one of our night fighters chasing a German bomber which flew low over our house along Granville Road. The bomber's engine exhausts were spitting flames. Before they disappeared over the house tops I saw the fighter send a stream of tracer bullets into the bomber. Then I thought of the young German lads so very far from home. I doubted they would see home again. I felt rather sad for them.

'HMS Halcyon' returns to the dry dock, which she had left the day before, after being mined.

# CHAPTER 9
# BUILDING ROYAL NAVY SHIPS
*Smith's Dock Shipyard 1939 -1947*
*The making of an apprentice marine engineer.*

I was thirteen years of age in 1937 when my mother submitted an application to Smith's Dock Co. shipyard for me to serve an apprenticeship as a marine engineer. The economy had hardly recovered from the crash of 1929, jobs were not plentiful. Many men were still unemployed. The steel works and shipyards had a father and son recruiting process. I didn't even have an uncle in the shipyard. I thought my chances were slim. War brought me the chance of a lifetime. On the thirteenth of September 10 days after the war was declared a letter arrived from Smith's Docks Shipyard telling me to report to Smith's Dock Ltd. South bank on Tees, report to a Captain Tee to serve a five year apprenticeship in marine engineering at nine am.

I took the trolley bus from North Ormesby six miles to the small town of South Bank and walked up a long rough road to the shipyard. I entered the open gate and was told to stand with some other young lads outside the personnel office of Captain Fred W Tee.

He was a nice chap, a bit of a toff. I formed the opinion he was not a navy captain, they don't talk posh. He had a bit of a limp, probably a retired Army type. He took about twenty of us young new starters around to the various departments. The first call was to the boilermaker's workshop, a cold draughty and noisy place, then on to the plater's workshop, not much better. The joiner's shop was more pleasant with the smell of pine wood, but it was covered with sawdust and not to my taste. The shipwrights, plumbers electricians, pattern makers and finally the engine fitters!

The last port of call, we were delivered to the engine works. This had been my goal, to build ships engines! Steam engines which our English teacher Pop Hornsby had taught us the working principles. Break your heart Fed Dibner. These engines were as high as a house and extremely powerful. I still have the Indentures listing the contract between Smiths Docks Ltd and the apprentice. It had been signed and a large red seal was attached to it. I was given a clock card, number 168. Now I had a five years commitment with three nights evening classes at Constantine College, Middlesbrough during the winter months. This was made more difficult with the air raids that seemed to take place regularly at dusk.

*Smith Docks Co. Ltd. South Bank-on-Tees 1928.*
*Factory ship Southern Empress alongside the dry docks with whale*
*catchers ships to the left. Southern Empress was torpedoed and sunk*
*with loss of sixty men some had been picked up from another casualty.*
*Factory Ship Pelagos is in third dry dock from the left.*

Captain Tee handed the last three of us over to the engine shop chargehand, Tommy Urwin. He was a dapper little chap in a light brown boilersuit and the ubiquitous cap. He had a slight geordie accent, spoke with a gentle voice through a full set of large white false teeth and he had big brown kindly eyes. When he very rarely took his cap off he was as bald as a billiard ball and his head was just as white! I made a faux pas by initially calling him "sir" as we were taught in school to show respect to our superiors. He looked querulously at me, I think he thought I was being facetious, but looking at my innocent face he told me in a fatherly like way, and confidentially that it was okay to just call him Tommy.

*Triple expansion steam engines in the engine erection workshop.*

Tommy took us around the machine shop which was open to the erection shop where the engines were built up, scores of machines big and small were busy turning out parts of engines, connecting rods, piston rods and all sorts of other items. We paused at a lathe turning what I thought looked familiar to that mentioned by our good old English teacher Pop Hornsby! The lathe was about fifteen feet long with a round piece of steel about two feet six inches in diameter, revolving in the jaws of the machine. Long shiny steel curls streamed out four or five feet from the hard tool biting into the front edge of the material being "turned".

The lathe operator said "I bet you don't know what these are" pointing with a grease stained hand to a couple of finished items lying there waiting to be taken away." Well, they look like eccentric sheaves to me" I said. I was fifteen years old, full of confidence with the knowledge Pop Hornsby had given me. The turner's mouth opened in surprise, the greasy belly of his boilersuit heaved as he laughed and said jokingly to Tommy "he's a clever young bugger!" It was very much later I learnt not to be so clever, it upsets dull people.

I went home full of speculation, my mother had a happy home, money was tight I was conscious of my trousers having been repaired with patches, sometimes darned. I kept away from kids who might make fun of me.

I enjoyed hearing my Mum play the piano and we'd sing all the old songs of the music hall, 'Nellie Dene', 'Just a song at twilight' etc. My Mum had lots of music in books and on sheets, they'd be worth a fortune today in 2005 .I was always happy to be home!

As a youngster I had been in the Cub Scouts at St. Aiden's Church. I went to the Church occasionally with a friend of mine, the "stations of the cross" at Easter and such like. Mum wouldn't go, she went to Mrs Scrafton's Spiritualist Church and I enjoyed going there with her. It had a friendly atmosphere and lovely hymns, I gave the books out.

I hadn't been very happy with the Cubs, mainly because I hadn't a dad like the other kids and when it came to going to camp, it cost seven and sixpence and I didn't think Mum could afford it so I dropped out of the Cubs.

I went to stay with Aunt Jenny and Grandma. I was happier at Hartlepool anyway, every holiday! Easter, Whitsuntide, August , weeks galore !

When I started work at fourteen there was very little leisure time. We worked 56 hours a week and on Saturdays from 7.30am until noon. The shipyards gave us only one weeks holiday a year and that was without pay! Half a Crown, or two shillings and sixpence was stopped from our wages every week and given to us for the holiday week.

A big problem for me was getting out of bed in a morning for work, or even not for work! We had an old alarm clock not very accurate to twenty minutes or so daily, fast or slow! I had taken the back off it a few times, to clean it with a drop of paraffin on a kiddie's paintbrush and adjusted the regulator, but the old clock seemed to have a mind of its own. I had relied on the works "buzzers" for a time check, now I had the wireless to give me a check, the horror of being late for work still remained with me for six days a week, up at six o clock. I didn't know of any house that had central heating in the 1930's. The winters were very cold but 68 Granville Rd was a warm terrace house, our house was never cold. Mum had a small gas fire that she burned all night in the kitchen when the weather was very cold. With a bit of "banking up" damping the red hot coals with coal dust or tea leaves from the pot, put aside for the purpose, we sometimes managed to keep the coal fire

87

going until early morning. It could be quickly revived with newspaper and a few sticks of wood. The coal shovel propped up in front of the fire with a newspaper blocking the air going up the chimney increased the draft through the fire grate, this made the fire glow and increase rapidly. The newspaper became scorched and if not handled carefully, it could burst into flames! Some unfortunate folks had the soot up the chimney take fire when the burning paper went up the chimney, often resulting in the Fire Brigade being called. We had the chimney swept every year so thankfully we never had a chimney fire.

The War Time Apprenticeship began on September 13th 1939.It was five years hard labour! I had to get out of bed at about six thirty am to get to Smiths Docks shipyard on the Monday morning at half past seven to start my apprenticeship. My mum got up to see me fed and off to work. This was going to be the routine for many years, it was a bit of a shock but most of the grammar school boys had been called up for the navy, army or the air force. Which was worse? We got harassed by the enemy at home and at work. I could have drawn the short straw again! The shipyard was about eight miles east of Middlesbrough near the small town of South Bank. To save bus fare I could go there on my bike but in winter I often took the trolley bus. I had a fifteen minute walk from home to North Ormesby to catch the trolley bus, then arriving at South Bank it was a mile and a half walk to the shipyard gates. The main gate was only opened for motor traffic early in the morning. Men walked through narrow alleyways to where their clock cards were in racks.

I didn't like the gateman, in his cheap grey suit he thought he was a cut above the men in their shabby work clothes clocking on. If the trolley bus was a bit late it was often a race against the clock to get in before the starting time of 7:30 am. There stood the important gateman, checking the final minute with his cheap pocket watch in one hand and the narrow entrance gate in the other. Looking at his watch through bottle bottomed spectacles when the second hand touched twelve he slammed the gate shut. Even if a chap was only a few feet away after running the last hundred yards, the gate was still slammed in your face! The man was locked out, humiliated to wait outside until eight o clock to be admitted. His pay would be docked for the half hour anyway with the time stamped on his clock card. It may have been the gateman's orders but he had a grin on his face as he slammed that gate shut! This happened to me a few times, otherwise I enjoyed working there. These poor working conditions could not last now with plenty of work and all skilled men fully employed

The bad weather created difficulties fitting out the ships with engine room machinery. A frozen crane hook became brittle and could fracture so the hook was lowered to the quay and a bit of fire with a paraffin rag was made around it to heat it up. But the men were not allowed to stand around to warm cold hands if a foreman came along! I suppose he'd think he was losing 'face'. We were obliged to move respectfully away. This attitude was slowly being eroded as the war exposed the need for all hands to work together to supply the ships for victory.

On my first day I walked into the engine erecting shop, big enough to house an airship! The three of us lads were Sid Simpson, cheery Harry Almond, myself, We waited to see the chargehand Tommy Urwin who quickly went round setting the new lads to work. Older apprentices knew who they were working with on the engine they were assembling or the assigned bench job working on the various parts of the engine such as the ahead and astern valve gear. I soon recognised the areas in the workshop where the many parts of the engines were being fitted accurately together from the machined parts coming across from the adjacent lathes, giant drilling and various machines.

The planeing machine had a flat bed that the part to be machined was bolted to. It moved back and forth with the cast iron part to be machined cut into fine cast iron chippings by the tool fixed to an overhead strong frame. The hard edged cutting tool doing the cutting was bolted into a clamp mounted on the frame. After each cut the bed moved again to allow the tool to bite again into the rough cast iron flat surface until a machined surface resulted. The operator set the tool to the required depth of cut to satisfy the design of the engine part and started the casting moving back and forth with tiny chippings of the cast iron coming from the stationary tip of the tool. The body of the tool was generally an inch or more thick of superior tough steel but the cutting tip was of even harder steel only a few millimetres thick and brazed, that is a form of welding with brass onto the body of the tool. Special grindstone wheels were required to shape or sharpen these tips as they were so hard. I thought it was a boring job once the cut had been set and the machine started. It could take quite a time watching the thing going back and forth, but I suppose it was a great responsibility to get the casting machined to a few thousands of an inch.

My first job was to polish engine handrails that were fitted between the cast iron columns of the open engine. These handrails were forged in the blacksmiths shop from inch steel bar and covered with a thin hard black scale, a "lug" forged at each end had to have a hole drilled in it to fasten the rail to the engine columns.

We were given an old well worn14inch flat file and putting the handrail in a six inch bench vice pushed the file back and forth with both hands in a swinging action to cover the roundness of the inch bar of the rail. It could take all day to do one! Doing this all day I went home very tired, especially so because we were given worn out old files which were no longer sharp. So we learned 'stickability', slogging on until the final handrail, polished with emery paper, was fitted gleaming to the engine standing in the workshop. Pride in the work was reward enough. It was a primitive way of making a hand rail. Polished steel tubing with lugs welded at each end would have been cheaper and easier to fabricate but old habits die hard with British managers. When marine engines were lubricated by oil pressure fed to the bearings, the whole engine was boxed in with steel plate. No handrails were then needed to prevent the engineer falling in onto the moving parts.

It wasn't long before we realised that some of our handiwork was being sent to the bottom of the sea by the German U boats!

We apprentices had to go to the blacksmith's shop to collect the handrails. This workshop was long and dark, a big shed without windows about a hundred feet long maybe forty feet wide. Down each side of the black coal dust floor area were ten hearths with glowing red fire, each reflecting the shadows of the blacksmith and his "striker" in their leather aprons working at the anvil. Round each hearth was a host of the Smithy's tools with a tank of water to quench the work as required. Some blacksmiths were making large numbers of stanchions and handrails for the deck and superstructure, others made chains of different dimensions, steel rings to reeve a rope through, steel wedges, 'drifts'for the platers to drive into a hole in the steel plate to line it up on the ribs of the ship being built on the stocks. A bolt would then to hold the plates in place before the plates were finally riveted together. These men could fabricate anything!

In the centre of the building stood four vertical heavy mechanical hammers, they were operated by compressed air. Often we passed a team of men, blacksmiths and "strikers" reducing a large red hot ingot of steel into some part of a ship!

It was difficult to tear oneself away from the ancient technology that went back to the bronze age, glowing steel, sparks, heat, noise and dust forging something useful from a red hot lump of metal.

Finding the handrails for our job, we had to leave the interesting spectacle of this inferno and wander back to our more sedate occupation in the fitting shop. Making sure we got the right ones!

Part of the equipment used in drilling metals with a pneumatic drill was called a 'stand'. They came in various lengths. This led to a trick played on a new starter. The young apprentice was asked to go to the store and ask for a 'long stand'. The storeman would know the score and say, 'okay son, wait there," then turn and get on with checking his paperwork. After some minutes the lad would tumble to the joke if he was bright enough! Returning to the squad, taking it in good part, he later enjoyed playing the joke on another new boy. A bit daft I suppose but harmless fun.

Another excursion for apprentices was to collect copper drain pipes for the main engine's three cylinders and two more sections for the reversing engine steam and exhaust pipes. They were one and a half inches diameter bore in various lengths being bent to fit under the cylinders to return the steam to the big steam condenser bolted to the back of the engine. These were made in the plumber's shop, bent to a template or sketch made by the plumber with flanges at each end to bolt to engine and condenser. The plumber's shop was a long walk from the engine works past the dry docks with war damaged ships being repaired. We gambolled over, pausing to see the gallant little merchant ships and the activity surrounding them. Cranes would be lifting steel, new sections of ship, winches in use and on a completed repair job, stores would be loading, to take the ship on it's next journey somewhere across the U boat infested sea.

Like the blacksmith's shop the plumber's shop was another magician's workshop. Copper when new is a beautiful rose/ yellow colour, soft and when hot makes gorgeous flames with colours of red, white, yellow and shades of pale green. The plumbers worked on various sizes of pipe from fifteen feet lengths of 10inch diameter to the ones already mentioned. To bend the soft metal copper pipe one end was plugged with a wooden bung, it was then filled with pieces of shiny black resin that melted and when topped up another bung was fitted. This to prevented the soft copper crimping as it was gently bent in slow curves to the required degree, stretching the outer side of the bend and allowing the inner side to squeeze over to compensate without distorting.

The heat was applied on what boy scouts call altar fires. The shop had about three of these hearths. Each had a hearth of fire bricks three feet square raised on a pedestal waist high. A small fire of coke normally just glowing gently was brought up to 600 degrees centigrade, bright red hot when a compressed air pipe valve was opened in the hearth to give the extra oxygen the fire needed. When hot enough the pipe was lowered onto a metal table that had adjustable metal blocks where the hot copper pipes could be coaxed round the blocks to the various angles required.

The pipes were suspended over the fire using chains attached to metal joists in the roof. With a temperature of six hundred degrees the spectacular colours now appeared. When the flange was to be braised to the end of the pipe it was placed flat onto the hearth fire with the pipe hung in position on the flange. When the colours appeared both flange and pipe were at the correct temperature. A flux of borax powder was applied to clear the metal of any oxidation and a brass rod was melted around both items to weld them together. It was a place apprentices liked to linger especially on a cold winter's day. The plumbers didn't seem to mind, even the boss would take an interest in us lads and ask where we were from and chat for a while.

The first years as an apprentice in Smith's Docks was to experience working conditions that had not changed since the Company established the shipyard there in 1910. It would be kind to call them primitive. Roads around the site were of hardcore from the abundant slag from the town's old iron works. Big mounds of slag abounded the area outside the shipyard in tub shaped concretions having been tipped there early in the 19th century.

Small steam cranes ran on railway lines around the shipyard. These 'Heath Robinson' cranes were cobbled together on a low four wheeled bogie using a coal fired small vertical boiler providing steam for both locomotion and to power the winch. The lifting cable ran over the jib which was hinged to the front of the bogie. The whole contraption was sheeted with corrugated iron to give shelter to driver, boiler, coals and any item the driver required such as an oil can, oily rag and his fire-irons.

A small tank locomotive engine moved heavy loads on low flat trucks such as ships propellers, steel plates and marine engines to the fitting out quay. The war made many improvements. Roadways were concreted and girls drove three wheel mini trucks with materials to the various plumbers, carpenters, stores and other workshops.

A busy shipyard produced more than ships. It trained many young men in numerous skills, shipwrights, engineers, cabinet makers, carpenters, plumbers and electricians. Pattern makers made wooden patterns sent to the foundry to form the moulds for steel castings. I am not sure where to place the draughtsmen. It is another category, skilful but has higher categories of design engineers who require a knowledge of stress and structure of metals. Formal qualifications obtained first at evening classes then on courses at some technical college.

We were expected to provide our own small tools, steel rule, inside and outside callipers used to measure diameters of shaft and the bore of the item to fit to the shaft, feeler gauges with fingers of thin steel leaves to measure clearances in bearings from one and a half thousands of an inch to twenty five thousands, and dividers to describe an arc or circle in marking off some item. These tools were expensive and prone to be borrowed by a fellow worker or become lost? We made templates of the larger spanners and the plater's oxy-acetylene burner cut them out in inch thick steel plate, which then had to be dressed to the size required. A complication here arose with our Whitworth standards and American nuts and bolts. This was further complicated when Whitworth standard 60 deg.screw threads became obsolete and the continental standard was introduced, all slightly different to 55 degree screw threads and nut measurements The British tools were still required to deal with work on machines built before the introduction of the Continental and USA standards. This triple standard often caused a lot of extra work and tool bags became very heavy!

We needed scrapers to scrape away the soft white metal when bedding in bearings to allow oil to reach the bottom third bearing surface. The tool smith Billy Atkinson made these for us from an old half round file heated in his fire and shaped on the anvil

Nowhere in the shipyard at that time were there any facilities for the workers to wash, eat or change. A canteen was available and I used it occasionally to help our meagre war time rations but at one shilling a day it was a lot out of my twelve shilling a week apprentice wages.

The Chargehand Tommy Urwin now put me to work with an older engine fitter. His name was Stanley Brown, Mucker Brown everybody called him but not to his face. He didn't like it, and he was a big strong

93

amiable fellow but not that amiable. About late forties probably one of the first apprentices when Smith's first started up thirty years before. Stanley had two teenage sons and he played cricket for the Smith's Dock eleven. Stan knew everyone in the Yard, and seemed popular although he had a  pedantic finger wagging attitude to the younger lads. Didn't swear only said , dash it but was a bit cute in avoiding any dirty jobs. One day going over the yard to the ship we were working on a smart gentleman was stalking past. He wore a brown bowler hat and wore a camel coloured overcoat. Not a manager I thought, Stan told me in respectful tones, that is Eustace Smith he owns the shipyard. He was known to all the workers as Eustace and I got the impression tthat he was not regarded as a Boss rather more as a Patron. If a manager was being a bit stupid about the job it would be said, I'll bet Eustace doesn't know about this!

The practice of locking men out at the gate came to an end one cold day in1943.

How it ever began was due to the attitude that arose with the serious unemployment of the 1930's. This allowed honest men to be subjected to such humiliating treatment.

The Company didn't lose anything to let a late comer in because each man had to put his card in a "time clock" and the time and day was stamped on it to make up his wages.
One minute over starting time and a half hour had been deducted.

This humiliating slamming the gate in a man's face had persisted until the very bad winter of 1943.

It must have been January when heavy snow fell all week end. On Monday morning the snow froze in ruts twelve inches deep on the road making it impossible for the trolley buses to operate because the trolleys wouldn't stay on the overhead wires.

Some men struggled to work on bikes riding along the ruts until it was crossed or blocked by ice, but I had walked two miles from home to get to the trolley bus terminus and had set off early to do so.

At seven o 'clock when I arrived at the terminus it was still dark. Usually a bus was waiting for passengers to depart when another bus arrived. I turned the corner of the street to find no bus but a crowd of about thirty or more Smith's Dock lads huddle together like penguins shuffling their feet on the frozen snow.  A low grumble rose from the moaners, wot's the matter with the buses? Grumble grumble, from unhappy characters. A voice piped up , the buses can't keep the trolleys

94

on the wires 'cos they're bouncing all over the ice, - - - was he a shop steward? Another voice cry'd what are we going to do lads!, Make him the shop steward! - - - then an older voice, there's a war on! Let's walk to work !. A low growl of assent in old English, a-y-e ! rose from every voice. The penguins tottered off from the far side in twos and threes stumbling along the frozen pavement, past the washer works on the edge of North Ormesby village then past the Cargo Fleet Steelworks, over the little railway bridge into South Bank, Turn left at Saint Peter's Church . We were past half way it was a grey Monday morning and well after eight o'clock. I expected to be sent home because no one was allowed in to start work  after eight o clock.

I must admit it wasn't just a patriotic gesture on my part , I had a base motive.

No work meant no pay, Mum needed the money. We reached the long straight road to the shipyard, I was pleased to find all the gates wide open !!! We clocked on and went to our places of work. In the engine works some local lads were already at work, we soon settled in and joined them.

Later that day word got around as it does in a shipyard like a bush fire. Eustace Smith, later Sir Eustace, had phoned in from his home near Darlington to ask how they were coping with the bad weather? He was told the men are walking in, but the gates will be locked at eight o'clock. Eustace gave the order, if the men are prepared to walk to work in this weather for the war effort leave those bloody gates open and never let them be locked again !

The gates were never shut on the face of a man after that, you clocked on and were paid to the next quarter hour. They didn't mind you starting work before that.

During this hard winter of 1943, when it froze all day every day for ten days or more I was walking over from the shipyard to the fitting out jetty to deliver some small engine part. As I passed the first dry dock I saw three men warming their hands at a brazier fire of old lumps of wood of which there was always an abundance. They were having a brew up with three cans of tea on the fire. Mr Cameron a shipyard foreman in his navy blue serge suit and bowler hat walked up and said, "what's going on here?" and kicked the brazier over scattering the cans and fire to the earth. The men just walked away , they dare not say anything. Before the war it would have been a sacking offence. No tea breaks were allowed. Shortly after the locked gates incident the union shop stewards met the management and were able to negotiate a ten minute morning tea break. Eustace had seen to making better conditions. Mr Cameron disappeared somehow ? Output of work improved Britain turned the corner, we started to win the war.. The war did have some good effects, better management was one of them.

# CHAPTER 10
# HOME GUARD DUTIES
*The Princess of Wales Alexandra's Own 1875 Yorkshire Reg't*
*The Green Howards 8th Battalion Home Guard.*
*Commanding Officer Captain William Lilly,*
*Middlesbrough Chief Librarian.*

Private Dinsdale, Headquarter Company Signals Aged 18 years, now a senior apprentice engineer . The difficulty of travelling in war time and in the very hard winters of the 1940's. As a teenager the important need to learn to dance the foxtrot and the waltz.

As if I didn't have enough to do building marine steam engines for the Royal Navy to win the war of the Atlantic against the German U boats, going to evening classes at Constantine College to prepare myself for a sea going engineer's job - - - Winston Churchill now wanted me to join the Home Guard!

At eighteen years of age in the shipyard I was expected to work overtime two nights a week and often eight hours on a Sunday. I was supposed to do three nights night school 7 pm until 9 pm. Nuisance air raids generally disturbed and often interfered with our evening classes.. I had to ask for time off to attend Sunday morning parade at the Home Guard Headquarters. This took place in the redundant general Post Office at Bright Street in Middlesbrough. Dressed in khaki battle dress I was told I was to be a signaller in the Headquarters Company. For the first few weeks the sergeant would march about twenty of us signallers to a field about a mile away. He was an office worker in his civilian job. He was a good chap and did his Home Guard job of Sergeant as a professional. We were ordered to space ourselves in open order. Far enough apart to swing red flags we had been given.

The flags were about eighteen inches square on a three foot long stick. A dot was given by holding the flag upright and swinging it left

45 degrees and returning it sharply vertical again. A dash was given by swinging the flag 90 degrees and returning it sharply vertical again. We accomplished this by learning morse code whenever we had nothing better to think about! We were expected to reach a proficiency of twelve words a minute but that was wishful thinking with the workload I had. It would have only been possible with daily use. Portable battery operated 38 voice radio sets were now issued to the Home Guard. These strapped to the signallers chest and had a metal ariel like a three piece fishing rod sticking up about three feet in the air. The microphone was strapped round the throat. A bigger command radio set identified as a 21 set could be strapped to a signaller's back for work in the field.

One night we were taken out in a pickup truck and dropped off at various locations round the outskirts of the town just after seven o clock. I couldn't get a squeak out of my 38 set, just a bit of static that told me it was trying, we had been told to be careful what we said in case the enemy was listening. That was more than we could do only a couple of hundred yards from each other. They were supposed to have a range of three miles. What a joke!

I waited until 9 pm, it was dark, I was cold and the transport didn't arrive so I walked the six miles or more to H.Q. The sergeant was waiting for me. "Hadn't I heard the message to meet the truck?" The others had gone home This was a repeat of my Christmas temp telegraph boy's late return story! We should have tested our sets before he left us at our stations. I didn't hear if the others had been more fortunate. We were later issued with Lee Enfield 303 rifles, they weighed 12 pounds without the 14 inch bayonet. Now the sergeant could give us rifle drill, one, two, three! As we flung the rifle up and grasped it by the trigger guard, one, two, three again as we flung it onto our left shoulder with the elbow at 90 degrees.

We were issued with five rounds of 303 live ammunition when our rota for H.Q. Guard duty came round. Our turn didn't happen very often as there were so many men in the headquarters company. One hour on duty at the main door and an hour inside. Time for a cup of cocoa. In 1944 when D day was expected we were given the five rounds of live ammunition to take home in case a German counter attack of paratroopers was made here in the North East.

On two occasions a dispatch rider on a motor bike knocked mum and I up at 1 am to tell me to report at Bright Street H.Q. I dressed in my uniform took the rifle from the hall umbrella stand and clattered off in my hobnailed army issue boots. I was a sitting duck to any German paratrooper, unless I saw him coming down first!

Saying goodbye to Mum it didn't occur to me at the time that we might not see each other again!

We had been taken to a rifle range to lie down on the grass and fire at a target at 250 yards range. The sergeant was a bit upset when I put the rifle to my left shoulder. This was because I couldn't see the end sight of the rifle with my weak right eye. It meant I had to change the rifle over each time I pulled the trigger to operate the bolt on the right side of the gun that pushed another bullet into the breach. In spite of this impediment I managed to put four of my five bullets in an eight inch target at 250 yards. The other shot was not a lot far out either. If push came to shove I didn't expect to use the rifle very much. We would have been no match against German paratroopers.

We had a couple of weekend camps. The first was at the little village of Seamer six miles or more south of Middlesbrough. We arrived in daylight on the Friday evening. Bell tents had been put up in a field for us. After seeing where we were going to spend the night we walked up to the King's Head pub only about a hundred and fifty yards away, more for the comfort than to drink. It wasn't a warm night and it soon got dark, We had no lights in the tents. I probably had a couple of pints of beer over the two or three hours we were there. Closing time was ten o clock, when the landlord called time three of us strode to the door passing the blackout curtain onto the pavement outside. We stepped onto the road but it wasn't there!

The pavement was alongside a ten foot steep grassy bank and in the intense darkness the three of us went head over heels in a heap onto the rough country lane below. Our eyes adjusted to whatever light there was and we felt around for our forage caps and limped a bit down to the five bar'd gate to the camp site. There was a big sticky mud patch to negotiate to pass through the gate and we almost felt our way to our tent. There was no ground sheet we lay on the grass with our feet to the pole, I used my gas mask case for a pillow and was asleep in seconds.

Next morning at daybreak I awoke with my head and shoulders outside the low tent wall. A gentle rain sprinkled over my face. Where my Headquarter's Company was I didn't know. I could not see the sergeant and only knew we were to do some manoeuvres but as signallers we didn't have radios or other means of signalling. I was out of the loop so to speak. I wasn't the only one! Another chap about my age was also adrift. We wandered over to the camp fire where porridge had been cooked. It was watery, hot and sweet. Strong tea, ladled from a white enamel bucket and sweetened with condensed milk, was very acceptable.

One of the three cooks, probably the sergeant, sleeves rolled up and not wearing his tunic, said, seeing as we had missed the manoeuvres he would kindly detail us to help with the cooking. We were given a couple of kitchen knives and a bag of potatoes to peel! "Just fill that dixie" he said! It has only now occurred to me that we two lads might have been hi-jacked by consulting sergeants. I'd never peeled a potato before in my life but it was a lesson in humility and did no harm. We had the last laugh when the cook tried to boil a dixie of rice on the camp fire. I realise now that he was no cook and had put far too much water with it to cook the rice The fire was also not hot enough to boil the water. He drained the rice and gave me a bowl full but it was far from cooked and hard. The rest of this episode did not register with me. I was glad when I got back to mum and home comforts, the shipyard and things familiar.

Our Headquarters Company had another weekend camp to do. This time it was to The Regimental Headquarters of the Green Howards, Catterick Camp in North Yorkshire. A formidable place for us to play soldiers. It must have been December 1942. Our Company assembled in Bright Street, Middlesbrough, about forty of us. I remember we were not carrying our rifles at this time. We got into the bus and off we went, the journey taking just over an hour. There wasn't much traffic in those days but the roads were pre-war and rural, to be polite. .

The bus arrived at the camp and stopped on an enormous parade ground. Our sergeant ordered us to form up in threes. I do remember we had been issued with great coats before this trip. These were long khaki overcoats with brass buttons and a high collar that sheltered the head and fastened up to the chin. We stood there next to another company who had just arrived. They stood like us awaiting a regular sergeant to march us away to the barracks on the far side of the parade ground. The host sergeant arrived and marched the other lot away. We stood at ease in the cold sleet laden wind for about twenty minutes. No host appeared. Our brave little sergeant stepped out of the ranks and ordered us to attention! "Left turn, by the left, quick march!" He marched us to a Nissan hut and we went in. There was a row of beds on each side. What took place next is rather vague but at some time that weekend we had a meal in the mess hall, eight men to a table. One man at the end of the table had to go for the shallow cooking pan and dish it up. Before we finished our meal a Regular officer with a junior officer in attendance came to each table and waving his stick demanded, "any complaints?" As if anyone would dare to complain? I was glad when we rolled up to our Headquarters in Bright Street and got home to my dear mum.

After Dorothy and I had started going out together I went over to Hartlepool quite often just to be with her for a couple of hours during the week One night I was going back home rather late to get to work the next morning. It was thick fog, never mind, I thought, it may only be local , I said goodnight to Aunt Jenny, got on the old motorbike I had bought and set off. A couple of hundred yards along Northgate I could hardly see the curb to find my way along the road. I stopped when a policeman asked me how far I was going, Middlesbrough I replied. The fog is all over the North he advised me. I decided to return to Aunt Jenny's and set off next morning early to get to work I was probably on two till ten shift next day so it was not a problem. Weekends I would stay overnight at Aunt Jenny's to be with Dorothy, calling on our friends. Sometimes going to a cinema together sitting in the dark with my arm around her watching a happy romantic film that were so popular then.

In winter I went to Hartlepool on the bus but many times with petrol being severely rationed, it was on my old push bike, with no gears!

It was a shorter distance to Hartlepool by going over the Transporter Bridge, from Middlesbrough in spite of having to wait for the platform to come over. The Transporter Bridge was built in 1911 and was designed to do away with the ferry that took workmen across the river to work at the shipyard on the north side of the river at Haverton Hill. At the time it was designed to allow steam ships that still had tall masts and carried sail if the conditions allowed. This was a unique design of bridge built with two towers of steel girders each side of the river supporting a steel carriageway crossing the river. On this high overhead carriageway a truck ran on rails with a platform suspended at road level pulled back and forth across the river by a wire rope wound round a giant drum mounted in an engine house on the Middlesbrough side of the river powered by an electric motor. The platform holds motor vehicles on its roadway platform with pedestrian passengers accommodated at each side with a sliding door to access the pavement after crossing the river. The Transporter bridge has been running now for ninety eight years at the time of writing.

Murphy's law says "it will always be on the opposite side to the one you arrive at!" The road from the north side of the river went through marsh land, salt flats and over Greatham Creek. Here during the war a few fishermen's house boats were still berthed alongside the creek. These house boats had been cobbled together from old ship's lifeboats with walls and roof of scrap tar painted timber with odd shaped little window frames.. A stove pipe sticking up through the roof at times gave notice of occupation with a thin stream of smoke, very rare now during the war. A lonely barrage balloon unit was the only signs of humanity for the seven miles along this road.

In the darkness of the blackout a far off air raid siren wailed a warning causing several decoy lights to appear on the marshes hoping the enemy planes would be encouraged to bomb them I suppose. To my knowledge, they were not deceived thank goodness! The headlamp of my pushbike had a device made from a discarded fruit tin with slots cut to allow the light to shine forward but not above where it could be seen by enemy planes!

I was always glad reach the Transporter. Sometimes if a head wind had delayed me and the last crossing had gone, I might be lucky and call over the foy (ferry) boat. The foy boatman, some old chap hoping to make a bit of beer money, would row over. Carrying my bike down a ramp to the riverside to the boat I was taken across for sixpence which saved me another five or six miles cycling round the road through Haverton Hill at midnight. Having to be up for work the next morning I was glad of the service!

On one occasion in cycling back from Hartlepool too late for the 11:30 pm last journey across from Port Clarence to Middlesbrough I had taken advantage of carrying my bike up the many flights of the stairway of the Transporter Bridge structure on the right hand side of the road, to the broad walkway over the top, then down the leg of the structure on the other side.. The next time I missed the last crossing, the gate giving access to the stairway was closed and locked with a padlock and chain. I then had to cycle the five mile long way around to Middlesbrough  The next months passed quickly, the anxious days retreated and very rarely did the German bombers keep us up at night. Losses were more frequent for the enemy.

At Brambles Farm, near the coast a battery of rocket guns sending up a box barrage of fifty rockets certainly restricted the enemy bombers, now we also had night fighters. Standing at our front door way I had seen a night fighter streaming tracer bullets into the poor lads who had dared to annoy us. They fled easterly for the coast back to the fatherland, if they were lucky! Hurricane fighter aircraft were stationed in speedy reach of Industrial Teesside and with radar, Mosquito twin engine night fighters made German planes' hope of returning home very doubtful.

At Smiths Dock one evening, at about eight o clock, an enemy plane came over very low and hit the wire of a barrage balloon situated just outside the shipyard gates. The plane crashed onto the railway lines a mile away, I was on two till ten shift that day. We had taken cover in long Anderson Air Raid Shelters that had been dug in the yard near the workshop. We came out to see what was going on .The sky was lit up with the flames from the plane; its ammunition was banging away for a long time. It gave me no joy thinking of those poor German lads dying so far away from home. I was only thankful their ammunition and bombs were not used against us. Mum and I had become weary of trailing to the part built Co-op Emporium on Linthorpe Road to shelter in the basement there, to bed down on the dusty concrete floor of the unfinished building. Mum and I carried cushions, blankets and thermos flasks of tea always ready for the air raid siren. Air raid shelters were eventually built on our road but brick and concrete again and not comfortable. We became bolder and when the air raid siren sounded we stayed in our beds. Our confidence was rewarded, very few enemy planes arrived.

As time passed my work as an apprentice became more skilful. We had specially shaped chisels, forged by the tool smith Billie Atkinson. We were trusted to use the chisel's cutting edge to make the small oil channels in the soft white metal of the bearings then scraping the metal to bed the bearing in we adjusted the metal to give clearance for the oil to reach the crown of the bearing. The crown then was bedded in onto the shaft using a blue oil to show the high spots. These were scraped carefully away until a satisfactory surface showed blue.

Using short lengths of 1mm thin soft lead wire laid on top of the shaft, the bearing was bolting up. Opening it up again, the thickness of the now compressed lead wire was measured with a micrometer to determine the clearance of the bearing. A thousandth of an inch clearance was given for every inch of the shaft diameter. These bearings were drip fed with oil from mechanical oil boxes with a wick feeding small brass pipes mounted over the engine for the few who may be interested? These "open" engines ran at a top speed of 250 revs per minute, throwing excess oil into the engine room so the oil had to be given with judgement, sometimes adding a few drops of water to create an emulsion thus keeping the oil in the bearing longer. When the engine had run for a few hours the soft white metal in the bearings developed a glass like hard skin. It was only a few thousands of an inch thick but with proper lubrication the bearings would last for years. Now who was the clever chap who discovered that soft metal would become as hard as glass after light running in for a few hours I wonder?

My apprenticeship now extended to being a member of the team installing engines in the ships hulls .The engine was partly dismantled in the erection shop by unbolting the three cylinders in one piece from the columns fastening them to the bedplate complete with their pistons. The Cylinders put onto a separate railway truck supported on big blocks of timber. The now dismembered engine was taken by rail pulled on the wagons by the shipyard railway tank engine to the fitting out quay. The bedplate with the crankshaft and connecting rods were lowered into the hull with a travelling tower crane. When it was near its final position chain blocks secured it and held the hull steady, which was floating remember. It was necessary to consider the tide, for if it was rising it would be necessary to raise the bedplate slightly until we had it in the correct position. Hand signals were given from the engine room to a man on deck he then signalled to the driver of the crane some fifty feet up. The cylinders were then lowered onto the engine. The next weeks were spent connecting up the engine and fitting out the whole ship. The work was a bit precarious but I never felt in any danger. We were brought up to be aware of the hazards and concentrate on the job. To look out for yourself!

The winters of the 1940's were very bad. In January 1943 one Monday morning we had a heavy fall of snow of about ten or more inches. I struggled to walk from my home to Smeaton Street, North Ormesby. When I got to the trolley bus terminus about thirty men were waiting for the trolley bus.

A voice shouted, "the buses can't keep their trolleys on for the frozen ruts in the snow." Another voice said "what are we going to do lads?" Some stalwart replied, "well there's a war on, so let's walk to work!" It was about eight miles to the shipyard gate. I didn't expect the gate to be open for us after eight o'clock, normally you had to go back home if you arrived after eight o'clock. Not a man refused to do the walk in the hard packed frozen snow. When we got to the shipyard the main gate was wide open! The boss Eustace Smith had phoned to ask what effect the snow was having on the work. When told the men were walking from Middlesbrough he said, if the men are prepared to walk in this, leave the bloody gate open and never let it be locked again. This coming from a "toff" impressed me. It wouldn't have been his idea to slam the gate in a man's face. It was the "gaffers" who treat the men badly, afraid to lose "face".

We had to clock on anyway and most of us could not afford to lose a full day's pay. Conditions improved after that. A morning tea break was allowed. Tea was made in a billycan of water on the stove with tea and sugar from home in a twist of paper in the sandwich box. Everything was severely rationed.

The Corvettes designed for coastal defence had been used on the Atlantic convoys and had only enough fuel to cross the Atlantic. The Corvettes top speed of sixteen knots was not enough to deal with the latest seventeen knot U Boats. Smith's Dock now began building Frigates with two Smith's Dock engines. These ships could do eighteen knots. Just enough to deal with the U boats but more would have been better.

On Bank Holiday Monday, August 1942, things were going badly in the war. We were working the holiday with extra pay. My pay at this time was about 14 shillings a week. An air raid was imminent, and managers came around the yard with megaphones calling "take cover" It was a bit late. I saw the German plane flying up the river at about three hundred feet coming in from the sea to avoid the barrage balloons. Then I heard a machine gun, it was slower than I had imagined, tac – tac - tac! Probably a cannon. I didn't think it would be one of ours, there was no guns of ours on the river to my knowledge. I dived into a cast iron cylinder for a second or two, but curiosity asked me where had he gone? I'd expected him to attack our ships one of which was about ready for sea trials. It was later that day I heard he'd bombed the railway station, which wasn't very clever of the pilot. Seven people were killed but the Station was up and running again in a couple of days. minus the ornate Victorian cast iron and glass roof. It would have been more effective for their U boat war of the Atlantic

104

if the German pilot had sunk a couple of our, near ready for sea, Royal Navy Corvettes! The German lads didn't get back home on that occasion either, shot down over North Yorkshire.

On the 22nd of June 1940 a corvette built for the Free French Navy "La Bastiaise" steamed out on sea trials with its French crew and twelve men from Smith's Docks. Enemy planes had dropped mines near the river mouth and the corvette was sunk with a loss of many men including twelve Smith's Docks men and five contractors. It was believed this was one of the first magnetic mines laid on the sea bed. The conventional mine required a heavy anchor, the magnetic mine was more suited to aircraft delivery. It would explode as the metal ship approached. This device sank other vessels in coastal waters until a means of detonating them safely was worked out. Ships were demagnetised with coils of wire around the hull. The apprentice who survived told me it blew the bow off the ship as she approached the mouth of the river. This older apprentice, Raymond Renwick said he was in the tail end propeller shaft compartment when the explosion took place. He managed to get up a vertical ladder and over the side before the ship plunged to the sea bed. Ray was in the sea with Alex Henderson an elderly engineer but Alex had told him he couldn't keep up and drowned before a boat came to pick up survivors. A favourite old friend of mine, Billie Pringle didn't get out of the engine room. He was a lovely old man. It was he who told me that as a boy he remembered when it was possible, at low tide, to ride across the river mouth on horseback!

Teesside probably wasn't a good assignment for the German lads. They had a long journey to get here and picked up on radar a fighter was scrambled from a nearby airfield sort them out.. What a daft business war is, the whole of Europe devastated by a few German clowns who enjoyed dressing up in fancy uniforms. They were encouraged by vast numbers of German people and lessons were eventually learned that appeasement doesn't work and people shouldn't encourage idiots to make war. The German people eventually discovered that.

When the war ended Mr Turner a manager of Smiths Docks, had left Smith's Docks and gone as an engineering Superintendent for Christian Salveson Whaling Company of Leith , Scotland, An Anglo Norwegian Co. I was twenty three years of age in June 1947 when I approached the Superintendent and asked if there were any vacancies for engineers on the whale catchers. He seemed quite keen to help me and asked for my name and address and said I would hear from the company. A few weeks later a letter arrived asking me to present myself to the Salveson Company offices 22 Bernard Street, Leith, Edinburgh for an interview.

The end of the war had brought some improvement to our lives, but not much! The country was bankrupt, food was still rationed because Britain couldn't afford to buy food from abroad and was having to send food over to Germany, which was a bit ironic. I later found out that Sterling was unacceptable abroad! The rations were now just adequate two years after the war ended. Mum could now get a few onions for the pot.

I had bought my first motor bike, second hand, from a guy in Newcastle which a cousin of Mum's had found for me. I paid £15 for this motorbike, a Douglas twin cylinder engine (fore and aft, not across the bike). It was a1936 model with an open flywheel and a gear change lever on the petrol tank! It had seen better days. I went to Newcastle to collect it and the vendor showed me how to start it, after a ride up and down his street I drove it, careered more like to Charlie Watts house, this cousin's husband. It was a lot different to a push bike but I was determined to master it, as a cowboy would break in a horse!

The Douglas motorbike had a long wheel base and it steered like a horse! Very reluctantly! I had difficulty judging my direction at the speed produced by the 350 cc engine, so different to my old push bike! I had been given a pair of goggles first world war type and flying helmet - pilot for the use of! It had a thin leather strap which fastened under my chin and with my old raincoat buttoned up to my neck I set off for Middlesbrough 50 mile away ; I skated through the city streets of Newcastle avoiding trams and horse drawn carts with abandon. The front halves of my coat blown away leaving my legs and nether regions open to the cold north eastern elements, I was numb! A hair raising development occurred crossing the high level bridge over the River Tyne. I entered the box girder bridge, noting the two sets of tram lines, then unwisely proceeded to overtake the tram ahead of me. The tramlines were set in wooden blocks which were greasy and cambered between each set of rails. As I came alongside the tram I saw another tram ahead of me entering the bridge from the south side. I had to avoid being caught between two trams which would have been a disaster since the Douglas handlebars were wider than the clearance between the two trams passing each other. The oncoming tram driver sounded his horn furiously! But I had no chance of getting back behind the tram I was overtaking! There was only one option left to me, by increasing speed I just managing to slip in front of the tram to my left before the other tram came level. I hadn't seen it approaching because of the bend in the road, skating along is the right word for it! On the greasy wooden blocks I slipped past the tram as the bike fortunately skidding the correct way to avoid certain death! I think it was an old but intelligent machine and in my years of dealing with machines I believe that some are more intelligent than others! Either that or the spirit friends are taking care of me, most likely?

After a few weeks I found a major problem with the Douglas. The engine rattled like a bag of hammers. The former owner had used badly fitting tools that had damaged the nuts and screw heads. Bolts holding the valve cam wheels were not properly secured and had loosened causing unrepairable damage. The chap responsible had used blunt screwdrivers as well as badly fitted spanners, this created difficulty dismantling the engine. Spare parts were unobtainable partly due to the war. My brother Jack who was working at Smiths Docks at the time came to the rescue. In a couple of days making enquiries he was able to tell me where there was an old Douglas engine at a garage near my home. I went round and paid £2 10/- for this but had no means of getting it round to Granville Road. It was only a couple of hundred yards so they kindly delivered it for me. I was able to strip this engine down for the parts I required. I was back to the old push bike that granddad had given me for my 13th birthday. I had removed the engine from the Douglas and stripped it down on the kitchen table. Mum was very good about it. She didn't complain about the smell of dirty engine oil. I think she enjoyed the fact that we were starting again where Fred and she had once been. Eventually I got the best half of one engine fitted to half of the other and still had a few bits over. I used it for a while going back and forwards to Hartlepool but now with a lot more knowledge decided it was time to move upmarket. I sold it for £45 soon after making it just road worthy and bought a 1939 250 cc BSA. I would have liked the new Matchless with teledraulic forks but it was £95 with a long supply waiting list and beyond my dreams. I had to use the push bike some of the time because the petrol ration wasn't enough to motor every day to work and I also wanted petrol to go to Hartlepool at weekends.

It wasn't all nose to the grindstone though, now turned sixteen we became of interest to the young girls in the time office. They would open their office windows and chat us up as we passed. "What are you doing tonight cheeky?" As two or three of us walked by. "Nothing much," we replied in the absence of anything better to say. "We'll be at the Saint Alphonsus dance at seven o clock!" "Ok we replied." I had to ask the friend who had replied, "where's the Alphonsus, shall we go?" "I can't dance!" "Don't matter they'll teach you, It's a good night. It's off Ormesby Bank, get such and such a bus." I told my mum where I was going. She was very pleased for me. She had enjoyed dances when she was younger. I polished my shoes and asked my mum "will these be alright to dance in?" "Oh yes they have a leather sole and they're not too heavy. Be careful not to step on the girls toes" she replied. I had a good walk before I got to the bus stop. I got off at the bottom of the bank and walked up. As I approached the hall the sound of the music guided me to its location. It was warming and very inviting. The band took the name of the leader, Jimmy Carr and his three piece band, Drums a saxophone and clarinet. The saxophone was playing a mellow tune to the swish, swish of the drummer's light strokes of the thin wire brushes on the snare drum. With his pedal he gently thumped the tempo on the base drum. Inside the hall couples of all ages were gracefully moving in pairs to the music. It was obvious that a few of the younger chaps were still struggling to dance to the music with the various rhythms, the waltz with its one two three, and others with a quick, quick, slow. It require concentration and left no time for misbehaviour, we all wanted the means to ask some pretty girl to dance! Four of the girls from the time office were waiting for us at the side of the dance floor. Two other lads of our crowd were already with them. As the music started again this big happy girl grabbed one of the boys and dragged him onto the floor. With his left hand in her right she pulled his right hand round her ample waist and jerked him round to the dum de dum of the music. With his eyes on his feet he stepped out valiantly and made his way round the dance floor being careful not to step on the brave girl's toes !. One of the other girls pulled another of us onto the floor and he bravely did his best. I was eventually taken onto the floor by the big girl, she hugged me to her ample bosom and almost lifted my feet off the floor. I was thankful when the ordeal was over. I promised I would take lessons from my mum. We had better fortune with the old fashioned dances with set steps that were easy to

108

remember. The Dorothy Waltz with three steps forward, three back, twirl a couple of times and reverse or something like that. At work next day in the dinner hour one of the older chaps would take us through the walz, one two three, one two three and the foxtrot. Mum encouraged me at home. In a few weeks I was able to do the basic steps but had to concentrate hard! It didn't take much to put a foot wrong, the secret was to keep going and give a hitch to put it right.

When I became efficient enough to be able to ask a girl if she would dance with me I would go to whatever dance I fancied. After trying most of the Church Hall dances I promoted myself to larger venues, Middlesbrough Town hall dance and twice went to a famous local dance in Stockton, The Maison De Dance where the renowned Jack Marwood and his band played the best swing music. At the Maison it wasn't easy to find a girl to dance with, the place was crawling with Canadian airmen with lots of money and fancy American style accents. They were based only a few miles away at Thornaby Air Field which had been an RAF base before the war. The girls loved them and they loved the girls so much so that many were married and sent to Canada with their babies before the war ended and the husbands were demobbed.

It was difficult to get home from Stockton. Fleets of double deck buses generally took the dancers home from the big dance halls but taking a girl home from the Maison was a problem if they didn't live in Middlesbrough.

I was fortunate to be able to go to Aunt Jenny's behind the cobbler's shop on a Friday night and stay over until the Sunday to spend a couple of days in Hartlepool with Dorothy. She in return had an Aunt Amy who lived in Middlesbrough and was able to stay with her on occasion so we could be together for a while. So we discovered each other's family. Our love slowly and gently grew firm and strong and will be eternal after 59 wedding anniversaries. Her father had died when Dorothy was fifteen years old. Now in our long courtship I had become the man in her life. I was determined to take good care of her.

There was never any misbehaviour at these dances. First the sixteen year olds had an object, to learn to dance! Secondly they wanted to emulate the twenty year olds who generally could ask any girl to dance and were socially upmarket. The third reason was the romantic calm atmosphere, the gentle music loud enough to make pleasant discreet conversation between couples. At the St. Alphonsus Church dance,

Jimmy Carr played the drums and sang the romantic songs of the day with a good imitation of Bing Crosby. With all those pretty girls to chat to who wanted to cause trouble? It was a sad day for young people when these dances were forced to close because a few stupid young men were allowed to wreck this atmosphere. It was the introduction of stupid novelty dances like The Twist that gave the dance hall entrepreneurs the idea that never mind the dancing, they don't need melody, a screaming guitar and drumming to get them on the dance floor to wriggle about. Flashing lights and high decibels of sound give a false exciting atmosphere that makes sensible conversation difficult and sadly encourages the foolish element of young people to misbehave. Many years later when as a parent I became a member of the local school P.T.A. the parent teacher association I was surprised to hear a lady teacher say that the Youth Club had a problem with the sixteen year olds and twenty year olds fighting when they had a Disco. In my day the sixteen year olds tried to emulate the twenty year olds who were good dancers and the girls were keen to dance with. With today's aggressive music, flashing lights and lack of need to learn to dance it is not surprising that chaos results in such an atmosphere. Music is now big business but teenagers today are being ripped off because music died when the aggressive guitar overtook the mellow saxophone. The Beatles matured to write good music and found it necessary to include violin backing for some of their more sophisticated beautiful music.

I had been to an all male school, I had girl cousins and knew of the secret difference between us, but I was fourteen before I accepted how babies were made. The country boys saw it with the sheep the cows and pigs. I knew about fish eggs but I was horrified when I saw two dogs locked together so I wasn't interested in sex.

I imagined if that happened to a married couple they would have to be taken to hospital to be separated, another of life's mysteries. The media didn't raise the subject of sex either which helped to avoid thinking about it. The News of The World ran some curious stories of scout masters and stuff but I couldn't connect it with anything I had experienced. Another older apprentice I was working with once surprised me by laughingly putting his hand out to fondle me. I was sixteen and the effect came as a shock, it took my breath away and my legs weakened for a few seconds, I wasn't offended, I liked George very much and it was only the once. I took it as a bit of fun, it was done in the open but other efforts to seduce me failed after George's warning fumble. The war and my apprenticeship filled my thoughts.

Now Dorothy occupied some of the day but in a kindly way. Some days in the dinner hour a few of us would walk the mile or so into the small town of South Bank- on- Tees. We could get a dinner at the British Restaurant where a war time meal could be had for a shilling and sixpence. On the way back each day I called in to the post office and bought a Winifred Atwell post card that had a soppy cartoon of two young cartoon child lovers and a funny verse one side. I wrote an affectionate note to Dorothy on the other side and posted it. In those days even with the war, it would arrive in Hartlepool the next morning. I found a little box in her wardrobe six months after she died with all these cards and a few of my letters, collector's items today, they were posted 1943 with postage stamps of King George VI. The year we first went out together. I suppose the mobile phone is used today, I see young people walking along talking away into one.

The holiday week was always the third week in July. Have I said it was without pay? This was so maintenance of the services could take place. Cranes were overhauled, air compressors to supply the ring main for the shipyard air driven drills and caulking tools were serviced. It generally rained that week! I went over to Hartlepool and stayed with my Aunt Jenny for the week and found company with my friends from childhood. Now Dorothy took a holiday the same week and our love was becoming stronger as we discovered eachothers habits. I had cycled to Hartlepool so we were able to cycle together to the lovely little village of Elwick to be alone for a few hours. We felt shy being together in Hartlepool, it's a small town and people gossip. We were not ready for that yet.

The holiday week over I was back at the shipyard on Monday morning, no more holiday until next year. At eighteen years old eligible to work overtime now. Even Sundays were to be either work or Home Guard. I did manage to skip a few duties and spend the week end with Dorothy.

The two Engine Works Foremen , with black bowler hats and navy blue three piece suits were Mister " Billie " Dixon, related to a past shipyard owner Railton Dixon of the River Tees, and Mister Tommy Brand. These were authoritarian figures with the power to sack a man on the spot, I suppose their job was to coordinate the materials and so forth, Tommy Brand seemed to be always walking around with a sheaf of papers in his hands looking worried to death whereas Billie stalked about to keep people busy. He was "retired" early because his ideas of constructing engines caused problems of changing spare parts. Spare parts like big end bearings and other small parts of the engine were bolted onto a large steel plate painted black with red paint under the spare part so that it was noticeable if a piece had been used when returning to port. This was fastened to a bulkhead in the engine room of all ships built by Smith's Dock.. Billie's method of fitting spare parts was not good for His Majesty's Ships at sea. He advocated adjusting the bearing instead of the connecting rod, it was easier to do but not standard practice. Not practical when a change of bearing was required, they had to be of standard dimensions. Tommy Brand's brother Stan Brand replaced Billie. Stan was a gentleman, easy to talk to and very kind. He broke the dress code of a foreman by wearing a trilby hat instead of the black bowler. When I had a wheel spindle break with metal fatigue in my 1936 Douglas motorbike and unable to find spares I took the pieces to Stan and within a few hours he had arranged a lathe to make me another one. I don't think he had any children but I would have liked a dad like him.

In 1945 after my apprenticeship I was working overtime on a Whale Catcher that had a Norwegian designed two stroke steam engine Smith's Docks had fitted, It was after eleven o 'clock at night The Fredrikstad Damp Motor had unusual pistons about two feet deep with segmented piston rings top and bottom. Preparing for sea trials we were working late on last minute jobs. The engine main steam stop valve was found to be seized only hours before the ship was to sail on sea trials. Stan asked me to go to South bank on my pushbike to call out a turner, machinist, to make a replacement part. It was near to midnight when I called at the turner's house and found lights still on, I knocked at the door, the chap answered, I told him the problem, he was taken aback and said, but I'm decorating the living room ! He considered for a few seconds, "I'll be there in twenty minutes,." I peddled back relieved to tell Stan the good news! I like to think it wasn't because of the Company's benefit he was willing to come in at such an inconvenient time but because it was his loyalty to Stan.

The shipyard only used air driven hand tools and had big compressors and air tanks which supplied the whole yard with compressed air by two inch steel pipes with tapping at intervals to connect various machines, a drill, rivet hammer or other machine tool device.

Steam engines required a lot of water and ships could only carry a limited amount of high quality water for the boilers, the answer to this problem was found in the early steam ships, the condenser! The steam after doing any work in the engine or the winches the steering engine or the cabin radiators was piped back to the engine room. These pipes carrying the used steam were connected to the condenser. It was here condensed on brass tubes through which cold sea water was pumped by a centrifugal pump, The pure condensed water then was pumped back to the boiler with a high pressure pump to overcome the boiler pressure of 250 pounds per square inch. The condenser was bolted directly to the back of the engine to accept the exhaust steam from the low pressure cylinder which actually operated on the vacuum created by the condenser. A job that taught the apprentice 'team work' was to assemble a steam condenser. This was a steel vessel about ten feet long, wider at the top where the steam from the main engine came in to condense on the seven hundred or more brass tubes. These tubes were fitted into brass end plates about an inch thick at each end of the steel vessel.

Where ever possible steam from the boiler was condensed back into water and any leaks of steam quickly sealed . In some parts of the world water was more expensive than fuel oil. The tubes were passed through the brass end plates that were drilled and threaded to form glands round the tube ends. One brass end plate was covered with a thick piece of plywood to prevent the tubes moving while the tubes at the other end were packed round with _ inch round lamp wick soaked in linseed oil. The apprentices had to make their own tools to stem this wick into the internal threaded glands that were machined into the brass tube plate. When each gland was tightly packed a brass ferrule was screwed in place to maintain a seal for the low pressure steam against the sea water which went through the tubes. This seal was vital. If the condensed water was contaminated with any mineral impurities such as salt from the sea water it could cause serious damage to the boiler!

A team of four boys cleverly selected by Tommy, worked in pairs, an older boy with previous experience and a younger boy in each pair. Each pair would take turns to prepare the thin round cotton lamp wick, cutting it to a suitable length for each tube and soaking the bundles in a can of linseed oil. The other pair packed the glands, fitted the brass ferrules and tightened them being careful not to shear the top of the ferrule for this would make it impossible to remove or tighten if it leaked when tested. If it did happen that a brittle brass ferrule sheared off, wails of denial arose! Help would be required from a more advanced engine fitter to pick out the broken part of brass ferrule embedded in the end plate, care taken not to damage the screw thread or further surgery would be required small picking chisels would be made to suit the job, time wasted! Each pair of apprentices would probably pack half a row of tubes, then change places with the other pair, until the whole end plate was complete. It took days. When one end of the condenser was completed the plywood bolted at the other end to stop the tubes sliding out during packing was now removed and this end was now packed and ferruled up tight. It was then necessary to test the work for leaks! This was a wet cold business in winter. All open branches on the condenser, which in the engine room were connected to pipes carrying exhaust steam to be condensed into boiler water were now blanked off.

The condenser was filled with water with a hosepipe. It took a few hours to fill, then the moment of truth! A bucket type hand pump took ages to pump water into the condenser up to about 45lbs per square inch! The condenser would normally operate at about 25 inches of vacuum. Under test it was filled with about five tons of water. Anxious lads waited for the leaks, it could take some time for the leak of water to creep past any badly compressed oil soaked wick. The boiled linseed oil, also used in making paint in those days, dried hard forming a good seal if carefully packed round the brass tube.

The first leak appeared. "it's one of yours!", the innocent party would shout. "We didn't do that row" would be the reply. A few more leaks would be found so denials were put aside and co-operation was made in order to avoid the horror of having to empty the condenser to repack the offending glands, then fill it again and pump it up.

A bit of gentle tightening would generally do the trick, "Mind don't shear off the brass ferrule!" The brass ferule was a thin round item that pressed the packing tight. It had screw threads cut into the thin outer wall of the item reducing the thickness even more. A ferrule broken in the tube plate had to be picked out with a thin picking tool made from a suitable piece of tool hardened steel. This was a delicate almost surgical operation care taken not to damage the existing thread in the tube plate. For rough lads this was a delicate learning curve, failure not allowed

Skilful discretion, a bit of useful competition to improve one's ability, and pride in a good job well done! Thus working with others was introduced, it was like a great big family! As such we were liable to a few rows but generally happy! I thought so anyway!

Quite a lot of chaps had amusing nick names, an apprentice in my year was called 'Blossom!' His name was Harry Almond, hence almond blossom! He was a lovely lad with rosy cheeks, always a happy face and temperament to match.

A machinist nicknamed 'Chocolate' was not so happy! An innocent apprentice who used the name to him would arouse his anger! His name was Huntley. Huntley and Palmer's made chocolate biscuits, I never knew his first name but had no cause to contact him, thank goodness. I wonder what my nickname might have been? I used to get 'Dins' from my friends.

Smith's Docks inherited probably a hundred years of experience from village blacksmiths building steam engines for masters such as George Stephenson who set up the first production line building of steam locomotives. Men who gained experience there would be drafted to others interested in marine propulsion. From the early uneconomical compound engines improvements eventually produced the ultimate triple expansion reciprocating steam engine. The skills were passed on through generations of apprentices. Smith's Docks inherited and created it's own 'in House' engineer fitters.

Company Chief Engineer Managers selected the men for promotion. Reliable strong in mind chargehands and foremen who they were sure would be capable of ensuring efficiency and had a thorough knowledge of the work. Education through evening classes with final examinations for sea going, Second and Chief Engineers Certificates were available for those able to study the requirements. The intake of apprentices at Smith's Docks had not been great because of the 1930s depression. Jobs were handed down from father to son, my chances of an apprenticeship had been slight, I had been fortunate once again, my Mum made the right decision for me.

One of the early jobs Tommy gave me was that of "fettling" steel castings of big ends, the newly cast steel bearings, later to be lined with white metal. This was then machined to the diameter of the crank shaft before we bedded them in as described above. The castings had to be ground to bright steel where the hot white metal was poured into the cast steel bearing round a mandrel to suit the size of the shaft. This was

115

accomplished with an air driven grinder applied to the rough steel until it became bright. Then the surface could be tinned to take the white metal, soldered in fact.

The shipyard only used air driven hand tools and had big compressors and air tanks which supplied the whole yard with compressed air by two inch steel pipes with tapping at intervals to connect various machines, a drill, rivet hammer or other machine tool. The grinder created lots of loamy sand dust and breathing masks were unheard of! We wrapped a length of muslin cloth round our faces, but it was expensive, so any old cloth would do! A good cough would produce lots of black phlegm. I still had my tonsils, that may have helped reduce any damage. This was not an apprentice's job, it was normally done at the foundry but I think there was a war time emergency of supply or manpower, and we got on with it!

In1940 a tool store was built along the length of the engine workshop. This was a big improvement. Billie the tool Smith was now set up here so he was readily available to forge any tool we required at short notice. The early engineers had made small drills to drill metal forged by the tool smith from round bar reduced in diameter and flattened at the end to from the two angled cutting surfaces. Smith's Docks were still using these home made flat drills invented by the village blacksmith of the 18th century. We had to grind the cutting edge on this thin end forged by the blacksmith to the size hole we wanted to drill. Then set the opposing angles of the two edges on the grindstone. This was time wasting and with no shank to guide it the drill made a poor inaccurate hole. Now we were supplied with high speed steel twist drills and good quality hacksaw blades. If there hadn't been a war they might still be using those methods.

The slipways on which the ship's hull was built were originally served with derricks each side of the slipway. Winches wound a cable over pulleys to lift the ribs and plates and other bits and pieces of the hull then manual chain blocks may be necessary to pull the part into its designated place. Now to serve the war effort investment was made, concrete runways were built between the slipways. The obsolete winches and derricks were replaced by swan-neck cranes that ran on rails along the length of the runway. making assembly of vessels quicker. Fitting engines into ships hulls      The first years as an apprentice in Smith's Docks was to experience working conditions that had not changed since the Company established the shipyard there in

116

1910. It would be kind to call them primitive.

I learned to bed in the white metal bearings for the main engine. This soft white metal scrapes easy to allow the bearing area to be limited to the bottom third where it runs on the crankshaft. We made scrapers from old half round files given to the tool smith who put them in his forge and shaped them with a gentle curve to form the cutting edges. The engine fitter then could grind this hard steel cutting edge to suit the bearing he was bedding to the shaft. Special chisels were also required to cut small channels in the bearing white metal to allow oil to get to the bearing surface. When forged by the tool smith some chisels had to have the cutting edge ground and then hardened. Older apprentices would show the younger lads how to do these jobs. Unlike the machines of today with oil pressure fed to the bearings the machined parts had to be fitted with appropriate clearances and bearing surfaces.

The area round the shipyard had been created by slag from the early Iron Works. This slag which is waste from the furnace after the iron has been melted from the ore had been used to reduce the river mouth which in 1860 was about a mile wide. By making the river mouth narrower with waste slag from the early iron works the depth at low tide was increased greatly by the river flow scouring the sand and mud from the floor of the river bed. At the present day at high tide a depth of forty feet can float large vessels into Teesport a modern docking area to unload various commodities. This rendered the dock up river near Middlesbrough obsolete and available for development.

On the 22nd of June 1940 a corvette built for the Free French Navy La Bastiaise steamed out on sea trials with its French crew and twelve men from Smiths Docks. Enemy planes had dropped mines near the river mouth. The Corvette had the bow blown off and sank with a loss of many of the men on board. The Free French Navy crew, the Middlesbrough pilot, twelve of Smith's Docks managers and men and five contractors. It was believed this was one of the first magnetic mines laid on the sea bed. The activity of the German planes at the approaches to the river had not aroused suspicion of some thick person on watch with no imagination ! The conventional mine required a heavy anchor, the magnetic mine was more suited to aircraft delivery. Laid on the sea bed the effect of the ships steel hull on the magnet detonator caused it to explode as a ship approached. This device sank other vessels in coastal waters until a means of detonating them safely was worked out. The apprentice engine fitter Raymond Renwick who survived the sinking told me it blew the bow off the ship as she approached the mouth of the river returning from a successful sea trial. Ray said he was in the tail end propellor shaft compartment checking the shaft bearings when the explosion took place. He managed to get up a vertical ladder and over the side before the ship plunged to the sea bed. Ray was in the sea with Alex Henderson an elderly engineer, Alex told him he couldn't keep afloat and drowned before a boat arrived to pick up survivors. Sadly I learned a couple of years later that Ray Renwick was killed when later serving as an engineer in the Merchant Navy his ship was sunk by enemy action. Billie Pringle, a favourite old friend of mine, didn't get out of the engine room, He was a lovely old man. He told me that as a boy he remembered when it was possible at low tide to ride across the river mouth on horseback! Many years later I confirmed his story when I read in The History Of Middlesbrough by Head Librarian William Lillie that at low tide it was possible to ride a horse across the river mouth in 1852 & 1862, records taken of the river then gave depth of the river at low water as two and a half feet and three and a half feet respectively. By 1960 due to banking up the sides of the river with waste slag from the iron works the depth at low tide was 40 feet. This was achieved not just by dredging, but mainly by the "scour" of the river flow. Billie Pringle had been in the engine room and had no chance to escape. He worked from a wooden cabin on the dock side and we apprentices loved to pop in for a gossip and hear his tales of the sea. On a cold day it was a warm oasis , he had a little pot bellied stove in his cabin and was always quietly humming some hymn or other. We would gaze at all the ships tackle hanging around the place. I was very sad to hear of his loss, he died on duty without a medal or recognition. His name with the others is inscribed on a plaque formerly in Smith's Docks Offices but they were demolished when the shipyard closed. The plaque is now at Eden Camp which is a war time museum in North Yorkshire. It should be in Middlesbrough Town Hall and remembered every 11th of November. There were other dens like Billie's  the occupant generally had a tale to tell and was probably well past retirement age but they were able bodied and valued by the senior managers for their experience, the petty rules would not be applied to them. At a small boiler house near the fitting out jetty the old attendant had his Jack Russell dog with him. He was delighted to show off its tricks. A cigarette and match was placed on a low stool and the dog taken outside. When asked to bring the cigarette it did so, held in its lips without wetting it ,and then the match .All done by love and kindness.

In 1938 when war was imminent, gas masks were being distributed at the nearest church hall, Saint Michael's Church in Victoria Road, (now a Mosque) My mum stubbornly refused to go for them. At fourteen years of age I went for the gas masks and the lady in charge of distribution didn't mind giving me one for my mum too.

The anti-submarine Corvette's had been designed from the whale catcher, and like the catcher the Corvette is a good sea boat in heavy weather, and although larger is still very uncomfortable! Originally they were designed for coastal command, anti submarine service. It carried a crew of about 90 men with guns and anti-submarine depth charge gear.

German submarines in World War Two were mainly deployed in the Atlantic. It was soon apparent the Corvettes were needed on Convoy escort duty but they only carried enough fuel to cross the Atlantic and lacked the range for effective long periods in Atlantic service.

When war was declared gas masks had to be carried wherever we went, but contrary to belief that there was a phoney war for the first six months, a few bombs were dropped on South bank near a railway bridge and the trolley bus shed , very early on in the war. I saw the crater of one of the bombs as the trolley bus went over the railway bridge. It was about fifteen feet across in some rough grass, not very deep, but not a bad shot for the railway line. This line was of low importance. A complete waste of war effort on the part of 'Jerrie.' I'd give him 2 out of 10! I think a cow in one of the fields was killed.

The only occasion I found mum upset was when she came in from shopping , trailing round the shops standing in queues to get what food she could. "What's wrong Mum?" This was 1942 at about the time when the U boats were winning. The desperation in her voice evoked disaster! "I haven't been able to get an onion anywhere! How can I make a meal without an onion!" I must say she loved her grub! There was nothing I could do about the onions. We did eventually get boxes of dried onion, from America I suppose.

Later brick air raid shelters were built in the street. They were cold and damp with a six inch concrete roof. Any improvement being we would not have to be dug out from a direct hit! We only used them a few times. By now Adolf had bitten off more than he could chew by invading Russia. He couldn't spare the planes to bother us. However, one night we were caught on the garden path by a bomb exploding before we reached the shelter. It destroyed a house about 100 yards away, the dust and cordite hit our faces and hair. Mum was more upset when windows were broken and soot fell down the chimney. She was a very stoic lady without self pity. The curtains were torn just a little. Well she'd seen it all before in the first war at Hartlepool with the bombardment by German battleships.

Another time, when I was sixteen years old, that I saw my mother upset was when I came home from work one particular Saturday. We worked from 7:30 am until noon as part of the 56 hour week, "What's the matter mum," I said. "That's our meat ration for the week", she sniffed! I looked on the table and there laid on the opened wrapping paper was a piece of skin the size and shape of a small hand, one half of which had half an inch of beef on it! I still had my coat on. I picked up the ration of meat and walked around to the butcher's shop. There were a couple of women in the shop. Mr Langstaff, the butcher, was a tall lean man with sharp sallow features, dark greasy hair combed close back with dark narrowed eyes, not a jovial type at all. I waited until they had been served and said respectfully, "this is our ration for the week, could you include it with a larger family's ration and give us something else?" He looked at me with a steady gaze for a tense moment, lips pursed. I feared the worse! "Yes son, I can," he said purposefully. I felt ashamed of the impression I had previously formed of him. He wrapped up a nice piece of lean meat, perhaps a bit more than our ration, I distinctly remember he didn't weigh it! I don't think he liked my Mum though! She was a jovial type and liked the men. I was relieved it was nothing more serious than this.incident which had made mum upset, but it made me realised how bad the war in the Atlantic was going. I'm sure mum gave me much of her ration of cheese, it was only an  ounce or so anyway. In the shipyard we all felt it! There was an air of desperation about the place, nothing but bad news.

The work in the shipyard was very manual. Big nuts and bolts required seven pound hammers to tighten the nuts with big spanners. Assembling the engine valve gear, steel levers (which moved the valve gear from ahead to astern) were heated to expand them a few thousands of an inch. They had to be forced with twenty pound hammers onto six inch shafts These levers had not to fail! The safety of the ship depended on the manouveres of the engine. We made the ships as good as we could for the men who sailed in them. The four dry docks were always full of ships damaged by torpedoes or mines which had managed to stay afloat. Some ships with holes big enough to drive two double deck buses through! In some instances holes near the water line were patched up with planks of wood and cement to get back for repair. It was very grim! It's all on record I suppose but sadly a generation passes and people forget.

Sadly Stan Brand died at the age of 52. He had had a heart attack, cutting his garden hedge .At this time, 1953 I had returned from a second whaling season. Avoiding the shipyard and river to subdue the urge to "ship out" again, I had joined I.C.I. Chemical complex at Wilton. Stan's funeral time coincided with the end of my six to two shift. I got to the church in Eston early and sat in a back pew, the church became full. The service over I came out of the church to find a vast crowd lining the path three deep on each side to the grave at the back of the church. The whole of Smiths Docks must have been there and probable most of the South Bank community. Stan Brand was very highly respected and sadly missed, what a pity my father was unable to receive the affection I had for the men who influenced me most. I couldn't hate my father but it was difficult to understand why he failed as a father. He had tried when I was a kid by having motor boats made for me but a hug was what was wanted, he had never been taught how to love anyone.

The shipyards are no more. Oil rigs are the business now but you can't sail the seas in them to bring supplies and they can't defend our Island.

We were saved by the skin of our teeth and by the United States of America. I will never forget the help America sent us. Food. Spam, the sweetest of meats at that time and tea with strange big tea leaves. We didn't know then that Britain had to pay for every bit. The final payment was made to the United States of America early in 2007. Not forgetting the munitions and ships we were given. An old American destroyer with four funnels arrived at Smiths Docks, one of fifty they had given us in exchange for the use of some bases in the Bahamas. It was refurbished and put into service.

Even with this U.S. assistance it seemed a long time before the threat of defeat eventually faded. All due to the stubborn courage and words of Winston Churchill, he gave us the will to carry on. People who now write of his faults have no experience of the times or of his heroic inspiration. Looking back I often wonder what courage he had knowing how desperate the situation was to rally the ministers in the cabinet who wanted to agree terms with Hitler. We paid a big price in holding the fort until help arrived from the USA, It was nearly too late. The effect of the struggle is still with us, we stood alone then. In my opinion we need to remain free. Europe has a desire to absorb us into a federal state with nations that have different ways of thinking to us. Both France and Germany have had designs to dominate Europe over the past two hundred years, both failed in Russia. Could they try again? They want to standardise us all. We seem to have no control over our usual way of life. Brussels decides how we are governed. I hope we never have to resist again, they are making escape impossible! When the war ended the whole of Europe and Russia was badly in need of food, millions of people had been displaced, crops and cattle destroyed. We were bankrupt and Sterling was not acceptable abroad. Something had to be done to improve the situation.

Whaling had gone on all over the northern hemisphere since man had created the means to capture this beast from the sea. The Basque fishermen of Spain and France were first recorded in the 13th century as putting to sea to catch the smaller of the whale species. I believe this is firm evidence that there was an abundance of whales concurring with a shortage of fish. Why else would fishermen resort to such a change of working. Whales eat not only krill, the tiny shrimp like creatures that swarm at times in the ocean and feed many other species. Whales also eat young fish like herring, oily fish that will produce the tons of fat that covers the whale inches thick under the skin. Fish spawn on the sea weed that covers parts of the continental shelves, the newly hatched fish when seeking a better food supply move out in large shoals to seek pastures new. The prehistoric whale that survived in the sea when the dinosaurs were wiped out know of the fish life cycle and have lately been shown on TV consuming tons of small fish in a few minutes. The early Basque whalers eventually developed skills and bigger ships in the monopoly they had for three hundred years until the Spanish Armada interrupted the sale of oil to European merchants. The Basque whalers probably took part in the Armada and many would perish as a result. The Dutch were first prominent sailing to the Arctic to catch whales with the British not so successful because of lack of experience. It was a long slow learning curve.

In the sixteenth century most European Countries with a seaboard had sent ships north in this dangerous work. Companies went bankrupt. Ships were lost. But gradually over the years a steady supply of the valuable products, particularly the oil were procured. By the end of the 19th century whaling in the Arctic with sailing brigs and hand pulled whaleboats was unprofitable. America had been the last to give up whaling early in the 1920's.

The last Square Rigger, a Brig named Wanderer with hand rowing dory's and hand thrown harpoons, left New Bedford, Massachusetts on the 25th May 1924. She anchored that night off Cutty Hunk Island dragged her anchor and was blown onto the rocks and was wrecked. The Right whale was so scarce it was uneconomical to hunt them and the other species were either too big and fast to catch from a rowing boat or sank when killed before they were able to tow it to the mother ship. Why would a Brig sailing ship skipper want to anchor near a rocky shore with the wind blowing onto the land? Even with a steam engine we were nervous being near the coast. Murphy's Law states that if you are going to have an engine break down it will be at the most inappropriate place and time. The Antarctic Ocean is a big and lonely place if you need help.

In 1900 a Norwegian, Sven Foyn, designed and built the first steam whale catcher, with a coal fired boiler. The mother ship, a sailing Brig was unable to carry enough coal to boil out the oil and was only able to steam the catcher for a few days. A limited number of about thirty whales were caught but these were the big whales seventy foot or more long. It proved that a successful expedition was possible. Further development would be economically viable if coal stocks were available. A Norwegian Captain Larsen sought financial backing to set up a whaling station on South Georgia Island. Only the Argentineans would finance him and in 1904 a whaling station was set up in a bay near the north east end of South Georgia. He named it Gryt Vicken, translated meaning 'The Pot Bay', from a few metal pots left there by early sealers. A stock of coal was taken down there and a factory was set up to extract the oil. Huts were taken down to house the men working there and a successful business was created.

Captain James Cook in January 1775 had sailed by the Island whilst on his way to the Pacific Ocean. He had with him one of Harrison's accurate chronometer clocks so was able to fix the longitude accurately to enable a ship to return there without wasting time searching. The

Harrison clock recorded the time at Greenwich when it was noon at the ship's position on the earth recognised by the sun's apogee, its highest point. A simple calculation gave the distance east or west of Greenwich in degrees. Captain Cook recorded in his ships log what a miserable place South Georgia was with snow covered mountains running straight into the sea even in the short summer days. On the 20th of January 1755 he went ashore with a party of men, named the place Possession Bay and claimed it for King George III of England. Returning to his ship he sailed around the South side to establish that it was an island. He then carried on his voyage west.

Captain Larsen had not thought to ask permission of the British Government and diplomatic representation was made. The British Government demanded the Argentinean Company pay a hefty licence to operate their Company on British territory. To sweeten the British Government, Captain Larsen offered to help the setting up of a British Whaling Station at Cumberland bay called Leith Harbour, South Georgia, 15 miles West of Gryt Vicken. The Anglo Norwegian Company operated under various names lately called Salvesen Co., 22 Bernard Street, Leith, Edinburgh. The Norwegians and British had built steam catchers from 1910 and operated from South Georgia Island on the edge of the Antarctic Circle.

Smith's Docks was given orders for steam whale catchers from about 1910. With the advent of the steam engine, ships could now go to the more profitable but equally perilous Antarctic seas. It was an eight thousand mile voyage from Europe to the Antarctic but if demand was there it could be profitable. The British had a head start with steam and territorial rights on South Georgia,

The National Government of 1944 decide to revive the whaling industry. Meat and other products from the dollar area were rationed for eight years after the war. Licences were given to the whaling Companies to design custom built factory ships and Catcher vessels.

We only paid off our war debt to America early in 2007. We didn't have dollars to buy enough food from abroad and were rationed for meat, sugar and other commodities for eight years after the war. Europe was devastated with fourteen million displaced people to feed.

Modern whaling was not the cruel business that is expounded by animal rights experts today. It was a professional job of necessity, an injured eighty ton whale on the end of a line is a danger to the ship and men. The gunners had to be as professional as the modern abattoir. The business is almost self-regulating because of the costs of seeking the falling stocks of whales in the great Southern oceans. Off the continental shelf of Norway the whales compete with man for the fish stocks. It is regulated by people who hopefully have considered judgement of the whales existence and man's needs of fish stocks

Before the war ended Furness shipyard at Haverton Hill had orders to build Factory Ships. Over the next ten years Smith's Docks built about forty whale catcher vessels for Salvesen Co. of Leith, Scotland and a Norwegian Company.

Orders for some merchant ships were built along with the whale catcher ship orders. The steel for these ships was produced on Teesside in the sterling area. Teesside's economy based on heavy industry was saved for a few years after the war until I.C.I. came along at Wilton near Redcar with a big demand for labour.

# CHAPTER 11
# JULY 1947, WHALING

*A chance to earn enough money to marry the girl, a ride to Leith, Edinburgh. Sailing on Southern Truce, a little whale catcher 8,000 miles down the Atlantic to South Georgia Island.*

I had been involved in building these whale catchers and now in 1947, at twenty three years of age, desperate to marry my sweetheart, I wondered if I could get a job as engineer on one of these little ships. It meant being away from home for nine months. One of Smith's Dock chief Engineer managers had joined Salvesen Whaling Co. as a superintendent. I would look out for him. I told no one of my idea.

I saw Mr Turner in the engine works one day in July 1947. I asked if there was any chance of a job as engineer on a whale catcher? "Oh yes" was the reply. "Give me your name and address and we'll send for you." In due course an invitation came from Salveson Co. of Leith, Edinburgh, for me to attend an interview for the position of Third engineer on a whale catcher. I travelled the 150 miles there on my BSA motorcycle, part of it along the ancient Great North Road. My great grandfather Francis Dinsdale may have done this run many times before as he was a coach driver. The interview wouldn't take long I hoped.

I set off from Middlesbrough at five am and avoiding Princes Street by approaching from the East arrived at Salveson's Offices 22 Bernard St., Leith, about noon, a seven hour journey. On the way passing through Newcastle and then Morpeth at about nine o' clock, I was ready for a break. I saw an isolated pub. "I wonder if I can get some breakfast there I thought?" The morning was beautiful, blue sky and no wind. There was nothing on the road as I chugged over to the door of the pub. I dismounted and pulled the bike up onto its stand and walked stiffly to the pub door. The landlord was sat at a bar stool in his empty pub, gazing out of the door admiring the sunny morn as I walked in. He must have wondered what I was doing walking into his pub at that time of the morning and was taken unawares when I asked if he could give me something to eat. I told him where I had come from and where I was going "Ayyyye" he said, while he considered how to satisfy a genuine traveller. He hailed his good lady in the back room, "can ye make this laddie a sandwich" - - -"will that de yeh?" He said to me as an after thought. "Aye, champion" I replied in the vernacular of my native Teesside. I sat at a small round cast iron pedestal table near the open door. The landlord's good lady brought me a thick beef sandwich. "What will ye have tae drink?" said the landlord from his bar stool as he looked on approvingly. I considered for a moment and decided that thirsty as I was a pint wouldn't go far wrong. This would have been illegal at nine am in England! I needed to restore myself to my personal comforts. After having eaten and feeling thus restored I paid the man. Then as I was fastening my coat he put a glass of whisky in front of me, "on the house" he said benevolently and insisted I drank it. It may have been a double or an unfamiliar Scottish measure! I was quite a bit tiddly for a mile or two. I kept giggling and running into the grass verge but it put some warmth into me and I soon recovered. A good job the A1 was not too busy for it was just a country road in those days and I had no problem following the route as it turned west to Musselburgh along the Firth of Forth to Leith.

Arriving at Bernard Street, I got off the bike and pulled it up on the rear stand. My legs were numb with cold and again very stiff after the long ride, travelling at a comfortable fifty or sixty miles an hour. I walked like a cowboy across the road to Salvesen's office. Mr. Turner saw me immediately. He seemed more interested in my mode of transport and kindly gave me a seat. The interview was a formality. I can't remember much about it. I signed some papers and was then "on the books". The pay was £28 per month with a bonus based on the catch. The crew faced the risk of a poor harvest that could arise with bad weather or any unusual migration of the whale. Nothing is certain in such a business. As an engineer I was paid five shillings for each whale we caught and ten 'ore,' a tenth of a Norwegian krona, about an English penny, per barrel of whale oil. About 50 to 80 barrels of oil were extracted from each whale.

I thanked Mr.Turner although I wasn't offered a cup of tea or any refreshment after such a journey. I walked across the road got back on the bike did a 'U' turn in the wide street and retraced my route south. The bike frame and petrol tank were quite warm from the engine's hours of running. I was feeling cold and tired by the time I reached Newcastle. I had not had anything to eat since the beef sandwich and pint of beer at nine am. Not being suitably dressed for such a journey, I only had some thin waterproof leggings over my trousers. I decided to call at my mum's cousin, Lily Watt and her husband Charlie, who then lived in Newcastle and she kindly fed me and put me up for the night.

I had told mum I might call at the Watt's on the way home but there was no way of confirming it as we didn't have telephones so mum would eventually realise I wouldn't be home until the next day. Mum took the news I had signed on to go whaling with stoic calm. I went back to the shipyard and that now I was on Salveson's payroll I arranged my departure from Smith's Dock Company. Dorothy took the news calmly too. I asked her if she would marry me and without hesitation she said yes.

I bought a nice little solitaire engagement ring in Middlesbrough. I chose it myself. Dorothy was a modest girl and would have chosen a less expensive ring. I was prepared to give her the best I could afford. The single diamond was in a platinum square setting I was sure she would like it. We were engaged! I suggested we get married when I returned from the whaling expedition the following May. I would leave it to Dorothy to make all the arrangements. We had to go around the family of aunts and uncles to receive their blessings. The next few weeks were a happy time.

In September 1947 an order came from Salvesen head office in Leith for me to join a whale catcher vessel "Southern Truce" at Smith's Dock. We were to leave on the 17th September to sail to South Georgia Island. Southern Truce had been at Smith's Dock for a refit as she was built in 1934. I was only aboard for transport to Leith Harbour, South Georgia. There I was to serve as third engineer aboard the 'W/C Sondra'.

It was unusual to service catchers at Smith's now because the catchers were serviced during the closed season winter months at the factory workshops on the Island of South Georgia. There was a dry dock and every facility at the whaling station. This service had been neglected for six years and had not yet recovered men and standards to operate a viable service. I was to sign on with Southern Truce as a 'supernumery' (not a member of the crew) in transit to South Georgia. The Sondra was a more modern whaler built in 1937.

With the crew, I signed on at a shipping agents office 'Cairns Noble' at the Exchange (now demolished) in Middlesbrough. I arrived at Smiths Dock by taxi, expenses paid. How different from the early days! I walked to the engine erection shop and had a last word with my friendly chargehand Tommy Erwin and one or two other old hands who had passed on their working experience to me for which I am greatly indebted. Then I went over to the jetty where Southern Truce was lying. A bustle of activity surrounded her as last minute stores and office personnel papers for the Chief Officer were loaded. I went aboard a couple of hours before she sailed, stowed my gear, and was on deck as the engine room telegraph rang "stand by". The deck stirred as the engineer on watch answered the command. Southern Truce looked very small to be going on such a long journey. From the bridge the command "cast off forrard", then the order to "cast off aft"! It appeared a nice mid September day, then "let go the spring!" This was a wire rope which allows the ship to swing away from the jetty.

From the North West a squall with sleet and hail blew up for a few minutes. The few workers standing on the jetty to see us off scurried away for cover. It did nothing for the trepidation I was already feeling, not a good omen? It occurred to me that I was going into the unknown for nine months! Eight thousand miles away down the Atlantic Ocean to the ice covered Island of South Georgia. What was I getting myself into? I didn't know anyone who could tell me. I was only doing what many fellows had done before. The telegraph rang again and Southern Truce moved slowly ahead at first, then at cruising speed, down river to the sea. Last minute delivery of engine room stores still lay on deck. The Chief Engineer detailed me to help stow the remaining stores away so there was no time for more contemplation. Before long we had got half the gear stored away in the "steering flat", the small after space where the steam steering engine was housed. The Southern Truce was then out into the open sea, bucking about like a young horse! Making matters worse, the skylight had been left open and the sea was now coming high over the stern pouring into the 'flat'. The whale catcher is definitely a wet ship! The door into the 'flat' was designed with a high sill to stop the sea from getting in. The sea having found another way in could not now escape and had to be bailed out. The skylight was slammed shut in record time but the seawater sloshed around with the roll of the boat up to our ankles at times and anything which was loose flew about until eventually feeling a bit sick and wishing I'd never joined, order was restored. Another lesson was learnt, "batten down the hatches before leaving port." The Chief Engineer should have seen to securing engineering spaces for sea and was probably a bit embarrassed to ask me to help with this job. I was in my home port and as a supernumerary I hadn't expected to have to "turn to", the crew having been on board for days. The stores should have been stowed and all shipshape, I had only joined that afternoon. I later found out that most ships depart like this, always a last minute delivery and scramble!

Passing down the east coast was quite nostalgic. I recognised Whitby and Scarborough. Then getting dark, when next I looked the coast became just twinkling lights. It occurred to me that those lights would be burning every night whilst I was away. They looked so homely and constant. Why did my life require me to go to the far end of the Atlantic Ocean? I knew the answer of course, I couldn't ask Dorothy to marry me without the means to provide a home for her. Money! We slipped by on the more southern, now calmer, sea and I went below to write to mum and Dorothy, letters which would be given to the coastal Pilot to post when he left us at Dover. I handed the letters over to him and that was it!

British men had been going to sea for hundreds of years. This is what had made Britain Great! We passed through the English Channel, it didn't seem very busy as far as I can remember but everyone was short of money after the war.

Crossing the Bay of Biscay things became really lively! Southern Truce bounced about like the biggest fairground ride imaginable! 'Topside', the lower deck, only three feet clear of the sea, was impassable and to get forward it was necessary to use the upper deck to reach the mess room amidships under the bridge. I was berthed up forward being aboard only for transport to South Georgia Whaling Station. Normally the engineer's cabins were aft on the starboard side. Here on Southern Truce I was in the top bunk in a two berth stoker's cabin, on the port (left) side, facing the bow. There was only room to walk into the cabin and climb into the bunks. Lockers were fitted on the narrow forward bulkhead.

Being in the bow of the ship in heavy weather, as the bow fell into the trough of a wave, about twenty feet or more, my body, laid in the bunk and floated weightless! Then as the ship lifted up on the next wave, my body weight increased several 'G's'. Somehow I managed to sleep. With the constant hanging on and staggering about all day on a heaving deck, sleeping wasn't difficult!

I had some experience of small ships at sea with trips on the wooden steam drifter 'Fisher Queen' which my Uncle Arthur had arranged for me. The shallow North Sea had been the worst seas I had experienced for a small vessel but the whale catcher beats them all. Designed for manoeuvrability, it has a flared bow to lift the ship and hence the gunner over a big wave. A ship like this was to be my home for the next nine months!

Southern Truce passed through the Bay of Biscay and headed south east. After many days of more moderate sea we arrived at Aruba, a small Island off the tropical north coast of South America. We only stayed here for four hours, to top up our fuel, water and fresh stores. A few 'bum boats' came alongside. The ship was moored off shore. I had been warned of boarders who might steal anything they could lay their hands on. Our cabin door was locked. I made a trade with cartons of 1,000 cigarettes, which cost £1:10/-, for a couple of bottles of brandy. I thought it might come in useful as medicine if things got a bit rough. I wanted to buy a wristwatch too, as the watch I had was not very reliable, and a spare would be handy to have. I leaned over the ship's side to examine a watch the seller was offering. The local police guard on deck came over, stopped me and said I should buy his watch! I looked at his mean swarthy face and the heavy revolver at his waist. It seemed to be a good idea! He wanted sterling for it, not cigarettes, but at £1:10/- it didn't seem a bad deal. My 'new' watch hung on a nail above my bunk for the whole of the season. I never wore it during the time I was at sea, for I always knew what time it was. Eight bells and I was on watch!

There were sixteen men aboard, maybe seventeen with me. The

cabin boy a lad of sixteen seemed to be constantly with the Skipper. Maybe he was family, son or nephew. The Skipper (gunner) turned out to be an alcoholic. I only saw him once in the thirty day trip, looking over the bridge, a horrible sight! His face glowing red, eyes swollen, unshaven and hardly recognisable from the chap I had seen when we set off. There were a few chaps like this in the Whaling fraternity who were "covered" by the other Officers. Frantic efforts were made to sober him up before coming into contact with higher management. Misplaced loyalty I thought but they probably knew their families and had sympathy for them.

Whale Catchers were not designed for long voyages or hot weather. We were sailing right through the tropics. We travelled at an economic speed of ten knots, the engine just turning gently, this extended the ship's range with care. Careless navigation or bad weather would have made it precarious. It takes more fuel to push through heavy seas. As we progressed South the skies cleared and I enjoyed glorious days of sunshine on deck when not on watch.

At Aruba, off the coast of Venezuela, as well as fuel for the ship, fuel for the crew came aboard in the shape of a very lively small black hairy pig! The pig was berthed in the low wooden " box " which normally held harpoons on deck and it was fed with porridge which we had every morning for breakfast until we were to have pork for dinner? I had fed the fish over the side with my porridge every morning for quite a few days but I always came back for my fried smoked bacon, I was delighted the first morning when the thin sweet condensed milky porridge stayed down! I was getting used to the food and the motion of the ship didn't bother me. The sea was fairly calm. Southern Truce was built in 1934, did not have a freezer or refrigerator aboard. The meat was salt beef in the port barrel or salt pork in the starboard barrel. There were tins of meat balls and corned beef, but not very often, probably subject to budget! Fish was of the salted variety and came dry, in wooden boxes. When the lid was broken open, it was difficult to tell what was fish and what was the lid! Salt fish of this kind looked like broken floor boards and was soaked overnight and made into fish soup. We ran out of bread after two days and it was replaced by ships biscuits. They were okay to eat, a quarter inch thick and three inches square, not too hard. I had good teeth in any case!

As well as the little pig about a dozen hens came aboard in open crates, the sailors used net cord to rig up a bit of a hen coupe round the emergency steering wheel and  binnacle on the upper deck.

The pig was the first to be sacrificed. He wasn't enjoying the trip on the fore deck anyway. The Norwegian sailors despatched him smartly and everyone not on duty or asleep helped with the ritual. A couple of empty tins were found to be the best tools to scrape his hair off, in a bath of hot water and he was prepared for the pot. The offal was thrown over the side, my Mum would have been glad of that, kidneys and heart, what a waste!

I don't remember any food being roasted! Stew was the 'plat du jour' and it didn't last long when shared among the sixteen crew, Although I was berthed forrard, I ate with the officers. Sunday main meal was 'smorgasboard'. The Cook's day off he set the table with slices of, to me at that time, funny big sausage, goats cheese and other continental things which after the war didn't bother me, I could eat anything and enjoyed what I ate! The goats cheese required me to have an education in the taking. I took a ships biscuit and cut a chunk of cheese from the piece, I sensed immediately I had made a mistake! The Mate very kindly showed me how to cut a thin slice from across the top of the piece, wafer thin, "that way you will get the most flavour" he said . He was right. It wasn't rationed I could take as many slices as I wanted, but it was nice and strong a couple satisfied me.

A few days later the hens were dispatched. I was asked by the Mate (Chief Officer) to give a hand and after he chopped the heads off I had to catch the headless bodies as they ran a yard or so flapping and kicking in danger of going over the side. I managed to get out of plucking them. Chicken stew was the result of our labours. It didn't have much flavour! Mum would have put an onion in it !

Fresh vegetables had only lasted a day or so, then we resorted to dehydrated potato and the like. The cook would make sweet soup with mixed dried fruit, which was kept in a hundred weight bag in the store. We were encouraged to drink 'Roses lime juice' every day to prevent scurvy. I had no problems with the food; there was plenty of it! A fresh apple was available for desert for a few days until they ran out.

By this time we were passing through the doldrums, the oily looking sea undulating with gilded swirls and blinding sparkling reflections of the sun as we glided gently past a background of blues and greens in the sea.

I had been put on the 'four to twelve' watch, (noon to four pm and midnight to four am) not to have duties but to avoid boredom on the month long voyage south. I suppose this got me into the steady rhythm

132

of four hours on and eight hours off seven days a week which was to be my lot for the next seven or eight months.

Coming off watch at four in the morning the sea being oily calm I would walk around the lower deck to pick up the flying fish which had, in flying to avoid a predator landed in the frying pan, on the deck, so to speak! This bonus lasted for quite a few days. There was never more than a dozen fish and only a few crew about.

At that time of the morning I would light the galley fire and share them with the sailor on watch for breakfast.

We passed through the Sargasso Sea. Being a small ship with low freeboard (deck level only about three feet above the sea) we were more intimate with the ocean, clumps of seaweed swirled passed us, not as much as I had been led to believe from books telling tall stories of sailing ships stuck fast in acres of thick weed. Old sailors tell a lot of weird stories.

Amazingly the weather remained fair for the whole trip down the Atlantic.

After many days at sea, I hadn't bothered to count them! It turned out to be thirty, one evening the engine telegraph rang "stop engine" In the middle of the Atlantic! I asked the Mate "why have we stopped?" He said quietly "It's getting dark, we will wait for daylight because we are afraid we may miss the Island of South Georgia, we are somewhere near." I knew enough about geography to know that if we missed the island we would be into the ice fields only a couple of hundred miles or so further south and the ship's fuel was low.

The navigation was very good. I have read that sailing down the meridian is not complicated, the angle of the sun being involved? I wish I knew more about it. The Norwegians seemed to navigate by the seat of their pants!

In 1946 a new whale catcher left Smith's Dock and never got to South Georgia because after taking bunkers somewhere like Aruba, they sailed 180 degrees off course and hit rocks causing the ship to be a total loss. An alcoholic error it seems.

It was a quiet watch that night, gently rolling to the swell. I sat in the engine room on watch. The shiny connecting rods of the engine stood still. I thought about the morrow, and relaxed, "what will be, will be!"

I came on deck at four a.m. it was just breaking daylight.

I scoured the horizon ahead and there on the starboard bow was the white saw edge peaks of South Georgia Island, ten thousand feet high glinting in the early sunlight. Only a hundred and twenty miles long, the full length of the island was visible in the clear crisp air eighty miles away.

We could have missed it in the night! The telegraph rang, the propeller churned the sea below our stern and the Southern Truce swung her bow to head to the Whaling Station of Leith Harbour South Georgia. I wondered if this was how captain James Cook had first sighted South Georgia on the 17th of January 1775? The island didn't have a name until he went ashore and found it deserted. He claimed it and named it apparently after King George III and spent three days sailing around to discover it was indeed an island and used his navigation skills to mark it on his charts.

Longitude had been a problem in charting accurately places on a map. Cook had for the past couple of years the use of the "chronometer" a clock accurate to a few seconds in months by which noon at Greenwich could be related to noon around the world identified when the sun was at its highest. The longitude was easily calculated. This "clock" developed and was built by John Harrison born in 1693 in Yorkshire. He was a Blacksmith by trade, another self-educated man whom like Cook helped to put the 'great' into Great Britain. He spent most of a lifetime creating this super clock to solve the problem of longitude and enable man to mark a place on a map and know with certainty how to return to that same place.

Captain Cook's maps were used until recent developments of satellite instruments as late as the 1990's. The sailors who accompanied him were very courageous to sail in those Antarctic waters with no engine to run for cover when a gale blows up! The icebergs or 'ice-islands' as Cook's men called them were dangerous too. Sailing too close to them on the lee side, the ship could lose the wind sheltered by the 200 feet high icebergs and then find it difficult to escape from colliding with the sharp edge of the giant icebergs.

January is the Antarctic summer. Captain Cook did not stay for long! As he observed, snow and ice covered the island of South Georgia for the whole year. Only three species of plant were found ashore whilst penguins and seals were the only creatures.

The Antarctic summer was a very short period of the year. Whaling had existed for centuries in the Arctic. Many whaling companies had gone bankrupt as the numbers of whales were reduced and severe bad weather made the hunting uneconomical.

*Southern Truce in action stalking a whale. Ice is forming on the lower rigging. The sea temperature is minus one degree. Snow floats on the sea for four hours creating a white out. It is not advised to swim down here!*

With the advent of the steam ship the Antarctic seas became more viable in which to hunt whales. For centuries the oil provided light in homes and cottages, margarine on bread and later from the 1910's fertilizer on the fields. Now the work of building the ships and the men who sailed in them long ago are forgotten.

The benefits whaling brought to Europe in general and Britain in particular are not appreciated now in a time of plenty. Thankfully the whales have been left to breed unmolested. Men have found ways to replace those benefits and no longer need to endure the hardships of many months in deep and dangerous waters.

Southern Truce only had two days fuel left in the bunkers and another eight hours steaming to go. There had been very little room for error. Eventually we entered the three mile long fiord at the end of which was the Leith Harbour Whaling Station. Southern Truce came alongside a wooden jetty and after thirty days at sea. I was to leave her to join the Sondra.

I have seen old photographs of Catcher vessels returned to Smiths Dock for repairs, and although they had steam engines they had rigged a sail from the forrard mast evidently deployed with a favourable wind to reduce fuel consumption to complete the long Atlantic journey.

I had my gear already stowed and wasted no time leaving Southern Truce. I hoped to sail with a gunner who was not an alcoholic! It was only a short walk along the rugged waterfront carefully giving a wide berth to a sleeping elephant seal to find my whale catcher 'Sondra'.

Three catchers, each a hundred and fifty feet long, were laid alongside each other at the short wooden jetty that stuck out fifty feet or so from the blunt end of the fjord. The jetty was short because the depth of water made it difficult to drive piles further out. This area is called 'Jericho', so named I imagine because the beach of scree, chippings of rock would be similar to all that remained after the walls of Jericho came down.

This was the whale catcher's 'bunker' jetty. Fuel and water (straight from the Mountains) and stores were taken on board here approximately every ten days. When we came in for bunkers it was my duty to fill the fresh water tanks with the crystal clear water from the mountains. It cost the company nothing, it was free!

The sailors transported the stores from the supply depot to the ship using a four wheeled flat bogey. This was pulled along a roughly constructed two hundred yard track of mud and scree. Snow was everywhere but had receded from the shoreline now as summer was approaching.

I left Southern Truce with little regret although it had been a pleasant thirty days trip. The Sondra was silent and appeared deserted. It differed little from Southern Truce in size, shape and level of accommodation. The main difference was the type of boiler used to raise steam for the engine. The forty ton of water drum boiler was replaced in Sondra with a seven ton water tube boiler able to produce steam with more volume than the Southern Truce. Like an athlete with bigger and better lungs!

Sondra was going to be my home for the next six months. So far so good.

# CHAPTER 12
# 1947 SOUTH GEORGIA. W/CATCHER SONDRA
*Third engineer aboard W/Catcher Sondra*
*South Georgia Island. October 1947.*

Sondra was alongside, the deck level with the jetty. I stepped aboard and walked aft down the side deck to the after accommodation. From the deck I stepped over a door sill into an 'L' shaped narrow passage way, the short leg of the 'L' across the ship. A door to the right opened to the steering 'flat'. A small steam engine in there moved the rudder with a toothed quadrant. On the opposite side of this short passage were two toilets. In the 90 degree. angle was a strong waist level steel partition to protect the almost vertical companionway leading down to four cabins across the stern of the vessel. Two engineer's cabins were on the starboard side. One was the Chief's single berth. A double berth, had two bunks for the second and third engineer, me! The centre cabin was for the Cook and mess boy, the port cabin for the First and Second Mates.

In 1941 all the whale catchers had been evacuated to Capetown and were converted to anti-submarine service for the duration of the war along the coast of Africa. Now converted back to a Whaler Sondra had just arrived back from Freetown. It was in a bit of a mess, probably as a result of the refit.

The Second Mate appeared, there was no one else around. I introduced myself. He pointed out to me that the bed was infested with little nasties. bedbugs! Small black things. The cupboard under the sink was alive with cockroaches. I had never seen things like this before in my life! It was difficult to believe that anyone had sailed in this filthy cabin all the way from South Africa. The Mate disappeared and came back with a tin of DDT. He showed me what the little bugs looked like and helped me to disinfect the place. The cockroaches were given the same treatment and in a few days the cabin was fairly respectable. He assured me that the cold weather would soon kill off any vermin aboard. By what I'd seen it could kill off anybody.

I did get a bite or two until the DDT took effect. The little devils didn't wake me up, but they left a few small red spots.

I met the Chief Engineer Anker Andersen. He was well built, a bit portly perhaps, hair thin on top, a full round rosy face with a pursed mouth as if he was going to whistle. He was quietly spoken. Weighing me up he said, "You can take the watch tomorrow." Silly question, I thought, and replied modestly, "I think so." He then raised his voice "You only think so!" "No of course I can" I replied. He had not understood the English understatement.

I made a mental note to be very positive when speaking to another national no matter how good their English was.

He told me the engine room commands would all be in Norwegian. The language isn't so difficult for an Englishman, the syntax is the same "jeg skal Har" in English "I shall have."

I was then instructed me in the engine room operations. "When you hear the cannon go off, the harpoon is being fired, and you must stop the engine dead. This is to prevent the harpoon rope wrapping around the propeller! Then start the luft pumpa." This was the air pump used to keep the whale carcase afloat until the natural gases arise. Perish the thought of having eighty tons of sinking whale meat fastened to a rope, wrapped around the propeller and dragging the ship down?

It was my duty during the midnight to four am watch when there was no chasing, to top up the boiler before daylight. Also it was my duty to change the boiler feed water filters and wash the removed filters in soda to remove the light deposit of oil ready to replace the filters the next night . During the midnight watch I would do any "dobeying" I had.(wash my clothes). I used a bucket of hot boiler water and dried the clothes  on top of the engine cylinders. This was not a duty but it saved me a precious few minutes of free time.

When the weather was moderate I took a 'bath' (not on my own watch) behind the boiler where it was private and warm. With hot water from the boiler mixed with cold, I first put one foot in the bucket and washed that side of me, and then the other foot in the bucket and did the other side. It became a bit tricky if a chase started as the ship swerved and the bucket slid across the steel deckplates with me tottering after it. I always managed to see the funny side of it! The washbasin wasn't much use for a good swill. Whalers had no bathrooms, refrigerators or freezers. However unlike the Herring drifter we did have toilets. The toilet floor had a drain hole to the deck for washing out purposes. In heavy weather a couple of inches of sea managed to slop in about ones feet in there .It ran in then as we heeled over it ran out, but came in faster than it went out!

I went to the cabin I was to share with Malbut the Second Engineer and sat on the day bed, an upholstered couch that extended along the bulkhead opposite the bunks. The bulkheads (walls) of the cabin were all curved to the cabin floor since they were the stern plates of the ship's stern. The paint used had cork chippings in it to reduce condensation. I didn't sit there long, it's not good to be alone too much at times like this and I was a bit peckish. I left the cabin and climbed the near vertical companionway (wide stairway) walked round the casement at the stairhead and went out of the port side door (at sea kept closed) onto the deck and walked along to the mess room.

It was now nearly six o clock. The steward / cook, told me where to sit. His name was Louie. He had dark hair parted and thin, stuck across his head. A full round soft face that reminded me of Stan Laurel's chum, Oliver Hardy! Louie had been in America for years and spoke with an American drawl in the same defensive manner as Oliver Hardy. He turned out to be an excellent cook with what was available. Louie, who also acted as steward and seemed permanently harassed, wore a slightly stained white apron that also served as a hand towel. He served the mess from the adjacent galley. I wondered what he was doing on a ship like this. Good cooks were always in demand especially in America. Was he a fugitive, and if so for what? That thought could apply to most of us on this rough little ship.

As the officers I had not already met came in to the small mess room I introduced myself. The Captain, (also the Gunner), Christian Christiansen greeted me kindly and asked me where I was from. A typical rugged blond Norwegian chap in his mid fifties, six foot four inches tall with pale blue eyes set in a wrinkled weather beaten friendly face. Each of his hands were as big as a shovel. Being out of Norway when the Germans invaded his country he had joined the British navy. He had been given the Command of a destroyer during the war. It may have been a Norwegian command. He was an authoritative figure. My place was to sit next to him on the inside of the curved upholstered bench seat in order to give him instant access. He asked about my background and wished me a good season. I suppose he needed a ship like a catcher, a boring merchant ship would be an anathema after the thrill of a destroyer in wartime.

In this small mess room we sat around the curved edge of the quadrant section three sided table. Our backs were supported by the rounded upholstered bulkhead. This meant that the two officers sitting at the ends of the curved bench seat attached to the bulkhead were able to leave the table in an emergency without disturbing the others.

A brass chronometer reading Greenwich longitudinal time and a brass aneroid barometer were fastened side by side to the bulkhead near the seaward door. They didn't mean much to me except to tell me when to leave for my duty watch! The weather would have its way with us and changed so rapidly around South Georgia that advanced warning was of little use to anyone.

A single nine inch glass porthole with brass turnbuckles gave a view of the foredeck.

The foredeck was a clutter of ropes, shackles and chains. Five pairs of bollards on the port and starboard decks were used to secure the whales with chains for towing. Amidships on the deck, a door set into a steel hood, gave access to the crew's quarters in the fore peak and also a door into the hold containing the port and starboard rope boxes. These boxes were four feet deep, six feet wide and fifteen feet long. The rope in these boxes passed through the deck to the harpoon and ran out with the harpoon when it was fired.

The harpoon gun was mounted on a platform at the bow. A narrow gangway with handrails each side ran from the bridge to the platform to give the Gunner quick access to do his job. A pedestal telegraph on the platform enabled him to direct the Engineer below in the engine room to change speed as required to make close contact when the whale rose up to blow. This ensured a safe and humane despatch of the whale.

The seating arrangement at meal times in the mess was for action stations, the Gunner to the bridge or gun, the Chief to prepare the massive winch. Meals were served before and after the watch change hour for engineers and deck officers.

There was a powerful steam driven winch situated on deck in front of the Bridge above, mess room / galley below the superstructure This winch had twin multi grooved drums on each side. The harpoon rope was wound around the V shaped grooves many times in order to get a strong grip when the time came to haul in a whale. The thick hemp rope used, was spliced to fifty metres of lighter nylon rope that was attached to the harpoon. The heavier hemp rope came from one of the two wooden boxes below deck on the port or starboard side of the hold. Normally only one rope was required unless a rope was lost due to some failure.

A sailor had to stand in the box to lay the rope out around the box as it was wound back in. He would get out smartly if it had to be run out again.

Below the harpoon gun was coiled the 'foreloper' the lighter nylon rope. This foreloper flew out with the harpoon. Nylon was a fairly new war time invention and improved the business. The heavier hemp rope then followed. It ran out through the deck by way of a wood lined steel 'mouth.' This prevented the sea getting into the rope locker. It then passed over a pulley high up on the mast. This pulley was suspended from a wire rope which itself went over a pulley fastened to the mast. The wire rope went down the mast through the deck and was wound around spring loaded pulleys in the bowels of the ship. This configuration made the mast in effect a big fishing rod. When the spring loaded rope pulley came down the mast with the load near to the breaking strain, the Chief would release the clutch on the winch and allow the rope to give way. As the ship moved slow ahead towards the whale, he could then haul in again on the winch. The strain on the rope was enormous with a whale of seventy or eighty tons and the bow rising and falling with the waves. However breakages were very rare. The business had been carefully calculated, as had the risks.

Being next to the Gunner I was under the scrutiny of his eagle eyes. One day trying to chew some tough salt beef, I gave a quiet ouch –toothache! He noticed and asked what it was. I made light of it. "Oh, nothing just a twinge" I said. Days later as we came in for bunkers the Gunner called me. "Mr Dinsdale, go ashore and see the Doctor!" I protested mildly, "Oh, my tooth's okay now" I said. My protest was ignored with a benevolent smile for he had radioed ahead. "The doctor is waiting for you. That is an order!" It's difficult to refuse such a kindly order but there was a steely edge behind the smile. The older Norwegians were in the habit of clicking their heels when addressed by the Captain/Gunner. I was his noon to four pm 'driver' on the engine. A busy time for 'chasing' and was not allowed to be off colour. I respected him and wasted no time in obeying his order. This was the kind of man he was, attention to the finest detail. I was influenced greatly by these characters I met in my journey through life, even if I was unable to reach the level they had achieved. Never leave things to chance! I put on my sea boots and heavy coat and stepped ashore. The deck was always fairly level with the jetty. I don't think there was much tide down there. I crunched my way along the muddy scree packed track passing the office and personnel buildings to the small hospital.

The male nurse was expecting me and motioned me to climb up into the chair. He was a man of few words from the Shetland Isle's. I didn't expect to be there long but it was forty minutes later before the doctor lowered the chair and I was able to get down.

The Scottish ex Indian British Army Doctor, was past middle age, strong dark hair parted near the middle, high cheek bones and a long nose. His breath smelt strongly of whisky. He brought out a red velvet lined box of dental instruments. Next he charged a syringe from a bottle of anaesthetic and injected me in the vicinity of the offending lower left sixth tooth. This seemed to freeze my face up to my eyebrows! Actually it was very local and in spite of the surgery I felt nothing for the full forty minutes. From a box of surgical dental instruments he chose a tool that looked like a pair of "side cutters" used by electricians to cut cable. The rotten crown of the tooth broke off and left a short stump. He tried one or two of the instruments from the box but was unable to get a firm hold of the stump. The Doctor looked around the surgery for some time. He was probably wondering what to do next, engineers often use the same manoeuvre hoping in the meantime the problem may go away. He apologised that there wasn't an elevator with which to remove the remainder of the tooth. He told me he was now going to sever the nerve, this would prevent me having any more pain with the tooth. Taking a scalpel and pressing it hard into the bone below the tooth he cut the nerve. Satisfied that this would prevent further toothache I was told that on my return to the U.K. I should see my dentist to have the stump removed. I thought he performed brilliantly and felt no pain. I had no more bother with it during the season. On returning home my local dentist removed the stump without difficulty. I then had a course of dental treatment to ensure there would not be a repeat of toothache at sea. It could have been very disagreeable.

In bad weather the cook had problems. First the table cloth would be wetted to stop the plates sliding about. In very bad weather, which was probably half of the time, wooden dividers were clipped to the table. When it got really rough, I'm talking of the bow rising and falling twenty feet or more, Louie lashed an enormous dixie onto the galley fire and made "storm soup" the Dixie being only half full, the soup wouldn't spill over! The mess room was kept shut off. The crew would stagger into the galley on the port side with rubber boots and oilskins, bringing in buckets of sea water with them on each occasion.

142

We could easily have six inches of sea water sloshing around the galley, up our sea boots! Two or three men would stand in the small galley hanging on to the ship with one hand, with the other hand we dipped a pint pot into the dixie and slurped a mysterious soup of salt beef and dried veg. With a couple of ship's biscuits this fortified us for the next few hours. Louie would be almost apologising for his meagre fare He was a gem, probably the most important job on the ship and on the go all day.

The cast iron galley stove was oil fired with "solar oil" a light oil, stored in a large tank outside the galley. A brass rail ran around three sides of the top of the stove to prevent pans from sliding off and the Dixie was tied to this rail. Coffee was the predominant brew. A huge jute sack of green coffee beans was kept in the food store. The beans were roasted regularly in the oven and a pound or so put in a tin for daily use. I was instructed how to put a handful of beans in the grinder and crank the handle, pull the little drawer out and tip the ground coffee onto the boiling water in the steam heated copper tank. The ground coffee landed on a muslin cloth which draped across the tank and sagged into the boiling water for a few minutes. The 'Norskies,' British for Norwegians, would fill a mug from a brass tap in the little steam coil heated boiler tank, pour condensed milk into the coffee, and sip it through a sugar tablet held in the teeth!

Louie would ask me if I would light the galley fire when I came off watch at four am each morning , grind the coffee and brew up for the lads. I agreed, and for this little service I was given permission to take a couple of slices from a whole side of smoked bacon hanging in the food store. This I fried for my breakfast after my watch each morning and would make myself a mug of sweet tea, provided the weather wasn't too bad. I don't remember ever having bacon at any other time, but of course I was never at the day time breakfast. Immediately after my bacon I went to my bunk and slept until called at eleven thirty am.

There was an enormous jute bag of dried fruit in the food store which contained dried apple rings , apricots, dates, prunes etc. I often took a handful and nibbled it on the way down to the engine room below. That bag would last two seasons and more. The cook used it to make what he called a sweet soup.

In bad weather I would have a tot from one of a couple of bottles of brandy that I had bought with cigarettes from the "bum boat" which came alongside in our bunker stop at Aruba. I think this "brandy" (kasash) was made from bananas but it eased the ache in the abdominal muscles that resulted from the strain of hanging on as the ship heaved and bucked! This wasn't sea sickness, just stomach muscles doing unusual exercises. I was sorry when my supply of spirits had gone because there was no general issue of booze but a regular tot was given quite often. The Gunner would send a bottle forrard for the sailors and a bottle aft for the officers if we'd had a bad day and that happened often. It was very generous of him. The crew had a lot of confidence in him, but he was the last one to run for shelter in bad weather and would stick it out. This was why we were "top boat" out working when others had run for cover! I was fortunate to be with the best Gunner / Captain, as my pay depended on the catch and a bit more rough weather was worth it. At times it seemed a bit risky, but these were Norwegians, descended from the best sailors in the world.

The Gunner's cabin and chart room was above the mess room and galley, the open bridge was above his cabin and the whole superstructure stood in front of the funnel. Behind the funnel were, on both port and starboard sides, big ventilators (without fans) which scooped air down to the engine room. The scoops faced astern, normal in the Antarctic regions, and could be turned with a spindle by the engineer from below when seas were breaking high over the ship.

The deck forward of the superstructure was the business end of the catcher. Winch, mast, harpoon box, ropes, flensing knives, bollards and fairleads to secure the chains round the tails of the whale for towing them back to the factory.

The Catcher could tow five whales each side from amidships forward. It only happened once in the two seasons I was there. We had had a good day. The weather was brilliant blue sky, the sea flat calm. We had caught eight good size fin whales each an average of 70 feet in length. It had seemed too good to be true! At the end of the day we had towed them quite a way to the Island when the cry went up "arr sett blost" "I see a Blast". We all used the Norwegian commands. The crew were horrified that the Gunner would cast off the whales we were towing to go chasing after another two. A gale can blow up in twenty minutes and all may be lost! Our bonus was paid on the catch! Our basic pay was paltry for the hours and conditions we worked, a seven day week for the six months season. The order was given, "cast off the starboard whales." Sondra turned in a big circle, then the port side whales were cast off, all with quick release shackles. Each whale

144

surmounted with a bamboo pole bearing Sondra's red number three flag and a battery operated white lamp for night time pickup. They looked like a troop of cavalry with lances flying forming a large circle. This was about a week's wages in bonus to me. I hoped we would be able to pick them up again before dark! Our luck held and within the hour we retrieved them and were back on our way to the factory. There was some anxiety about towing such a haul in case a storm blew up and the whales were torn away from the ship's side The engine at full speed now moved the ship at little more than four knots as we slowly towed the ten whales the last few miles. The weather held good and we entered the fjord with ten whales much to the delight of the shore gang too, as their pay was also based on the catch.

Now let me get back to that first introductory meal. I was told we would sail at midnight. I was on midnight until four o clock in the morning, so thankfully there would be no hunting action, 'jager' (in Norske) for my first watch.

I went below and stowed my gear, there wasn't a lot of locker room, I didn't need much, I wasn't going anywhere! I arranged for the mess boy, Jamie, a sixteen year old Scottish lad to call me with a pot of tea at eleven thirty pm, in case I overslept. Jamie came with a good brew on the dot! He was a bright lad I was glad he was British. This made six of us. Malbut (Geordie), Davie the deck hand from Arbroath, and two 'North sea-Chinamen' sailors from the Shetlands, lovely lads, who normally spoke Gaelic, and me from Teesside. The full ships complement was eight officers, four sailors. cook, mess boy and two firemen making sixteen in total.

This was to be my first watch in charge of an engine room. At ten minutes to midnight I went below to take over the watch from the Assistant engineer. He was lean, strong, and over sixty I would say. He spoke fairly good English, through big yellow teeth, long white hair that had once been blond brushed straight back with a long white bristly face to match. He taught me quite a bit of Norwegian during the season and was very helpful. Although my first impression of him was that he was a bit doddery, he kept a good watch. However he did once manage to get the harpoon rope around the propeller with an eighty ton whale on the other end. I was on deck and noticed Sondra was going astern being pulled by the dead sinking whale. The method of freeing the propeller from the heavy hemp whale line was to turn the propeller anti clockwise. I had gone down to the engine room and helped to engage a worm gear into the gear wheel attached to the engine main shaft. This enable us to manually slowly turn the engine anti clockwise using a four foot ratchet fitted onto the worm spindle, thus unwinding the rope and allow the winch to haul in the catch.

The assistant engineer climbed out of the engine room leaving me in charge. I would be doing this for six months, four hours on watch and eight hours off, seven days a week. I decided to get on with it one day at a time. I smiled at the fireman. He gave me a quizzical look. I had to show him I was up to the job.

The telegraph rang "stand by" The engine cylinders already warmed with steam by the Assistant, I put a bit of steam to the engine with the brass wheel of the steam control valve, just enough to move the engine slowly and blow out any water through the cylinder drain valves that may have condensed in the cylinders. Water trapped in a cylinder does not compress and could do a lot of damage by breaking the cast iron cylinder head! This did happen to a careless engineer on the Salvesen oil tanker Southern Opal a few years later. I enjoyed the smell of steam and oil, it reminded me of the giant traction engines of the fairground but it was even better in the confines of the engine room. The telegraph rang again "slow astern." The valve gear already astern, I opened the throttle to the 'slow' indicator on the throttle spindle. I felt the checker plates under my feet sway as Sondra moved away from the jetty. Now a clang of the telegraph indicated "slow ahead."

I had to move the valve gear to the ahead position. I opened the steam valve to the six inch single cylinder engine, bolted to the main engine near the main engine control valve. The little engine chugged around quite quickly driving a gear wheel that moved the three sets of 'Stevenson's' valve gear connected by a shaft that ran along the back of the engine. The three sets of valve gear swung over to the ahead position. Now I opened the main steam control valve to start the main engine, "Slow Ahead it is."

The fireman nicknamed 'Gandhi' lit extra burners to fire up the boiler to make more steam for the expected next command. Sondra turned at the head of the fjord, then "half ahead" for a few minutes, I opened the control valve more. I could visualise the action on deck.

The crew stowing ropes carefully away and clearing the deck for sea. Now "full ahead" down the three mile fjord. The sheltered smooth water of the fjord changed to a gentle heave as the bow cut into the open sea. The season had 'begun'. I don't believe in lucky charms but

146

I hoped a spirit friend would be looking after me!

It was a quiet watch, a 'moderate sea.' Gandhi the fireman, (stoker or boiler attendant) already on watch was a petite cadaverous white haired Norwegian with a big floppy white moustache. His real name was Sigmund Johanson. We all had nicknames.

He only wore a singlet and jeans in the engine room which exposed his pale skinny physique. The crew had called him Gandhi! He looked very much like the Indian statesman apart from his colour! The name was only contradicted by his bright blue eyes and a magnificent Red Indian chief tattooed on his left upper arm. He was a very cheerful chap in spite of his looks and good at his job. I was pleased when he gave me an encouraging 'thumbs up' sign as he changed watch with Johansen the other fireman. As a new boy I had met his approval, and he was an old hand, word would get round the crew. The firemen changed their watch during my four hourly watch. They were 'watch and watch about', six hours on and six hours off, seven days a week. Like me they didn't have a heavy job, the boiler being oil fired. Just being on a small ship like this 24/7 for six months was heavy enough. However when chasing whales, the manoeuvring of the engine required the oil burners to be shut off and on at each change of speed. The burners to spray the oil into the furnace had to have the spray tips cleaned often as the residual oil contained a small amount of clinker (carbon and sand.) Likewise I had to adjust the engine speed to suit the Gunner's telegraph as he tried to get close to the whale when it came up to blow.

The other fireman, Johansen, was Swedish and about twenty eight years old. They both spoke fairly good English. Johansen, quiet but friendly was tall, thin and gaunt and like Gandhi, had very poor teeth. Must have been the years of ship board grub

My first watch was quiet but I was tired and ready to be relieved after the long and hectic previous day. We often chatted about our experiences. Johansen told me a hilarious tale of a trip ashore in South Africa. He'd had a fair bit to drink (Swedes were like this away from Sweden!) and a local black girl invited him home to stay the night! When he woke up next morning he was in a mud hut!

Malbut the Second engineer relieved me at four am, he was a "Geordie" a native from the Newcastle area. I think it was South Shields. We shared this two berth cabin above the propeller in the after accommodation. Fortunately we never seemed to be in the cabin both together, owing of our watches, as there wasn't much room. Malbut suffered very much from a gastric stomach. Taking over the watch he didn't check the engine room status before I left, he just sat on a box and lit a cigarette. This was contrary to engine room procedure. He had no conversation of any quality. I soon realised he was a sick man who relied heavily on milk of magnesia for his stomach ulcer. I was going to have to 'carry' him somewhat. He often came down a half hour late for his watch. I had some sympathy for him but each minute of free time was precious to me in the rough lifestyle which we lived. I would spend a few minutes with Malbut and then climb out of the engine room (literally up a vertical steel ladder) and go up for'rard to the galley to make a pot of tea.

Before daybreak there were only two sailors on watch, one on the bridge at the wheel, the other in the galley to spell him off. They did an hour each at the wheel. It seemed to be the routine on an open bridge in Antarctic waters. On bad days the sailors on deck had a bit of frost bite on their cheeks. I came up one morning at four am to find both sailors in the galley! There were no icebergs about but the gunner would not have been happy about it. I didn't say anything. As I say, we had to trust one another. I went aft and turned in to the bottom bunk, Malbut had chosen the top one. The propeller throbbed under the cabin, the engine room noises told me what was going on below. The boiler feed pumps whining as they forced water into the boiler at two hundred and fifty pounds pressure, the rumble of the main engine and the hum of the steam driven electric generator told me all was well! I slept okay but woke to hear the telegraph 'double ring.' This was an emergency ring for 'full ahead' not full cruising speed. This meant Sondra was chasing. I use the word loosely because a whale blowing could be seen two or three miles away. Full speed was used to make our approach quickly before careful stalking for a professional kill. It was counter-productive to miss a whale. I don't remember the gun firing the harpoon in this instance. It may have been a protected species of whale they had seen? The Gunner would look closely through binoculars to identify its status, female with young , protected species or under size before approaching closer.

I must have dozed off to sleep again. I'm a good sleeper, next thing I knew, it was eleven thirty am. Jamie, with a mug of tea, gave me a shake! A quick wash with the water swilling about in the wash basin, and up onto the upper deck coming down amidships to the messroom for a meal before my watch. I paused for a few moments to see what was going on, there was never a dull moment on a whale catcher. There were a few icebergs in the area. We steamed along at cruising speed, all free hands searching for a "blow". The man up the mast in the barrel generally saw a whale blowing first, "Arr sett blost" would be the cry! After a bowl of soup and some cheese I would have a couple of ships biscuits, for there was no bread (the ships biscuits were fresh, no weevils and not too hard on the teeth)

The main meal of the day was at six o clock. As it got near dark business was suspended. I went below and took over the watch from the Assistant Engineer, Harald I think his name was. I didn't see much of him because of our watches.

The engine and boiler room aft of the fuel tanks was all one space and took up half of the ship's length and all of the beam (width) Some of the auxiliary machinery, pumps and generator were fitted on platforms up the curved sides of the ship's engine room.

The officer's accommodation aft, was built over the propeller shaft above two fresh water tanks built into the tapered stern each side of the shaft. There was room to work on the propeller gland which contained soft packing to control the sea leaking into the ship around the shaft that ran through to the propeller. At sea this gland was eased off to allow a trickle of sea water to lubricate the shaft running in a long hard oily wood 'lignum vitae' lined bearing. The gland was tightened up in port to stop the sea leaking from the propeller shaft to save having to pump the ship's bilges out

Going down the almost vertical steel ladder into the engine room, past a steel gantry (a grating walkway) along the engine cylinder tops, down to the lower deck plates there was a narrow steel plate walkway between the side of the engine and the boiler water feed pumps mounted on a small platform welded to the side of the ship

Here at the for'rard end of the engine was the small box desk below the full size telegraph indicating engine commands from stop to full ahead, opposite to the main engine steam control valve and a few pressure gauges. This was my operational post.

The desk was never used for paper work. In action there was no time to write anything down. It generally contained a tin of brasso and some hand rags. We took pride in the brass gauges and other fittings and give them a polish now and then. I also kept a round tin of fifty 'Ship's Woodbines' in the desk drawer. The best cigarettes for flavour, I would light one have a few puffs then go to check a pump or another item. When I returned the cigarette had burnt away, forgotten.

The telegraph hung above the desk, a "clock like" enamel face divided into ahead on the left side and astern on the right. A segment 'finished with engine' at the bottom with segments from slow to full, left and right. A big brass pointer and loud clanging bell indicated the desired engine action, this was operated by thin wires with chains to go round corners in ducting from the bridge and also the gun platform. Directly over the desk was a ventilator two feet in diameter, above deck it was turned aft to keep the spray from drenching the engineer. At times the sea came down regardless! I had an oilskin jacket and sou'wester, a large brimmed oilskin hat, which I used to put on in a heavy sea.

I soon had the opportunity to practice the instructions I had been given. A double ring on the telegraph meant we were chasing. The whale was probably two miles away when sighted. We went at full speed to get near to the whale but then the gunner on the bow platform telegraphed me a speed that would stalk the unfortunate animal and bring us close to the whale as it came up to blow. I opened the throttle, the engine room deck throbbed and bounced as the ship sped forward at full speed of sixteen knots. Then various speeds, half, slow, a few minutes full then slow again until a professional kill and kindly despatch of the selected animal was affected.

The engine was not enclosed. The crankshaft and connecting rods were a glorious sight as they spun round at full speed, 250 revs a minute. The bearings had to be lubricated by hand using an oil can most of the time. There was an automatic drip feed system but it was necessary to supplement it.

The automatic drip feed system dripped oil into brass cups on the crossheads. The crossheads thrashed up and down with the pistons and connected rods turning the crankshaft. This oil should run down thin brass pipes to the bearings but with the ship heeling over the drips could not be relied on to hit the cups!

Being an open engine with only a nine inch toe plate and a handrail at waist height, it was a case of one hand for the ship and the other for yourself!

In a merchant ship's main steam engines, oil was measured at a rate of a pint per watch on the slow (70 revs per minute) big triple expansion steam engines. We could not have a bearing run hot for lack of oil

*The author aboard the 'Sondra'*

during a chase so there was no limit to our use of oil.

The chase could often last forty minutes or so. First the ship had to draw near to the whale, then the difficult job of stalking the animal to be close enough to make an efficient hit when it surfaced for the few seconds to blow.

Aiming and choosing when to fire was good judgement between the gunner on the bow and the sailor up the mast in the barrel who could, if the sea was smooth enough, see the whale approaching the surface to blow. I was involved with instructions from a telegraph on the gun platform for different engine speeds the gunner demanding to be in the best place to make his hit.

When the harpoon cannon was fired it was heard all over the ship. I then had to stop the engine dead! I spun the steam valve shut, reversed the valve gear to astern and put a bit of steam on the engine to hold the engine in astern against the 'way' of the ship so that the propeller was still. This action prevented the rope trailing under the ship to wind around the propeller.

The fireman only a few feet away from me in a lower well sunk in the engine room deck, shut off the burners at the front of boiler. There was then a pause, the whale having surfaced and been spotted by the deck crew, 'slow ahead' was telegraphed. This was to put Sondra's bow in the direction to approach the whale and haul in the rope. After some minutes I had the order to 'stop'; the whale was under the bow coming alongside.

My next job was to start the Westinghouse air pump. Compressed air was injected into the carcass to keep it afloat until natural gasses took over. The whale was now cast off with a four metre bamboo mast stuck into it with a red flag bearing Sondra's number and a battery lamp clipped to the pole below the flag.

At the end of a day, we were sometimes sixty miles from the first whale we had 'flagged off'. Keeping a close eye on the weather Whale Catcher Sondra turned to pick up the other whales for towing back to the Island factory.

The wind can blow up to hurricane force rapidly and, as other whales are strapped to the bow bulwarks, our way through the sea is reduced considerably. It required good judgement on the part of the Gunner as to when to call it a day.

Somehow the Mate retraced our course, (after chasing in all directions) to pick up the whales. I am told a navigation aid was to draw the outline of a nearby iceberg and come back to work from that.

The icebergs all looked alike to me, like flat topped ice islands. A radio beacon gave the course needed to return to the factory. Usually we only caught a couple of whales in any one day, and sometimes many days could pass before a whale was sighted. Approaching darkness we towed the whales at night for several hours to a buoy anchored near the factory and returned to sea each time unless we needed to come in for fuel.

After a few weeks I had need to see the Doctor again. I had been bothered for three days with diarrhoea. It was no trouble when cruising but on two occasions when chasing Johansen had to cover for me when the Gunner had rung for a change of speed and I was in the toilet (conveniently just near the top of the engine room door)

I had reported my problem to the Mate and he had produced the "medical chest." This was a box about 18 inches square the inside being divided into about two dozen compartments. Each compartment contained a bottle. The inside of the lid had a diagram with a number for each box. A book to accompany the chest listed the ailment that each bottle was for. My ailment was listed as number nine! I was given a dose each day but it had no effect.

When we came in for bunkers and stores I went up to see the Doctor who had been radioed to expect me, The doctor took a tapered measuring glass and poured a clear liquid into it from a winchester medicine bottle. It was castor oil! "Hey!" I said, "my Mum always gives me some orange after taking that stuff!"He laughed, "well we 'ain't got any oranges here" he said, "well I can't take that without something" I replied. He was easy to talk to and asked his "Sheltie" assistant to bring a tin of condensed milk from the kitchen and a tablespoon. With this spoonful of condensed milk at the ready I downed the castor oil. The sweet condensed milk was as good as the orange at taking the sickly taste of the castor oil away. I thanked the Doctor and his assistant for their kindness. I strolled back to the Sondra at the bunker jetty but galloped the last twenty yard and just made it to the loo! The astringent number nine should be changed to castor oil! It cured me immediately in one go!

The daylight watches were always busy but sometimes we had cruised around for ten fruitless days. When foul weather at sea made sighting the whales impossible, the Gunner would decide when to return to base and refuel. After taking fuel and stores he did not always return to sea immediately. It was to rest the crew, but he only gave us one night alongside. I was free to go ashore, there was a "Kino"(cinema) which had hard bench seats. I went once or twice. They were silent films, continental with sub titles and not always in English! Schubert was one!

I was fortunate to see the live Variety show the shore lads put on once or twice in the season .The Kino seated about two hundred and had a fair sized stage. It was surprising the talent among the people down there!

A seventeen year old Norwegian lad, blond, tall and slim, dressed up as Carmen Miranda, lipstick and Spanish skirt slashed up to the thigh showing a pair of beautiful legs. He gave a terrific sexy mime performance to the Carmen Miranda record. Being naïve at the time I thought it was just a bit of fun again! He was nicknamed 'Josephine' by the lads. I was beginning to realise some lads were like this. Later in the season I heard that because of some embarrassment with the Chemist and photographs he'd taken of 'Josephine' in the lab, the Port Captain, the factory manager, was going to send Josephine back home on the next ship but Josephine had friends in high places! He settled for a move to another factory of Salvesen's in Newfoundland. I wonder if it was a promotion? I still wasn't sure what all the fuss was about, nude photos of a young bloke didn't seem a sin. I'd never heard the word homosexual until I was about thirty years old!

In Hartlepool, I had been skinny dipping with my pals. What's wrong with that? Some apprentices would grope their mates openly over their trousers in company for fun, it was common enough with teenagers teasing eachother. I didn't think it was more than that.

Aboard a whale catcher vessel, sex never entered my head. Food, sleep, work and the weather were priorities. A drink was always helpful. There was no booze allowed unless issued.

On one of Salveson's transport ships I was once in some company where a 'brew' was going on! The fermentation took place in a cut down forty gallon oil drum. This was steamed cleaned, a few gallons of water, with dried fruit, sugar and yeast from some galley. It only took five days to ferment, creamy with the yeast it was sweet tasting. Two glasses put a warm glow in one's body! I walked back a bit unsteady to my own ship but no one would notice because all Catcher men walked with a rolling gait. Coming ashore it took days to lose the rolling gait created by the constant heaving deck.

Here near the bunker jetty was a bit of a wooden shack office for crew who had problems or who wanted to send an important message home by expensive telegram. It was sent by morse code to the UK and then on to the recipient by the Post Office telegraph service. I didn't realise when I had done the job of Christmas telegraph boy seven years before that I would be using the service from such a place as South Georgia Island , eight thousand miles away.

I was a bit embarrassed the day I went into the office to send Mum a Christmas telegram. It was the 18th December 1947. I didn't remember that at the time but it was on the telegram and I still have it saved by my dear Mum and found in her treasured possessions.

A young Scottish lad, about my age, was in the office crying to get off his Catcher, "ah canna sleep, ah canna eat, get me off that boat!" He was desperate, tears streaked down his anguished face. I didn't wait to hear more. I was shocked that anyone could get into such a position without knowing what he was getting himself into. The season had just begun. He didn't appear to be suffering from sea-sickness; that makes people helpless, he seemed more scared? I left the office and strolled around the 'amenities' and saw where the sauna was. I used it twice during the season. It was good to feel super clean. I then found the 'slop chest' (general store) where I bought a zipped cardigan for off duty wear. Cigarettes were £1:10/- for a 1,000. I bought "ships woodbines" not that I was a heavy smoker Ten a day was about my limit. No money was exchanged. All transactions were put on account and deducted from my pay when discharged in the UK. I returned later to the office to send the telegram; the poor lad had gone. I sent a Merry Christmas and Happy New Year telegram to a dear mum who had brought me up to live a good life. It cost £3/10 shillings, half my weekly basic wage of £7 per week. Communication with South Georgia by post in those days was rare as few ships called. International morse code by wireless was expensive.

In her 1947/48 diary Dorothy relates to writing me twenty three letters. They would have been sent to various ports the Leith Office would tell her of in South America, where a ship might be. Possibly it was calling at South Georgia. Some letters may still be lying there as I received very few.

Imagine sailors and their families in Captain Cook's time, away for two or three years at a time in faraway undiscovered places.

During my time at sea on the oil tanker Atlantic Duke in 1952

I met young Greek men who had been at sea for five years, with no holiday pay or home leave. One said he was fearful of giving his job up because his place would be filled by another of the many unable to find work. One chap told me his pay kept his family fed and he was providing his sister with a dowry. The owners were multi-millionaires. We must thank them for creating the jobs by their ability to find the people with money to build the ships and pay to have the oil traded. Life is very complicated these days but our sailors are out of sight sadly neglected when at sea.

# CHAPTER 13
## OCTOBER 1947
## START OF THE WHALING SEASON

The first weeks of October at sea in Antarctica is late winter. Hunting for whales was difficult in the rough seas.

Did the young chap in the office pleading to be off his catcher know something we on the catcher Sondra didn't know? Shipping Companies keep the loss of a ship quiet. It is not good for recruitment of ships crews. I discovered many years later in a list of ships lost that the Catcher Simbra was reported lost in heavy seas. Feasible but not true. The Chief mentioned to me that the Company had ordered us not to use the centre fuel tank and continue whaling. We had to return to Leith harbour to refill the port and starboard fuel tanks. These were changed over every day to balance the ship. To me that inferred that the stability of the ship was in question. Generally stability is corrected by loading ballast to weigh the ship down to enable it to recover from an extreme roll.

A story was going around that a catcher had done exactly that whilst turning at speed. According to the rumour only the messboy was saved because having all got into the lifeboat the men had surrounded him to keep him warm as they died of hypothermia. The catcher ships were very lively in a bit of a sea but before they left the shipyard they were tested for stability. I'd seen it done myself. The shipping Companies keep bad news quiet. I don't think the young man anxious to get off his catcher could have heard anything, he just wasn't fit for the rough conditions. Stories like that are bad for morale even for chaps who will put up with the salt beef, salt pork salt fish no fruit and dried vegetables in 1947. I heard no more of this tale and when Sondra rolled over and dipped her skirts in the sea she always came back again.

*This was a good day. Lines of 'bergs laid out like a giant chess board*

One afternoon and on watch at about two thirty pm, Sondra was only steaming at half speed, whilst the men on the Bridge were seeking the shelter of a big iceberg. We were ploughing into very high seas, the bow rising and falling twenty feet or more and rolling very heavily. Like policemen, there was never an iceberg about when you needed one. I was stood, hanging on is a better description, by the steam throttle valve in case of an emergency. Johannsen, the Swedish boiler man was sat hanging onto the railing surrounding the well in front of the three boiler furnace burners.

He worked in this shallow well, where he would  clean the burner tips in a vice mounted on a small bench when they became choked with residual sand from the oil wells of Arabia. However on this occasion, we couldn't do much as we were being thrown about like two small mice in a great big tin can of an engine room. The telegraph clanged, an emergency double ring, 'full speed ahead!' In a sea like this full ahead seemed suicide! My home guard training kicked in! Obey the last order you are not paid to think. I quickly opened the throttle to give full steam to the engine, the connecting rods flashed up and down the crankshaft became a blur of oily blue movement, at maximum revolutions of 250 revs per minute, all the engine parts, eccentric sheaves, valve rods, top end bearings with their brass oil cups were thrashing about at the same time rolling and heaving with the antics of the ships dance of the giant waves. The reaction was immediate. Sondra reared up by the bow and rolled over onto her port beam. The engine room deck was now near 60 degrees from horizontal. My feet slid towards the engine toe plate. I hung on to the engine column that supported the cylinders. In this moment I glanced up at the engine

*W/Catcher Sondra with W/C. Sorcera, at the Bunker Jetty.*

room skylight which was always partly open, from the floor of the engine room I was able to see the top of the enormous waves of the wild sea. The ship had reared up a giant wave, probably the reason for the bridge to ask for full power to climb up the wall of water. The ship recovered from the extreme roll and as it did so the telegraph rang again for half speed. Thank God! It was fortunate I had been able to hang on there to be able to close the steam throttle valve. Now back to half speed we slugged on for another hour, then in the lee of South Georgia Island we found a more moderate sea. The telegraph rang 'full ahead,' I opened the steam valve to our full cruising speed and soon we came into the three mile long fjord where our whaling station Leith Harbour lay sheltered by the black snow topped mountains of this barren place.

When we were tied up at the bunker jetty the telegraph clanged again and the brass indicator swung around to the bottom section of the clock like face, 'finished with engines'. I tidied up the engine room, putting away oil cans and checking the boiler water level was okay. Everything was ticking over smoothly in the engine room before going up the vertical steel ladder giving access to the narrow passageway opening out to the deck housing. Therein was the companion way to the after accommodation and another to the second deck above. I went onto the upper deck to walk forward to climb back down to the main deck and the galley to make a mug of tea. As I walked past the port lifeboat I saw that the chocks the boat normally rested on had been broken away by the sea, the boat was hanging from the ropes on the davits. The davits are there to swing the boat out to launch it. The lifeboats are stored on the top deck, that's how far over we had rolled! If we had been low on fuel with poor stability we could have suffered the same fate as the crew of Simbra and failed to recover from the roll.

It was nearly sixty years later that I learnt the truth of the Simbra capsizing. This was when I received a book, 'Shetland Whalers Remember.' I read the two page memoir of John Leask who was the sole survivor of the loss of the whale catcher Simbra (see picture on page 32). In this book John Leask wrote that the loss occurred in January 1947 eight months before I joined Sondra. Our Chief Engineer Ankar Andersen did not join Sondra the next season, was he being a bit wary? I had decided I would a second season because I needed the savings it made to my bank balance. I knew it was risky. Then I thought, lightening doesn't strike in the same place twice, or was it the big cheque that made me find a reason to balance the risk?

In September 1939 many Norwegians did not want to sail on British ships because of the German U Boat threat. An appeal was made to the men of the Shetland Isles and was well rewarded with good seamen. Shetland then had only fishing and cutting peat for employment and something like whaling where the opportunity to make savings was just what was needed. Ninety men and boys eventually went to the whaling over the next years. The men of Shetland were able to buy tractors and start other ways of earning a living during the time between seasons. When whaling finished in 1963 Gibby Fraser who lives as far north as it's possible to get in Shetland got the lads together and asked them to write their memoirs.Fifty one of them did so and Gibby, Gilbert Fraser published the book. I was sent a copy by my

159

nephew Cliff Thornton, President of the Captain Cook Society of the Captain Cook Museum, Marton, Middlesbrough. I'd almost forgotten about whaling until Cliff who has known me since he was three years old started kindly pestering me to write my memoirs.

I e-mailed Gibby Fraser for permission to use John's story in this book and he kindly agreed. I copied it as John Leask wrote it. The Shetland English is unusual but understandable to us north country folk.

## SHETLAND WHALERS REMEMBER
*An excerpt, word for word of John Leask's account of the loss of the whale catcher Simbra. September 1946*

I joined the whale catcher Simbra in Smith's Docks, Middlesbrough in England, the same place as I joined the Southern Wheeler for the previous season. Except for a steering problem crossing the bay of Biscay, the voyage was uneventful.

After arriving at Leith harbour, South Georgia, we took on supplies, whale ropes, harpoons, stores, etc and left in company with eleven other catchers and the new factory ship the Southern Harvester. After two or three days we started whaling and worked our way into the Weddell Sea area of the Southern Ocean, this would have been approximately early to mid November.

After about two months fishing, on the evening of the 11th of January 1947 the Simbra was lost. With a lot of high speed chasing, fuel was taken on every four to six days. On the morning of the 11th we delivered whales to the factory ship then went alongside for bunkers and stores but we were refused bunkers as the factory ship had a tanker alongside replenishing her tanks. It is possible that, with normal procedure, the Simbra might not have been lost for with full tanks the stability of the ship would have been much better but as it was we carried on fishing with what bunkers we had left.

The crew were all Norwegian except for the deck boy who came from Edinburgh and myself. I was on watch that evening of the 11th from 4pm to 8pm. We had caught and flagged two whales close up to an area of pack ice. It was my hour in the crow's nest from 6pm until 7pm. We were running before the wind chasing the rest of the pod which had taken fright so it took like a long chase to catch them up. Perhaps that is why, as I was looking around, I saw the skipper on the bridge talking to my watchmate probably telling him to turn round and go back to pick up the two whales we had caught before dark because at that moment she started coming round to starboard into the wind and. As is normal when turning sharply, she started keeling over to port – But this time she just kept going over. As I realised that things were not right I got out of the crows nest to come down the rigging but she had keeled over so far I had to come down the rigging head first, on my hands and knees. As I looked down the sea was starting to pour down the hatch. I got down to the ship's side and to get aft to the lifeboat I had to shuffle my way along the outside of the ship which I managed by keeping a grip on the bulwark and going down crabwise along the ship's side. When I got to the lifeboat the crew were already there. They had got the covers off and my watchmate was cutting the boat adrift from the davits as there was no chance of getting it launched. By this time the sea was coming down the engine room skylights so we all got on the side of the ship ready to jump. That was a bad moment because with no distress signal sent out and no lifeboat launched, when we all had to jump it was just like jumping to our deaths. The shock of the cold water was bad but I managed to get hold of the lifeboat strongback, the wooden spar that the covers are fitted over. The skipper and my watchmate also got hold of it. The lifeboat luckily had floated free. It was quite close but upside down. We started paddling towards it but the Skipper soon lost his grip and went under. It was slow going against the wind so my watchmate let go and swam towards the boat. I could make no headway myself as I wasn't a swimmer but I struck out and made it. The fact that I was wearing a kapok lined coat gave me the buoyancy to get me there. The wireless operator also made it and between the three of us we managed to heave her over. After getting on board we pulled another four of the crew on. The boat, of course, was full of water. We tried bailing but it was no use – the sea just kept slapping over the side. Three of the men died very quickly so we put them back over the side. Nobody else made it to the boat. The deck boy kept shouting my name but he, too, soon went under. We tried bailing again but it was no good. By sitting right up on the stern of the boat I managed to get out of the water, except for my legs below the knees. I had lost the mitten of my left hand but it wasn't long before my hands and legs were numb. I saw the smoke of a catcher as it was getting dark. I set off a flare but it wasn't seen.

The three men left in the boat with me didn't last long. The wireless operator, the fireman and the mate soon died. It was probably no more than an hour, hour and a half. The mate was last to go. I was alone, it was a cold night just sitting there. Thankfully the wind had dropped. An iceberg floated past close by and a couple of whales went past. I must have been in a semi-conscious state when the sound of a harpoon gun going off brought me to my senses. I looked round and a catcher no distance away had just shot a whale. I managed to get to the middle of the boat and although I had lost all feeling in my hands and feet, I managed to get an oar with a bucket on it and placed it where the mast went. They saw me and it wasn't long before they had me on board – that was about 11am. I spent some time in hospital on the Southern Harvester. My knees were badly bruised and I think it was a week before my legs and hands came right although it was a fair while until my left had got back to normal.

*Author John Leask*

Gilbert 'Gibby' Fraser sent me an e mail to say that John had died in 2004 This was before I had read the account of John Leask's dreadful ordeal. Gibby had published fifty of the men's memoirs in the book Shetland Whaler's Remember. This book is a tribute to the Shetland sailors who served in the British Merchant Navy suffering serious losses during the 1939 – 1945 war. Then Britain bankrupt, the pound Sterling unaccepted to buy food from abroad. Orders were given to build whaling fleets of ships to feed a devastated Europe and the men of Shetland Isles with the tough men of Norway sailed in them for as long as it took to restore the Birtish economy. They worked long hours in poor conditions for little pay.

*Commander Christian Christiansen, taking aim for a professional kill.*

162

*Helicopters were not a success. Pilots got lost and ran out of fuel*

On board Sondra at the officers mess table I heard many stories of the 1939 whaling season when Britain had a big need for whale oil. It was a source of making glycerine, necessary in the production of explosives for munitions.

The Germans had converted a first class merchant ship named Kandelfel into an eighteen thousand ton auxiliary armed cruiser. She was renamed Pinguin, 'Penguin' in English, and was capable of seventeen knotsfast for a merchant ship in the 1930's. Fitted with guns from an old battleship and capable of laying mines she caused havoc with British merchant shipping. Pinguin sailed from Germany in June 1940 when Britain was at its darkest hour and she was able to reach the Southern Atlantic without British interference. In 1941 the Norwegians were well aware of the Pinguin and her Captain, Ernst-Felix Kruder. He took his ship down to Antarctica where the Norwegian whale factory ships were working and in January 1941 captured three factory ships and eleven catchers. The Germans could have bought the whale oil from Norway but that was not Hitler's way of doing business. He invaded Norway and they acted as pirates on the high seas. These whaling ships were sent back as prizes to occupied France arriving in March with a large stock of whale oil for the German war effort. As well as this success, Pinguin sank thirty two British merchant ships, a

163

formidable score. Eventually the German raider Pinguin was hunted down by the Royal Navy cruiser HMS Cornwall. They found Pingin and cornered her in the Indian Ocean. On the 8th May 1941in an uneven sea battle Pinguin was sunk by shellfire from the British heavy cruiser. Many of the 400 crew and 200 prisoners were killed when a shell exploded among the mines that Pinguin carried. Sadly for some reason the Pinguin Captain Ernst – Felix Kruder did not surrender. The Royal Navy deplored enemy warships sailing as neutral commercial vessels, no quarter was given. Seriously out gunned by HMS Cornwall, the massive explosion blew the ship up. In the book Shetland Whaler's Remember there is an account from a sailor who was on a British whale catcher from South Georgia, they had witnessed the capture of the Norwegian factory ships and had run at full speed into a fog bank to avoid capture themselves. They then steamed at full speed back to South Georgia to raise the alarm at the British whaling Company. This ended the whaling season 1940 – 41. All the useful whale catchers were escorted by the Royal Navy to South Africa to be converted to anti-submarine and mine sweeping service in that area.

The Leith Harbour factory was defended by a six inch gun mounted above the factory and twelve volunteers of Salvesens Company men, mostly Shetlanders. They were given Government Status and guarded the place until the war ended. They lived off the fish caught from the sea and the occasional deer which were plentiful but because of the terrain were not easy to hunt. This history is well documented in the book containing fifty one stories written by Shetland men who went for many years working on South Georgia Island. The 1940 -1941 season ended whaling until 1946.

The Government decided in 1944 before the war ended because of Britain's bankruptcy that we needed to work within the Sterling area to feed ourselves and also Europe. Most of the slow old modified liners converted to whaling factory ships had been sunk by German U Boats.

Orders were given to shipyards on Teesside to design and custom build large Factory Ships well capable of providing the vast amount of fresh water from the sea required to cook out the whale oil. The few whale catcher vessels in South Africa were then refitted out from Anti-Submarine work back to whale catching. Many more were going to be required and Smith's Dock Ltd, South Bank, Middlesbrough built them. They were not a lot improved on the pre-war catchers. Still no refrigerators or freezers were fitted so food was not considered too important. Economy and efficient steaming was important so water tube boilers were fitted. The old drum boilers held forty tons of water and required more fuel to raise steam. A water tube boiler only held seven tons of water and was more economical but did it affect the stability of the ship? The ship's hull was the same design. The answer was to use aluminium plates to build the superstructure instead of the heavier steel plate. This would lighten the topside of the vessel.

Sailors passed the time at sea when there was no radio, telling stories. If you were lucky some chap may have had a musical instrument to entertain the lads. There was no time for such things on a whaler during the season, it was all bed and work, only very bad weather stopped us hunting for whales.

During the midnight to four am watch when all was quiet I had various duties to prepare for first light when the whales might be seen. It was my duty to change the boiler feed water filters. These trapped any oil that had been carried over with the steam from the engine into the condenser and then as water pumped back to the boiler. It's a bit like your electric kettle in the kitchen. If the electric element is covered in lime scale it will take longer to boil. With a ship's boiler at two hundred and fifty pounds pressure oil fouling the boiler tubes can cause tube failure with serious explosive problems. The dirty filters were washed in a bucket of hot water with soda to remove the light deposit of oil. The engine piston rods had to be oiled occasionally and this was the cause of the problem. The filters were cleaned every night.

I deliberately did not have a calendar or keep a diary. I made notes from time to time in order to have something to write home about but knew I had 130 days or more to live on this little ship.

The catchers working for the Leith Harbour factory were allowed a six months season. However the catchers working for the Factory Ships were only allowed a three months season, because being able to steam around the icecap in that time the catchers had less distance to tow the whales to the factory. We were only allowed a certain quota of whales.

One day coming off watch at four pm I saw the Chief Engineer, Anker Anderson smartly dressed and shaven and I remarked on it. He said, "Christmas Eve, we celebrate! Tomorrow Christmas day we stay in and have the day off!" I didn't even know what day it was. When I went along to the galley for a mug of tea the cook was preparing a bit extra special table. We were steaming along the South Georgia coast turning to run into Cumberland Bay and the Leith harbour Factory. I went down to my cabin went into my little cupboard and brought out my luggage. In my canvas and leather grip I brought out a heavy round biscuit tin sealed with sellotape. Dorothy had given me this for Christmas. Her dear Mum had baked me a pound Christmas fruit cake, now nicely preserved with a smell of brandy. I took it along to the cook and told him to half it, send one half to the eight crew who were quartered for'rard and the other half for our eight man mess, Captain, 1st mate, 2nd mate, Chief and other three engineers. The cook was included in our mess. We made a little effort to celebrate this important meal but I sensed our hearts were not in it. I have seen better funeral meals. Like me I suppose, we tried not to think of home, if you can imagine such a profound conundrum.

The Chief later asked me if I would kindly relieve the two firemen's duties by taking care of the boiler on Christmas Day? There was no great demand for steam with the engine idle. Only the little steam electric generator and the boiler feed pump were working with some demand of steam for the cabin heating radiators. The regular Norwegian whalers most of whom were from Tonsberg in Norway wanted to visit friends ashore or on other ships also in harbour for the day. I had no one to visit and I was pleased to just have a quiet day and accept the duty. I was supposed to be on duty from midnight until four in the morning. Anyway, I was alone in our two berth cabin, my room mate engineer Malbut disappeared without saying a word. I wrote a couple of letters to Mum and Dorothy, there was little to write about, but I was quite well. I felt very strong although I only slept in snatches of a few hours at a time. In heavy weather I was never in a deep sleep, half of my brain was conscious of the throb of the engine and the drumming of the propeller beneath our cabin. I was glad of this day off, but I was now Duty Officer in Charge aboard so I kept a routine inspection of the ship's deck as well.

The weather was improving now for about four weeks of Antarctic summer. I went down into the engine room every hour or so and checked the boiler water level, the pressure had gone down to about 150 pound per square inch, I lit a burner in one of the three furnaces and waited ten minutes or so until the pressure came up to full pressure of 250 P.S.I. I climbed out of the engine room and went on deck. It was a beautiful night, no wind and a clear sky. Christmas night on South Georgia Island 1947!

I'll always remember that night, not a soul about, very quiet except

166

for the lapping of the water against the ship's hull. I was the only man aboard. I suppose everybody was with their friends or relations from their home town Tonsberg, asleep or drunk by now as it was after midnight. The sky was very black dotted with bright stars that didn't seem to twinkle. The stars of the Southern Cross stood out in the blackness. I knew Dorothy would be under a different sky with the North Star, if the sky was clear at all back home. I was conscious of my responsibility. The deck officers had not asked me to keep an eye on the mooring ropes but I checked them when I went to the galley to make a pot of tea. I found some old English magazines and read for a while. The time passed, every hour checking the boiler and raising the steam pressure until daybreak.

At eight o clock the assistant engineer came down to relieve me. I had a bit of breakfast and turned in. No sign of my cabin mate Malbut. I got up again at eleven thirty to maintain my watch at noon. Surprise! We were asked to sail around to the Argentinean whaling station Gryt Vicken with the Leith harbour football team. One of the firemen came down to attend to the boiler while I operated the main engine. It took about an hour to sail the fifteen miles to Gryt Vicken.

Some of us accompanied the team; we left the ship and walked up to the football pitch. I was one of about a dozen spectators. This football pitch was one of the few places flat enough to play football. Even then it had crevasses and tussocks of coarse grasses growing in smaller cracks in the black rock. I watched the wild footballers for a few minutes then standing in the exposed cold windswept ground moved back to the lower factory area. With another chap from Leith Harbour we walked into the little cemetery. I stood beside Ernest Shackleton's grave, and read the head stone and noted the well kept state of the grave curb stones containing the white marble chippings. A wreath of laurel fashioned in thin copper sheet lay at the head of the grave. I stood there for a few minutes in contemplation. If only more of the public were reminded of such a man today and equally the men who went with him on his perilous journey. But the majority of people don't seem to care! I then decided to return to the Sondra, my nice warm ship. Gryt Vicken seemed in better shape than Leith harbour, better walkways around the place, not so rough, a bit of concrete, investment made. Argentina had not suffered from the slump of the thirties it seems. The match over, I didn't hear who won? Both parties in a match like this I suppose! We then sailed back to Leith Harbour by which time my watch was over.

The cook was having a day off too! He laid on a Sunday lunch. Smorgasbord, a meal of cheese and cold meats, those big German sausages full of white bits of fat! I ate it, after the war we were never fussy eaters. We had no bread, but the ships biscuits were good and we had plenty of beautiful butter.

Next day it was business as usual, hours of cruising, hunting for the elusive whale. By February the weather was turning bad again. Force ten gales with high seas. Caught out on the south side of South Georgia the Gunner took us into an old sealing station for a night's shelter. It was in a narrow fjord with jagged cliffs reaching high into the darkness of the night. We tied up to a small wooden jetty built by the sealers of 1850's. I said to the Mate, who was checking the mooring ropes, "I don't like the look of those big rats there on the jetty, they could come aboard on the ropes." Big ships put a steel collar on the mooring ropes to stop rats coming on board. The Mate replied "don't worry the rats do not come aboard the whale catchers!" He was right, the rats didn't like us! What did that say about us? Now darkness increased the wretchedness of what was an eyrie place.

Nothing decays or rust in Antarctica. The little narrow railway track and tubs that ran along the jetty the sealers had used in their dreadful work were still stood there from when they had been left perhaps a hundred years before. The wind broke the silence now and then with the rattle of a loose sheet of corrugated iron, somewhere higher up the fjord. It seemed far away like a ghost moaning for some lost soul. I had a few hours restful sleep in a cabin that was still. At midnight I went down on watch. All was quiet so I took a bucket of water from the boiler and with some shives of the common brown soap I washed a few clothes. I hung my washing over the handrails at the top of the engine room. They dried in a couple of hours.

Early next morning the gale had abated, I was asleep in my bunk I didn't hear the engine room commands or the propeller throbbing below our cabin. It must have been a deep sleep on that occasion. I woke to the rise and fall of Sondra as she ploughed through a more than moderate sea to continue the hunting. Twice in the season there was venison from the herd of deer that had increased to two thousand from the original twenty deer that had been taken to South Georgia in 1910. Like everything else it was stewed. The cook never did a roast for some reason but at that time I couldn't tell him how to do a roast either. I was just pleased to eat fresh meat instead of the salt beef, salt pork menu. This herd of deer in 1947 had thrived and were culled to keep the numbers down and provide us with fresh meat. The Gunner or the Mate insisted that they saw us drink the lime juice provided that was available each day as scurvy was a possibility. We had enough problems with cuts going quickly sceptic so we drank the "Rose's" lime juice and stayed healthy! There was no chance of catching a headcold during this time as we were rather isolated which was a good thing !

My Mum had given me the hair cutting scissors, steel comb and shears she used on me to take to sea with me. She had used these to cut my hair since I was a baby. This became quite an asset! I made good friends amongst the crew, going for'rard to cut the sailors hair, mainly in bad weather when there was no chance of chasing whales. In the crews quarters up in the bow of the ship the deck rose and fell twenty feet or more in a heavy sea. To cut a man's hair we would sit together on a long stool with me behind him, It was surprising how well this method worked! The men who worked on deck wore their hair to the shoulders normally with beards to match. This helped to protect their faces from frost bite. Long hair was not fashionable in the 1940's, so I found this unusual. During my first six weeks, because the weather was so rough, I grew a beard but found it uncomfortable. I left the moustache, much to the amusement of the boiler man we nicknamed Gandhi as we tried to see who could grow the longest! He won at seven inches tip to tip! As 'the hairdresser' I was in big demand, more at the end of the season, and it had earned me a few tots of spirits from the Gunner. The sailors made me a thick sailcloth sea bag, hand stitched to get the extra gear I had bought at the 'slop chest' home. I was even cutting hair as we sailed up the River Mersey to pay off in Liverpool. It would save the guys valuable drinking time they said!

The weeks in the South Atlantic went by, the days were now getting shorter and the weather deteriorated, by that I mean there was more of it, bad that is. When it snowed, the snow floated on the minus one degree sea and made a "white out" for about four hours. January was the best month, some days could be considered perfect, with bright sun and blue sky. Towards mid-February the cloud cover thickened again grey and wet, the norm. Whales were scarce and difficult to see in a rough sea, they could move faster than the ship in the big seas.

At night, about six o clock, we stopped and drifted until daylight at five the next morning. Some nights we lay amongst a field of icebergs set out like chess pieces on a giant chessboard as far as the eye could see. Occasionally the sea was free of 'bergs!

I suppose the Sondra moved around a lot in the South Atlantic! We did get within sight of Bouvey Island a couple of times which is about three days sail east of South Georgia. We cruised at normal full speed as long as it was light. At cruising speed we would range for about 120 miles. I never knew what part of the ocean we were in, North or South of the whaling station. There was always the danger from the small 'bergs (as big as a house).They were particularly dangerous as there is not a lot showing above the water surface, big enough to do a lot of damage and difficult to see in rough weather! At intervals during the night the sailor on watch would telegraph for slow ahead as we drifted close to a 'berg then stop again until our drift required another move. On one stormy night drifting, waiting for daylight, twice a hundred or more seabirds came down into the engine room attracted by the ship's lights. These Terns, I think they were, came down the two big engine room ventilators which acted like scoops, the wind blowing them down to flutter about in all the awkward corners of the boiler and engine room machinery. The boiler fireman Johannsen and I spent an hour with sacks bagging them up and taking them on deck to return them to the sea, the daft little things were easy to handle but their nice white feathers were a bit sooty!

I disliked going onto the top of the boiler. It was hot, badly lit and the risk of a steam leak at 250 pounds pressure would create a painful shriek and was invisible at the source of the leak. It was easy to receive a burn especially on a rolling ship. The pipes were insulated with pads of asbestos cloth lagging. The valves had to be exposed to give access for adjustment and although we wore gloves we generally had bare arms. The boiler was a 'five drum water tube' and built by the Yarrow Company. It was constructed of two inch diameter steel tubes connected to two steel drums about three feet diameter at the bottom taking up about two thirds of the width of the ship. Two more similar drums were above closer together with the third larger steam drum above them. These drums about fifteen or more feet long were connected by rows of two inch tubes that crossed from the bottom drum to the opposite top drum forming a triangular furnace area about eighteen feet high. A thin steel casing enclosing the boiler was lined with two rows of firebricks insulating the casing from the burning oil which was sprayed into the inner triangle formed by the tubes. The temperature was bright red hot! During a stop to secure a whale after a long day at full speed Johansen called me over to the boiler furnace inspection holes. The engine being shut down, the oil burners were turned off. The furnace still glowed red hot. I didn't know what I was supposed to see. "What am I looking for?", I asked Johannsen. The inner row of fire bricks are melting, he said! It was always the case with steam engines, the engine when fully opened up could always take more steam than the boiler could produce. It just went faster! Speed being the most important part of catching whales more speed required more steam so bigger oil burners were fitted than were designed for the boiler. I reported it to the Chief who reported this to the factory by radio and when we came in shore workers came aboard to replace them. The large top steam drum had two sight glasses showing the level of water in the boiler. This level was important. The boiler only held seven tons of water. If the main engine was taking steam at full throttle and the boiler feed water pump failed to pump the condensed water back to the boiler it would only take a few minutes to lower the water level and create serious damage. Today with automatic control any fault would automatically shut down the furnace but our design engineers had not got as far as that at this time .A centrifugal fan six feet diameter powered by a small steam engine blew air into the furnace fronts around the burners to aid the combustion of the oil. This was termed 'forced draught'. The early ships with coal fired boilers improved the draught of air to the furnaces with tall funnels. In a pitching sea, a high water level caused water to carry over with the steam. Water getting into the cylinders of any steam engines in the engine room that operated the electric generator, the condenser sea water cooling pump or other vital machines especially the main engine, could do serious damage to the machinery. It was difficult in a rough sea to gauge how much water was in the boiler. With the ship pitching and tossing the sight glasses were full one second and empty the next. I estimated the level by counting, one two three 'full' and, one two three 'empty.' This might have indicated a half full glass, however it seemed to work. At the end of my watch with daylight approaching, in a moderate sea I would top up the boiler water level to 7/8ths for the Second engineer coming on watch. It was less for him to do if a whale was sighted and different engine speeds were required in stalking the whale.

One morning at three am with a calm sea, I spent twenty minutes topping up the water level in the boiler. To ensure the water did not contain salt or other impurities it was evaporated in via a steam heated "evaporator" to the condenser. This ensured its purity. I saw with satisfaction the sight glasses were 7/8 full. I was anticipating the end of my watch when we ran into a heavy pitching sea! This happened so suddenly, I was taken by surprise it was unbelievable but this was the wild Antarctic. The electric generator steam engine cylinder started slapping badly with boiler water coming over with the steam! Water cannot compress in the cylinder and can crack the cast iron cylinder especially being at 250 pounds pressure. My dreams of an easy end to the watch evaporated. I had to blow the boiler water down a bit! This would waste precious boiler water! I pulled the steel floor plate away from the bottom of the boiler to get at the blow down cocks, two interlocking drain cocks to ensure it was not possible to have one leaking or left part open. A special socket spanner was needed to open these important cocks .I opened first one, this allowed me to open the second one and I heard the hard earned boiler water blowing into the sea. I had put the socket spanner onto the floor plate near where I was sat with my feet dangling in the bilges. Guessing I had blown away enough boiler water to reduce the level enough to avoid water carrying over with the steam I went to pick the spanner up to close the valves. The ship gave a heavy roll. Bilge water was running up the side of the engine room. It passed the steel decking which was a couple of inches short of the ship's side. On the return roll, the bilge water couldn't get back down the narrow gap quickly enough and the foul water swept across the deck plates where I was sitting with my feet in the bilge space to my wet smelly discomfort! The essential spanner skidded down into the bilges. It slipped down to the keel plate and was sloshing about in the bilge water. I dived under the floor plates and grovelled about fishing for the thing. The boiler all this time was losing it's precious water! If things went too far we were up the creek without a paddle or in this case a boiler so to speak! Wet through in stinking bilge water I quickly found the spanner and closed the valves. I just had time to feed a little more water to the boiler to a suitable level before my watch relief came down. I had not taken a calendar with me, not even a diary and lost track of the days. Perhaps it was for the best, just take one day at a time whatever it throws at you!

The constant strain of hanging on to the heaving vessel or risk of being flung to the deck was beginning to tell. At times I felt nearly exhausted, not seasick just weary! Stomach muscles ached with straining to stand upright. I saw the funny side of it, one never knew which way we would be thrown next. It was difficult to predict and amusing when taken by surprise! No wonder ships are called 'she' We love 'em and hate 'em!

Jamie had called me one morning at eleven thirty, he didn't bring a mug of tea since I normally went straight for my lunch. I woke up just in time to go on watch! When I saw the time I was mad! I couldn't remember Jamie calling me and I had to do without my lunch! Coming off watch at four in the afternoon I went to the galley for a brew and gave Jamie a bollocking, "you didn't call me!" He was a grand lad! I couldn't believe I would have to do such a thing. He responded very gently and said in a hurt voice, "but you sat up and said thanks!" I was stunned and apologised. I realised how all on board must be feeling. The end of the season couldn't come too soon! There was still a long way to go! A few days later a Royal Navy cruiser H.M.S. Glasgow arrived in Leith Harbour fjord and stayed to show the flag. Maybe our Gunner Christiansen being an ex Royal Navy Commander had friends at the Admiralty. I hope H.M.S. Glasgow steamed past Gryt Viken the Argentinian Whaling Station to let them know they were present.

The days passed. One time when we came in for bunkers the Mate who had been up to the office, handed me a telegram. It was from my Mum, just a few words printed on a strip of ticker tape and stuck to the telegram to say my sister Sybil, who had contracted polio at five years old and was paralysed down her left side had died at the age of thirty two years. It was a tragedy of a tragedy! I don't want to write about it. I felt the deepest sympathy for my Mum and she would know my thoughts would be with her. I can't remember much of my reaction to it now, there was little I could do. It was maybe a blessing in disguise. I couldn't even send a telegram. I went on watch and kept busy. My Mum's brother the cobbler Uncle Arthur, had given her his New Testament Bible, Royal Navy issue 1914, for her to give to me to take to sea. Now and then I would open it at the book of Saint Matthew chapter 5 'The Sermon on the Mount' and read the words which I tried hard to live by.

Down in the engine room when the ship shuddered and dug into the great seas the boilerman and I just hung on physically to a handrail or valve wheel mentally and dumbly for hours until the lads on the bridge could find some shelter, the lea side of a large iceberg would do. I felt a bit claustrophobic down below, but it was cold and wet topside. It was a bit better below but it could be cold when seas breaking high often came down the ventilators. The hull of the vessel was only ribs and single plates riveted together, the higher plates a bit buckled between the ribs from the pressure of the giant waves weighing fifty tons or more of sea water hitting the ship. Not much to have between men and the worst ocean on earth. It was some comfort to see "Cargo Fleet Middlesbrough" embossed every couple of yards along each rib!

We very rarely saw other whale catchers but one very wild day somehow four of Salvesen's catchers were hove too on the lea side of a massive 'berg perhaps half a mile long and a couple of hundred feet high, a 'flat top' as they were called for obvious reasons. It was flat calm here on the lee side of the berg. One of the boats had a whale in tow and using it as a fender went alongside the berg at a convenient place and made fast (don't ask me how-these were Norwegian seamen) then the other three boats tied up to him. They had been in radio communication with each other. There was a lot of too'ing and fro' ing between the boats as the crews visited friends and probably neighbours. As I have said the Norwegians with Salvesen Company nearly all came from the town of Tonsberg. We had a nice quiet evening and I had a restful sleep before going on watch at midnight. I did my routine jobs in the engine room changing the boiler water filters and pumping out the bilges. then did a bit more 'dobeying.' Nothing lasts for ever! At about three in the morning the weather had swung around and the sea was going wild on our side of the iceberg now. It's not a good place to be alongside an iceberg in bad weather! Voices were calling to cast off! Engine telegraphs were clanging as the outside boats got clear. The weather had abated somewhat as we all went our separate ways. In the due course of the season the Factory ships Southern Venturer and Southern Harvester with their escort of catchers returned from their excursion around the icecap. They came into Leith Harbour, South Georgia, their season ended. They were restricted to a three months season because they had more flexibility. Their catchers had less towing distance. The shore based factory catchers had a six months season. The factory ships would depart before us, and this was an opportunity to send letters home, not that there was much to write about!

Weeks after the factory ships had departed with their precious cargo of oil to make margarine for the rations of the people and guano for the farmers of Europe, another ship arrived. It was named 'S.S. Saluta' and was to be our transport home. I had been asked if I wanted to 'overwinter' and work through the seasons overhauling the catchers during the Antarctic winter. This meant being away from home for eighteen months! I couldn't imagine a worse job in the world! I said I had to go back to be married but would consider it after the next season. The weather was now atrocious for the last weeks. I think the whales had all gone away for their holidays!

Finally Sondra came in, the season ended. I packed my bags and without sentiment stepped from Sondra's low deck and walked along the fore shore past one or two bull elephant seals that thought they owned the territory. They did I suppose! I arrived at the steep angled gangway of S.S.Saluta and climbed aboard. I reported to the Chief Steward who allocated me to a two berth cabin. I was to share it with an old third engineer Jimmy Rankin. Jimmy was about sixty five years old a dour Scot with a "fine" philosophy and dour sense of humour. He complained of the cold and had the cabin door air grill sealed up with brown paper and the door always firmly shut. The cabin was a fug of steamy cigarette smoke. When visitors arrived they were told to "shut the bloody door!" However he was always pleased to entertain them with his pessimistic view of life! He was really amusing! After a few days assembling the lads going home, Saluta set sail. The first days at sea I was dubious as to how long the ship would last in these waters. I think Saluta was built about 1890 something or even before that? The forty ton Scotch boilers were not in good health the steam pressure had been reduced to 180 P.S.I. (pound per square inch).Very slowly she put on a few miles each day hoping for a favourable wind or current, maybe doing about six knots, no more! Looking over the side I imagine I could have walked faster. When S.S.Saluta was younger with boilers at 250 PSI she would steam at a comfortable12 knots. Traversing the cold roaring forties we socialised in the saloon. I think the ship had been a cargo / passenger vessel, a fine ship in her day. It was quite comfortable after a being on a whaler. Having reached better weather in a more Northern Latitude the Chief Engineer set us to work. The ammonia refrigeration plant was in a serious state with the ships supply of meat in danger of waste and something like a couple of hundred men to feed. The ammonia compressor automatic control was unreliable so the Chief put us on three watches to control it 24 hours a day. The steel freezer coils in the freezer rooms were rusted badly and leaking. We managed to keep it going until we reached the tropics. I'm not sure what failed. It was antiquated and clapped out! Finally the sides of beef and other meat had to be put over the side. We had a good feed of meat for a day or two, then I think it was bully beef. The next major problem was with one of the boilers. The triple expansion steam engine was most reliable and would run for a hundred years with little attention. Boilers were more of a problem! We catcher engineers were now put to double up the ships engineer's watches. We repaired one boiler by plugging up a couple of leaking tubes. This was a hot job in the tropics. The boiler fires were extinguished and under a reduced pressure of 90 PSI we had to enter the furnaces to get to the back of the boiler fire tubes. It was very hot and we had to use a plank of wood to keep our feet from the hot furnace shell plates. We worked as a team staying in the boiler furnace a few minutes at a time with wet towels and sacks until we were successful in putting the plugs and tie rods in place. The boiler was back up to it's pressure of 180 PSI in a few hours. Now I thought we stood a good chance to get the old girl home if nothing more happened like the propeller dropping off which fortunately did not happen. I always tried to see the funny side of things. Saluta made a stop over, I'm not sure where, possibly Tenerife for stores. We were able to buy full stalks of bananas here in exchange for cigarettes. The Chief Steward carried a good stock of cigarettes for business purposes that were paid for on our account. Many days later I was told we had passed the Ushant Light off the northwestern coast of France. We eventually entered the Irish Sea. The engine ground on at about seventy revs a minute pushing us up to the Mersey River. At the mouth of the Mersey we stopped to pick up a pilot. Then panic stations! A swarm of ten or more Customs officers came aboard all dressed in boiler suits. They were armed with screwdrivers and sharp prodding instruments. They proceeded to take the ship to pieces! Panels were removed from the cabins. They searched tanks and vessels in the engine room! What did they expect to find? We'd come from Antarctica and been nowhere to get contraband! A few cigarettes or a few tins of tobacco was all we had. One poor sailor who voiced an opinion had his sea bag emptied over the deck. It felt as though we were criminals! I thought it was wrong that British seamen who had been at sea for nine months on Her Majesty's Business supplying food for her subjects should be treat like this. We had been warned of their arrival and told what we were allowed to bring into the country. I didn't expect them to behave like that, I hadn't the cash to pay duty on a tin of tobacco I had bought for Dorothy's Uncle, what was the point? Reluctantly I threw it over the side. The stick of bananas I had bought with cigarettes from a bum boat on the stop over raised no objections! Bananas had not been seen in the shops in England since 1939. We gave them to our neighbours' children.

# CHAPTER 14
# HOME TO MARRY JUNE 1948
*The sailor home from the sea to marry his sweetheart!*

After nine months away I was going to marry the girl I fell in love with when I was five years old. It had not occurred to me that Dorothy had not been happy living with her Mum who was now married to this Mr Jimmy Davidson. He had worked as a draughtsman in the shipyard drawing office for Mr Fell, Dorothy's father. Her mother had been a widow for six years, when Jimmy Davidson's wife died and following this he wasn't long in visiting Mrs Fell, taking her out in his old Jowett motor car. Sally as I affectionately called Mrs Fell, but not to her face, thought Jimmy was very kind. He would take her in his car to North Yorkshire villages for afternoon teas. It was not long before his intentions were obviously to be matrimonial! Dorothy's married sister, Marnie tried to persuade her mother that after six years of independence she had adjusted her new life well and was comfortable as she was. Although only sixty two, she had no need to marry him. I think her decision was partly based on the fact that Dorothy and I were to marry and she was afraid of living alone. Nothing that her daughters said would change her mind.

Jimmy turned out to be a disaster for Sally even before their wedding. After accepting Jimmy's offer of marriage, he lost no time in managing the situation to his advantage. "You sell your house Sally," he said, "and we'll buy a new car." For him to drive! "I'll sell my house," an old Victorian monstrosity, "and buy a more modern house." But the house was in his name only. The car would depreciate and Sally would have nothing, His house would appreciate especially in 1946 after the war. Sally would have nothing to leave her daughters in her Will. Without discussing it with her family he had persuaded Dorothy's mother to complete these transactions even before their wedding! Dorothy, her sister and I were now fully aware of the type of man he was. Dorothy's Mum also realised the mistake she had made. The Bowling club ladies who Mrs Fell had enjoyed playing bowls with every Saturday afternoon also knew of the disaster that had befallen their gentle friend. However with whatever regrets she had, Sally was too proud to dissent and went through with the marriage. She was a captive woman but after selling her home she now didn't have much option. Jimmy had gained a 'live-in housekeeper,' a new car and a better house! This was a few months before I joined Salveson Whaling Company in September 1947.

Dorothy was now living with her mother and step-father and things had settled down and appeared normal.

Dorothy had done a good job of arranging our wedding and honeymoon under the war time rationing that had continued after the war had ended. Her choice of a small boarding house in Harrogate was not my idea of a honeymoon venue. I would have chosen somewhere like a hotel in Scarborough but Dorothy was unable to communicate with me 8,000 miles away. She booked the same boarding house her sister had chosen during the war when she married her soldier boyfriend Fred Hawks. We made the best of it and found plenty of things to laugh about in Mr.Suter's boarding house.

Mr Suter would spend a long time studying the sport's page. Chaps would come in and make confidential conversation with him. I suspected he was running a Book on the horses. This was illegal until the Government realised they could tax it and allowed betting shops to open. I never saw money or betting slips change hands but the boarding house was a perfect cover for such an operation, men could come and go at will without raising suspicion. Harrogate wasn't such a bad place even in June 1948. On the spur of the moment we went to a dance somewhere at the Pump rooms. I took Dorothy in and then went back to our room to change my shoes that had rubber soles and were unsuitable to dance in. When I got back she was dancing with a very handsome young man! I had to sit and watch them chatting away as he waltzed her around! I was a bit miffed at first but the fact that she was mine and he had fancied her made me feel very proud of her. We laughed about it because we hadn't consummated the marriage the first week of our honeymoon. The first night I waited until Dorothy had had time to get into bed before I left the lounge downstairs. She had been a bit upset for the first few nights and had a few tears.

I thought any upset was because of the enormous responsibility we had undertaken, to set up home and care for each other. It was more likely she was worried about leaving her Mum with the miserable Jimmy Davidson who I read in her diary, didn't bother buying her Mum a birthday card. With my arm around her we drifted off to sleep. I was always tired at the end of the day with all the walking we had done so sleep was never a problem. I wasn't used to walking after being on such a small ship as Sondra. I guess I was right about the situation at her mother's home so I comforted her and we went to sleep.

A nearby bus stop took us to York and for a few days, we explored the Minster, the City walls, Clifford's Tower and the river. I had never had a proper holiday in my life before our honeymoon. Travelling by train and having a room with a wash basin with hot and cold water was a luxury I never had. Onboard Sondra the washbasin was never used when at sea, for water would have been all over the cabin floor.

The happy days seemed long and passed slowly. We now had confidence in each other's ways and how to please each other. If she was a bit grumpy I made her laugh. I knew she loved me when at times she would tease me. We never grew tired of each other. I often wonder how we managed it, were we just lucky? No it takes patience! We had many difficult times ahead but helped each other to get over them. Dorothy's troubles were my troubles and vice versa. Life would be boring otherwise.

I had become totally isolated from my father's family. In 1954 we had been married for six years and had bought a little house behind the Albert Park, 34 Newstead Road. Sadly living there I was never told that my Granddad George Dinsdale was in a nursing home only a few hundred yards from my house. He eventually died there at eighty four. My brother Jack told me he had died and I took my eldest brother Eric to the funeral. Eric had learning difficulties. Mum said it was due to oxygen starvation, he was too long in the birth. He could read and write and go messages but that was about all. Eric had been taken to live with my mum, with a gratuity of £1:10 shillings per week. It appears Eric had been a nuisance in Fred's household after his grandparents died. There was no one to look after him. Fred was perhaps realising what a stable marriage was worth, and that housekeepers were no substitute! It may have been cheaper to have provided his wife with a home for his family in the first place! In any case after I left home to be married Eric was company for mum and it was good for both of them until she couldn't manage the house because of her weak condition due to cancer. This eventually led to me seeking help from the social services.

Eric was placed in a Roman Catholic Home in Chorley Lancs. run by Brothers of Charity, to whom I am very grateful. I arranged with my father's secretary for the allowance for Eric £1;10s to be sent to them. The social services put Mum into a Council Home in Nunthorpe, We paid the rent on No. 68 Granville Rd for a year until she settled in. It took the best part of two weeks to empty the house. Mum eventually spent her last three years in Nunthorpe Hall and accepted it with dignity and in fact enjoyed getting the bus to go into town to see the friends she had made at Mrs Scraften's "Temple of Light" Spiritual Church. She usually called at our house for her tea and I would take her back to the Hall. I gave the old piano and the sheet music to the family next door to mum's as they had two girls who wanted to learn to play. It was a watershed to me, but I still cherish the memories and often one of Mum's old songs comes into my mind and the words of Nelson Eddy and Jeanette MacDonald singing 'sweethearts' brings Mum close to me.

It was on Thursday 27th May.1948 when S.S. Saluta came into the Mersey River and the Ships Agents came aboard in Gladstone Dock. Discharge papers were given out with travel vouchers and we were free to go. One of a fleet of taxis took myself and another chap who was going to Redcar near Middlesbrough to the city centre. I telephoned Dorothy from a call box there to tell her we had arrived and I would see her next day. A taxi took us to the station. A porter collected my luggage from the left luggage depot and saw tired me and the luggage onto the train for Middlesbrough. Like all drunken sailors, just a little, I had tipped him well for the service! After nine months away from civilisation I was worried I may get on the wrong train. I slept most of the way.

Sadly I don't remember getting home to my dear old Mum but I'm sure it was good. We'd been through a lot together and I slept in my own little bed again. The next day I went over to Hartlepool to see the love of my life Dorothy. There was no great emotional display but we both knew that nothing had changed. Our love for each other was as strong as ever. There were lots of things to do to make the final arrangements for the wedding. We arrange to go into Lynne Street to buy the wedding ring. I only read about this event in Dorothy's diary six months after she died. She wrote, "Saturday 29th May.1948. Raining hard today, Arthur and I went down to town, bought the ring in Lambs (jewellers) Don't know if I have done the right thing not getting a fancy one. Arthur thinks it's lovely, but if I don't like it over the weekend, Lambs say I can take it back on Monday." The ring was a war time austerity wedding ring, very thin but it has four little bars of platinum on the outer edge. She would never replace it in later years when her friends were buying thick replacements. I offered to buy her an eternity ring to put with it but she gently refused. She was happy with the ring we had chosen.

May 1948. Being at sea away from home for nine months had changed everything. I had been my Mum's life's work, I wonder how many lunch boxes she had packed for me. In the war, rationing had made this very difficult. I remember the first days as an apprentice going off to the shipyard in a boilersuit several sizes too big for me, with the legs and sleeves turned up "you'll soon grow into it" she had said, and I did. But I have a sense that during the hard times when food was short she had gone without. I was given a mother's love with nothing asked in return. The black enamel pan full of lamb stew, made from lamb lap, the cheapest cut. It simmered by the fire on the hob for a couple of days. It was thick with barley, lentils, marrowfat peas, carrots and the fatty meat. It was allowed to go cold. The white fat was then skimmed from the top of the stew. A pan full would last us a couple of days. This recipe was certainly handed down from her mother who as a girl had learnt it from the previous generations of thrifty Scots. This phase of my life was now over, our relationship was more distant but nothing lasts for ever. I had written to her at sea and thanked her for all the years she had taken care of me as a child and for the values I had learnt from her of thrift, honesty and love.

Mum was pleased with Dorothy, who had been over a couple of times to stay with her for the weekend. It was thoughtful of Dorothy who could have stayed with her Aunt Amy, her mother's sister who also lived in Middlesbrough. I think Dorothy would have confided to Mum her anxiety about arranging the wedding.

I had felt guilty leaving home to marry. Now the guilt turned to compassion. Mum had made some difficult decisions arising from her marriage to my selfish father. She had to leave four of her kids with her mother in law while she went off with me a baby to avoid his cruelty and make a life for herself. Her little chick had flown the nest! I knew a woman like that would not break down. I had learnt from her how to get through hard times. She would still play the old tunes on the piano, it was what I would always miss, her happy hour. Little did I know she wouldn't be alone for long when a few years later my eldest brother Eric was lodged with her by the family. Eric had learning difficulties but was able to go messages and do a bit of shopping for her.

Dorothy had done well with the wedding invitations and catering venue. At the Co-op in the bakery office where she had worked and was well regarded, her boss Mr Hart had ensured Dorothy had a good reception in spite of the rationing. I read in her 1948 diary that the wedding cake had been made at home by her mother. Dorothy then took it to be iced in the basket of her bicycle, the three miles to her Mum's friend a retired baker Chrissie Markum who lived in a cottage by the 14th century Town Wall of Hartlepool. I'll bet the iced cake didn't travel back in the bicycle basket! It would be on a trolley bus.

We were to be married at West Hartlepool on the 16th of June 1948. Dorothy had everything under control, all I had to do was be measured for a suit and be there! I must say Dorothy looked stunning as she came down the isle of Saint Luke's Church in West Hartlepool. She was what was called a strawberry blond. I was later told that it was 'unusual' in those days for the bridegroom to turn around to see his bride come up the isle to join him. I was eager to see her again, I wasn't nervous about the ceremony. I'd been away nine months in dangerous waters, what was there to be nervous about!

The Reverend Goldie conducted the ceremony, he was not old or stuffy, when he was finished I was sure we were joined together, until death do us part. The night before the wedding I had stayed at Aunt Jenny's in Middlegate St. in the Ancient Borough of my beloved Hartlepool. The morning of the great day I had breakfast with my Granny in the old house behind the cobbler's shop. We sat at the dining table in the best room, with the best china. This would probably be our last meeting. My dear old Granny, Margaret Ann Wright, nee Scot, died the following year 1949, aged eighty seven.

Dorothy's cousin Walter, my "best man" arrived to escort me to the church. I decided not to shave myself on this important occasion. Walter accompanied me to Mr Kirtley the professional barber to be shaved. His shop was just across the square leading to Sunnyside where the Salvation Army before the war had stood and played every Saturday evening. Above the shop door was the "barber's pole" white with a red stripe curling round from top to bottom. It should have been a warning of what was to come! Mr Kirtley gave me a hot towel facial then after stropping up his open razor on a strip of soft leather hanging by the chair, he lathered my face rubbing the soap up first with his fingers then used the brush to produce a firm lather. I gazed in the mirror watching as he wielded the cut throat razor. It came down my face from the top of my ear on each side. Before me, around the washbasin were the tools of his trade, coloured bottles of hair lotions one I was familiar with, a brown liquid 'bay rum' A hair dressing very popular, probably the only hair dressing in those days. I don't suppose there was any rum in it? I thought I would ask for the lavender aftershave, I didn't think there was any other! Now the cut throat razor was going round my chin. I obliged by pulling my face into various grimaces at the suggestion of his thumb and fingers. The result was he gave me such a close shave my face was oozing blood in several places! I thought I could have done a better job of it myself - probably not! At Granny's there was no bathroom, hot water came from the copper kettle on the fire. The mirror was high above the mantle shelf. My previous years at 14 Middlgate Street I had no hairs on my face. Mr Kirtley apologised, he said I had "a very tender skin!" In truth there were no cuts. Being a professional he applied his skills to stop the bleeding and I walked from his shop smelling of the aftershave of my choice, lavender! It stung quite a bit! My face feeling smooth, tight and fresh as a daisy!

Walter got me to the church in good time. I was surprised at the number of people there! Dorothy came down the isle on her stepfather's arm. Standing facing the altar with Walter I turned to see her, she smiled at me, and I knew there was no doubt at all in her mind. The day impressed on me the responsibility I was taking on. Rev. Goldie said marriage was a state not to be taken lightly. I understood that but realised I needed all the good fortune there was going!

Jessie my Mum looked very smart with a new hat, brown with a wide brim that framed her heart shaped face with the soft brown eyes. A fashionable fox fur draped around the shoulders of a brown two piece costume .She stood next to me in the vestry as I signed the register. This was the parting of the ways. This was the only wedding she had been invited to attend of her three married sons. I was surprised to become quite upset signing the register. My eyes filled with tears when I thought of the change that was now taking place.

183

Mum understood, we all have our own life to live but it was hard to think that now she was on her own. We had gone through a lot together during the war but even then there had been happy times. We had many a happy hour around that old piano as she played all the old Victorian favourites nearly every night following our dinner. Now she was composed and if there was any emotion in her thoughts they were for my happiness. That was the kind loving person she was .I never heard her say a wrong word about anyone. True! She never even bad named her erring husband Fred, but she did scorn the woman and her family who had led him astray. I don't think even then she realised what a weak stupid fellow he was. Jessie always expected Fred would one day tire of the women who had usurped her rightful place and she would return to end their days together. I don't think Mrs Scrafton had seen that in her messages. One message was of a Victory, I realised later that this was a euphemism for my Mum's final hour. It did no harm if it gave Jessie something to comfort her. In hindsight I wish I could have done more for her but she wasn't the clinging type and had her own friends and ways.

I took a deep breath and turned to my bride. Now we had to face the world and start a new life together. I was glad when the rationed austerity reception was over. It had been a trial. I made a formal speech thanking Dorothy's Mum and stepfather Mr Jimmy Davidson. I wonder to this day if he paid for the wedding reception, it was never mentioned. I thanked Walter and his wife Mary who had been Matron of Honour and the friends for being there, but after months of isolation. I was mentally exhausted of meeting people and was pleased to get away.

We went to what had been Dorothy's new home with her Mum and step father, near the church in Weldeck Road. There we changed and picked up our luggage. Dorothy was in her, going away costume, powder blue Harris Tweed. Me I can't remember, Dorothy might know, probably in grey flannel trousers and a jacket. Walter her cousin, my "best man" ordered the taxi and accompanied us to the railway station. He was brilliant, everything well organised, his army training probably. The smell of the railway engine as it steamed into the station, "bright coal smoke" and oil impressed me with its assertion of power. Steam engines with their moving limbs seem to be alive. I had spent months in charge of a much larger mechanical beast. Could it get addictive? I hoped not, I didn't want to spend my life at sea only coming home for short leaves. As the steam train slowly huffed and puffed its way along the platform Walter waved us off, his responsibilities to us were over. We didn't know it then but he only had a short time to live, he died a few years later from a heart attack at forty eight years of age.

*Our wedding day, 16th June 1948*

We, the happy couple, spent two weeks in a quaint boarding house in Harrogate. It wouldn't have been my choice, I would have preferred Scarborough near the sea but it didn't matter as long as Dorothy was happy. Mr Souter the proprietor was a funny little man. Both he and his wife did the cooking and waited on table. As I have said, he was very keen on the "horses". Betting on them, not riding them, he seemed to make a science of it, sitting a long time after breakfast with the sports page conferring with friends who came and went. They were not boarders? Street betting wasn't legal then, it was a furtive business. A boarding house would be a good cover for a "bookie, just a thought, I wish I had investigated further, I admire anyone who can beat the system and that system was to protect the Bookmaker Companies. He knew we were newly weds because Dorothy's ration books were in her maiden name and her wedding ring was crisp and new. I was only twenty four years old and Dorothy twenty two. There was a frisson of nudges and nods from Mr Souter to the other guests when we came down to breakfast that first morning. We were a happy couple so it pleased me. Dorothy looked beautiful in the dress she had bought for this occasion, I was very proud to be her husband. This was the girl I first fell in love with when I was five years old! Despite coming from a 'broken home' the difficulties arising in my education and the uncertainty of my place in the world, I had married her, what a lucky lad I was! I was to spend two seasons bashing about the Antarctic seas in order to do it. What was I going to do to follow that?

The honeymoon days were spent exploring by bus the City of York. I had been interested in Roman remains since I was given a slim book on the subject as a kid. I admired those ancient Romans who had arrived in this country and shown the tribal ancient Britons how to build roads, organise and do business. There wasn't much that interested me in Harrogate. Not even the toffee! York had plenty of interesting places. It was better than Scarborough! The magnificent Minster, I felt privileged to walk into it and think of the men who had built it. Down in the undercroft can be seen the massive foundation stones weighing many tons each. One wonders how masons in the year eleven hundred even envisaged such an undertaking. Also exposed down there are the remains of the Roman fort of Eboracum, The Roman name for the Viking City of Yorvic, which we call York today. A trip up the river in the morning, and a visit to Clifford's Tower filled in an afternoon. This was new to me. In my past life I hadn't had the opportunity or the means for holidays which cost money. Dorothy on the other hand had been used to a carriage to the station and the train to Scarborough as a child. The trunk of clothes had been sent on ahead. They would be happy days with her Mum and Dad. He had died in 1941 when Dorothy was fifteen years old, the happy days had ended. Mr Fell's savings had gone on operations for his illness. She was trusting me to take care of her as long as we both shall live and I did that and more as I cared for her mother when she needed help. Maybe that's why she chose Harrogate, because they had holidays there when Dorothy was a little girl? There was a bus stop nearby that took us to Knaresborough. The river was neutral territory for man and wife! I wasn't very interested in shops. I took Dorothy for a boat ride on the river, me showing off my skill at rowing, not very exciting but relaxing. We decided to go to an afternoon tea dance in the 'pump rooms' in

Harrogate. This building originally was the 'pump room' where people took 'the waters' as Harrogate was and still is a Spa town. Water could be dangerous stuff in its many forms! I tried it, a horrid sulphurous taste I remember.

I drank the occasional pint of bitter but it was not available aboard ship and spirits became my tipple. Just for medication purposes.

The gardens in Harrogate were very colourful, a refreshing change from the many days I had spent at sea. South Georgia had no trees or shrubs. Sometimes when returning to the ship I would pull a few coarse grasses from along the snow's edge where it grew in sheltered north facing places. It was nice to have a bit of green even if it was just grass! I would put them in water in an old mug and keep them in the cabin to remind me that there were such things growing in the world. They didn't last long when it got rough.

I had 'paid off' from that first season with a cheque for roughly £800. It had been well earned being away for a total of nine months working seven days a week. With the bonus per whale it was an average of £22 per week. We worked two four hours 'watches' a day plus any extra unpaid hours that could be designated safety of the ship. There was no holiday pay and no pay until we were working aboard ship again.

Following my first season whaling I had a few precious weeks of leave with the girl of my dreams. We stayed a week or so with Dorothy's sister Marjorie, given Marnie, and her husband Fred, then stayed a few days with my Mum then Dorothy's Mum, Sally and Jimmy, Dorothy's step-father. Dorothy wrote in her diary that we were like two homeless strays. She was obviously wanting to start a home of her own. This idyllic life couldn't go on. We had a few more relaxing happy weeks visiting Dorothy's Uncles and Aunts. We sat and watched her Mum with her friends on a Saturday afternoon playing bowls in beautiful healthy Hartlepool. Now she was married, Sally was coming over from West Hartlepool in the electric trolley buses that served Hartlepool people so well and after the bowls would sit with her friends on the breakwater that ran out to sea from the promenade where her old home was in Rowell Street. Then before returning to her new home and the husband who had exacted such a price to marry him she would often have afternoon tea with her old friend Gertie Sunderland.

1948 was a good summer with blue cloudless skies. It was enough for us to be together, content, lazy in fact but nothing lasts for ever. I received a letter from Salvesen's Office in Leith, Edinburgh to say that on Monday 2nd of August they would employ me "working by" the factory ship 'Southern Harvester' at Middle Dock on the River Tyne at South Shields until the start of the next whaling season. This meant I had been two months without pay, now the average pay at sea with bonus worked out to £18 per week. This included the bonus working on Sondra the 'top boat'.We caught more whales than the other four catchers serving the Island factory. It was more than I could earn at home but the conditions were very different. If the bonus had been any lower it wouldn't have been so attractive. Something to be said for a good steady job ashore! Being ashore I wasn't eligible for unemployment benefit. I was in a state of limbo, if I went to another shipping company I wouldn't be available for the next season. It didn't bother me, I was enjoying the time off. In any case I didn't anticipate spending the rest of my life at sea. There was plenty of work ashore at this time.

During the war the pay of a British seaman stopped from the time the ship was sunk by enemy action. Time in a lifeboat sailing home didn't count. Wives and dependants allowances were stopped the day the ship sank.

The days flew by, June the 29th my 24th birthday, four more weeks during which we visited Dorothy's Aunt Amy a few times then it was time to join the factory ship 'Southern Harvester'. I packed a small case and took the train to South Shields and made my way to the docks.

The factory ship S/S Southern Harvester was in dry dock, 'Middle Dock.' It stood alone. Where the other docks were I don't know. 'Harvester' with its two side by side funnels painted in Company colours, white with the top third red, mounted above the after accommodation. Down in the dock the twin propellers were visible below the after slipway that led to the flensing deck. Harvester was enormous, her stern close to the dock gates indicated that she had nearly filled the dock. I stepped up the gangway that had been put from the lock gate up the stern slipway and reported to the 'Second' engineer. He was a Scot. I was allocated a berth cabin, and eventually met the other engineers as they came forward to 'meet the new guy!' They were all about my age, broad Scottish

I was the only Englishman aboard. They gave me a run down on the job and the day to day drill. Down below to start work at eight, smoko (coffee break) at ten, lunch at 12 noon, finish work at five, dinner at six.

188

Dorothy with her mother and step father lived now in West Hartlepool during the time I was working on the Southern Harvester. They had a telephone so I was able to ring up from the ship and we arranged to meet for ease of travelling in Sunderland for a couple of hours during the week, I was working 'days' coming to Hartlepool each weekend. It was like courting again, a walk in the local park. Just passing the time, until it was time to say goodbye and go our separate ways. Then back to the great ugly ship, read a magazine in the mess room for an hour have a bit of supper in the Engineer's pantry and turn in to awake next morning at seven o clock to have breakfast. This was good! I feasted on kippers, bacon and eggs, toast with lashings of real butter and marmalade with strong tea, a wonderful treat after years of rationing which was still enforced.

Our work on Southern Harvester was only desultory in the cathedral like engine room of this big vessel. A shore gang of 'Geordie' workmen came aboard each day for the overhaul work. It was bedlam! A couple of Geordie's had a way of working that seemed to require they yell at each other from one side of the engine room to the other in the high pitched unintelligible vernacular. It may have been partly for our amusement, if so I was embarrassed for the impression it made on my Scottish colleagues. I hadn't been used to this. At Smith's Dock the men were a phlegmatic lot. The Yorkshire boundary came as far as the river. The motto was 'hear all say nowt!' Here we were 'on the books' and there was little work to do. I pottered around the engine room. It was interesting. The engine room extended from the 'double bottom' of the Southern harvester to the skylights in the top deck. It was a vast space, the sides painted white with an overhead crane capable of running from one end of the engine room to the other. Sections of steel ladders led from the accommodation deck via gantries to the lower deck. The 'double bottom' of the ship served a dual purpose as it gave strength to the hull and formed tanks to store fuel. On these 'tank tops' stood two large triple expansion steam engines, port and starboard with their controls amidships. A row of generators provided electricity for the ship and factory. The switchboard on a half deck above them, duplicating the switch gear for each generator, extended nearly the full width of the vessel. The ship was like a small town. At sea the men worked 12 hour shifts in the factory. A half deck (mezzanine) at the other end of the engine room was home to a large number of 'evaporators' used to make vast quantities of fresh water from sea water. I didn't fancy working on a ship like this. It was a tricky job managing an evaporator, no automatic control in those days but an alarm to indicate if salt was carrying over to contaminate the steam if control was poor. I was my own boss in charge of the watch on my small catcher vessel! At this time working by in this vast engine room we did nothing more than adjust a few valve glands and liaise with the Geordie chargehand's simple request to open or close a valve for him to drain a vessel or seal off a line to accommodate their work.

We spent a lot of time going up to the Engineer's mess room for coffee and a smoke. This operational duty called 'smoko' was held in the Engineer's 'Pantry.' where we only had to wash our hands and didn't have to dress up There were about a dozen Salvesen Engineers like me 'working by' but I was the only Englishman! The other lads being Scots I was subject to a bit of leg pulling in spite of my maternal grandparents being Scottish! These Scots could recite reams of the poetry of Robbie Burns and I was given the full book!

Thursday was pay day at £7:00 per week! The food was excellent! Britain was still rationed for butter, sugar and meat. It wasn't because it was scarce, England was bankrupt remember, and could only afford to buy essential food. What was brought into the country was not the best quality either! England saviour of Europe was destitute!

Hopefully our work would be a great help to get the country back on to its feet! The whale would feed Europe until the people could restore the normal supplies of oils and meat. It cost millions of pounds to send a whaling expedition to the Antarctic Ocean It gave work to thousands in the shipyards and the local economy benefitted. I have read of the many whaling expeditions over the past years that went bankrupt. In a way the business was self-regulating. When the numbers of whales reduced to make it unprofitable to search the ocean looking for them, the whaling stopped. The food chain readjusted itself. There was then more food for the surviving whales. They would multiply again. Man would find a more economic way to replace the products lost. Certainly there were safer and much easier ways to produce oil for margarine.

Two young Shetland stewards waited on at table. It appeared to be their first trip with Salvesen Whaling Co. probably having been on fishing boats prior to this. There was some amusement at dinner one evening when the two young inexperienced "Shelti" lads served the gravy as the first course soup! I didn't like the way a young Scottish engineer sneered as he instructed them in table etiquette. These lads were obviously from a simple fishing community in the Shetlands, they were being employed 'working by' like us until they were put to the job they had signed on for as deck hands or mess boys. Good lads to have on small ships. The guy who sneered at them was a big ship man. Had he been used to the standards of an Atlantic liner? Another new experience for me was being with an all British crew. In spite of my first season I was very naïve.

On Thursday nights after the evening meal we would all go to the 'Rose and Crown' just outside the Dock gate. I never had more than three pints of the local draught beer, it wasn't as strong as Teesside beer or so I thought! The first week after a visit to the Rose and Crown, next morning,a Friday, I came too as if from a coma! I vaguely remember the mess boys coming in; they left without making the beds. This was a four berth cabin I shared with a nice guy Ian McEwan and other two engineers. The Chief Steward then made a short appearance. He said something unintelligible to me. I was not capable of receiving visitors! I came round about ten o' clock when my cabin mates arrived in an agitated state! They got me down from the top bunk, "come on you've got to muster." They were getting me into my boilersuit. I was half carried along the corridor to the door of the engine room still protesting, "I can't, I'm not well!" "You must make a show or you'll get the sack." This stiffened my resolve a bit but I was very confused as to what was wrong with me. They took me down the many flights of steel steps to the engine room deck and sat me in a corner where I was allowed to doze until it was time for lunch. "Oh I don't want any lunch," I wailed. My protests were ignored, "come on get up, the Chief will wonder why you aren't at the table!" (the dialogue was in a strong Scottish accent) Now I was dragged, pulled and pushed up again to the accommodation deck. It was necessary to remove boilersuits and clean up to appear in the saloon. By this time I had recovered consciousness and was aware that my presence in the mess room would be under the eagle eye of the Chief Engineer. He was a dour Scot not a man to trifle with! I could be in big trouble! I sat having difficulty focusing on faces trying to appear interested in what was being said at the table. Voices seemed to come through a muffled engine room voice pipe! I picked at the food, had a strong cup of coffee then sat back in the dining chair trying to keep my head from drooping onto my chest. I accepted a cigarette from one of my 'keepers' and took a few puffs. I sat well away from the Chief at the other side of the long mess room table. I suspected he knew of my condition as he viewed me with a suspicious glare from under heavy bushy eyebrows. We got up to return to our duties, me stumbling but managing to walk out of the mess without bumping into anything. I only wanted to go to my cabin and sleep but it was impressed on me that it was not a wise thing to do! I got below and went back to my corner. My keepers kept coming over to see if I was okay. I was beginning to sense a collective guilty conscience, "best to say nowt," as they say in Yorkshire. It's nice to know who your friends are. I might have recovered quicker if I could have been sick but bouncing about on a whale catcher for many months makes the stomach sphincter muscle very strong. I hadn't been sick since my first few days at sea. I managed to get the day over and was later catching the train to Hartlepool for a precious weekend with Dorothy.

I climbed up the several landings and flights of steel stairs from the engine room feeling a bit better, relieved my trial was over. I went to my cabin and freshened up. I packed my weekend case and walked down the accommodation corridor. As I passed the Second's cabin he was waiting for me and called me in. On a big ship the 'Second' would have a Chief's 'ticket'(certificate), he was the executive engineer. I was given a warning "drunk and unable to muster, serious, etc. etc." He could stop my weekend leave, but would let me off this time! There was a hint of amusement in his manner. Only a hint mind! Another Scot! He must have known I had been slipped a 'Micky Finn' I think he was warning me to be on my guard another time. I thanked him for his consideration and went ashore.

Dry dock was still known as 'going ashore.' If only he knew my reaction to the day. There was no way I wanted another day like it! I was still a bit weak that evening when I got home. I'm still not sure if I was drugged or not? The following week I discovered the reason for my discomfort. Whisky slipped into your pint when one went to the gents. Hard to believe as the beer didn't taste any better or different. I never left a pint on the bar again unless it was empty. I don't object to anyone buying me a dram. That's a friendly thing to do. I learnt the Scottish habit of a 'half and a half' a whisky chaser and half of beer.

Dorothy's diaries show that we had often been to the cinema, we seemed to like the same things; that was a promising start. I was very happy but always at the back of my mind was the thought that I had to go back whaling for another season. I didn't have to! But the Company expected it as engineers for catchers were in short supply. It would hurt my pride to back out now. Being newly married, a better reason was I needed the money. It would be almost impossible to save any money working in the shipyard. I was prepared to take a calculated risk.

There was always some element of danger on the catchers, but this was reduced by the skill and experience of the entire crew when on watch. In severe gales a small mistake could jeopardise the whole ship. It didn't even take bad weather. In 1947 the Simbra had overturned on a calm sea for reasons unknown. A whale catcher is designed for manoeuvrability, it has poor stability and heels well over when turning at speed. Simbra was returning to the Factory Ship Southern Venturer for bunkers and to deliver two whales. The Gunner of Simbra was told to wait until Southern Venturer finished taking fuel oil from an oil tanker. Whilst waiting Simbra sighted more whales. They set off at full speed and turning, heeled over. Being light of bunkers the ship went so far over she was unable to right herself. She lay on her beam ends. Engine room sky lights were probably open, the sea entered the ship. It would not stay afloat for long! How this was discovered I didn't know at the time of writing. There may have been time to send a 'mayday' message while the ship's lifeboat was put into the icy water. This was all speculation on my part. I only found the truth a few years ago when I read John Leask's story.

We were given orders that all whale catcher boats must not continue whaling when both port and starboard fuel tanks were empty. They must return for bunkers using the centre tank. I was prepared to do another season and chance it. I received permission from Gilbert Fraser to publish the full story of John Leask's survival.

The next entry in Dorothy's diary was that I had received a letter instructing me to go to Salvesen's office in Leith to sign a contract for the coming season. On the 15th of August 1948 we took the train from Hartlepool to Edinburgh, changing at Darlington. Owing to floods on the East Coast the train had to go via Carlisle. It was late in the day when we got to Edinburgh. Every hotel we called at in Edinburgh was full. In 1948 it was the beginning of the first Edinburgh Festival. Just my luck I thought! Eventually we found the last available room at the 'Kings Commercial Hotel' in Leith, not a long walk from the top of Princes Street in Edinburgh. The room was most unsuitable for a newly married couple whose husband had soon to be going to sea for nine months! Just my luck again! Two single beds were situated foot to foot in a long narrow room. We were able to sit up and wave to each other! We saw the funny side of it and stayed two nights, taking the opportunity to see the sights of Edinburgh. A last short holiday for a while.

I had been given orders to report to the S.S. Polar Chief, berthed at Bidston Dock, Birkenhead on the River Mersey. On the 17th August we took the 10:15 am train from Waverley Station, Edinburgh to Liverpool. It was only a short journey from the busy Port of Liverpool across the Mersey to the Wirral where we had been invited to stay with relatives of Dorothy's who lived in the little village of Upton.

The following morning Wednesday 18th I reported to the Chief officer of the 'Polar Chief'. There would be a couple of hundred men aboard on the 22nd when she sailed down the River Mersey taking men and supplies down to Leith Harbour, South Georgia. I was returning there to join the whale catcher 'Sondra' Another season as third engineer. Leaving my young wife for nine long months, what a terrible thought. I was able to stay with Dorothy with her friendly relatives in Upton for the few days before S/S Polar Chief sailed. The ship was over forty years old, originally a passenger liner built in 1892. As a passenger ship she was the Liner "S/S Montcalm" the sister ship to the S/S Montrose, the ship that Dr. Crippen, who had murdered his wife, and to escape arrest, had taken his young lover dressed as a boy to sail to Canada. In 1910 he was the first person to be arrested by use of a wireless as a means of communication! The Captain of the Montrose saw through the disguise of Dr Crippen's lover and sent a radio message to the U.K. A detective took passage on a faster ship and arrived in Canada in time to make the arrest.

After a long history of service through the Boer War and World Wars One and Two the S.S. Montcalm had been converted from a passenger liner into a whale factory ship with a slipway at the stern to haul the whales onto the deck. Made redundant now, the slipway was obsolete and roped off. The factory equipment, boilers and so forth had also been removed. The space was now used to transport fuel, stores and spare gear to the factory on South Georgia Island and to transport whale oil and other products of whaling back to the UK.

Cabin accommodation had been modified to accommodate the crews of the catchers and factory workers. None of the splendour remained in the cabins. Panelling and furniture had been stripped out and probably sold. The Company men were in metal bunks four to a

194

cabin. The dining room we used was probably a second class room and remained in its 1892 state with very comfortable soft seating along the saloon wall with tables firmly fixed to the floor. My cabin had a porthole and a small ventilator which could be turned to the wind. The bulkheads were painted with cork chippings in the paint for insulation. There was nothing fancy in the way of a cabin washbasin or air conditioning. Communal toilets, showers and washbasin rooms were the order of the day. Fresh water for washing was limited to a couple of hours each day. Landlubbers ask "why didn't they make fresh water from sea water using evaporators?" The answer is it uses expensive steam, and that costs money!

## CHAPTER 15
## 22ND AUGUST 1948
*Leaving Dorothy, sailing from Liverpool*
*for a second season whaling.*

I said goodbye to my pretty wife Dorothy on Saturday, it wasn't an emotional parting although we would be parted for nine months. Dorothy knew whaling wasn't an ordinary sea going occupation and we maintained an unemotional attitude to our last few hours together. I had been given permission to stay ashore for the few days previous to the date of sailing but had to be aboard the day before we sailed. On Sunday the 22nd of August 1948 S/S Polar Chief with the assistance of two fussy tugs one for'rard and the other with a tow line aft left Bidston Dock and sailed down the Mersey to the sea. I'm not quite sure why we two catcher engineers were asked by the Chief of this big old tub to assist the Second engineer in the engine room, as he had his own assistant engineers with him. We were signed on the ship's papers as 'supernumery in transit', not as crew members. Best not to argue, we obeyed orders.

These big ship men didn't like to think we were passengers. There wasn't a lot to do. Unlike the Southern Harvester this English Second Engineer was friendly enough, he seemed to be a bit nervous! We performed small 'big ship' duties such as making a note in the log of each telegraph instruction, passing through a bulkhead to the boiler room to check the boilers. These fifty year old boilers were 'double ended' and very long with three furnaces at each end. They were natural draught probably coal fired originally, now modified to oil fired.

The fire tubes were blown clean with steam each morning to remove the soot. Naturally we were given this dirty job when on duty. The firemen were a bit sloppy and tended to let the steam drop a few pounds. One Glaswegian chap read kids comics and had a pile of them! Where was Rabbie Burns?

The two tugs steadied us down the river. After a while the pilot telegraphed down for slow ahead. The three cylinder steam engine as big as a small house, responded to the steam and turned ponderous and slow as we moved down river. Later as we reached the river mouth a signal on the telegraph clanged and the pointer went to 'Stop.' This created a problem for the main steam control valve to the triple expansion engine had seized! Having been renewed during the refit by the shore gang, the brass screw thread, probably a nice fit when cold, expanded slightly with the heat and seized on the steam valve spindle. It refused to budge! Further telegraph signals from the Bridge could not be answered. The engine room telephone began to ring! " Bridge here! What the ******* hell's the matter?" The 'Second' was busy, The third Engineer waited to pass the phone to him. He ignored it, in desperation the 'Second' put the engine valve gear in the midway position. Being half way between ahead and astern the engine finally stopped! The telephone message from the Bridge seemed to make the receiver red hot the way the Second was now holding it! The squawks it made sounded like an angry Donald Duck! The steam control valve had been badly repaired? Not the Company engineer's fault! The powers that be on the bridge decided S.S. Polar Chief must return to Bidston Dock for further repairs. A Board of Trade inspection found other items below regulations. There was a lot of waste oil under the boilers. We arrived back at Bidston Dock. Not a good thing, I'd just about spent up! We didn't think we needed money where we were going! The repairs would take a few days! They didn't give us a departure date! The Chief was too busy to need us. I imagine he got an "ear wigging". A shore gang came aboard to do the work. I bet he checked their work this time!

According to Dorothy's diary she had gone home to Hartlepool on the 22nd. She would be surprised when I telephoned on the 23rd with the news that we were back in Bidston Dock! On the 25th I phoned her

196

to send me some money! She sent me £4:00, about thirty pounds today. I had bought a small Phillips radio. It was about the size of a shoe box, one of the first miniature valve sets, the transistor hadn't been invented yet! It had medium wave, long wave and short wave stations. Things like this were now coming onto the market. The wartime austerity was fading from our lives as long as you could pay for it! There was none of this 'buy now pay later.' I had to buy a converter to power the radio from the ship's 110 volts to the required radio's 250 volts. The money was probably for this. When I discovered I needed a converter. I was able to buy this in a city like Liverpool.

Finally on the 29th August we left Birkenhead docks for the second time and were on our way again, down the great Mersey river. At the wide river mouth the pilot left us and we turned to steam down the Irish Sea. Again the Chief engineer pressed us into service doubling up watches with the ship's engineers. It was interesting to walk around the big open space of the engine room. The Main Engine bolted down onto the tank tops rocked quite a bit. This I was told was because the steel plates of the ship's 'double bottom' were rusted a bit thin. The engine cylinder tops moved back and forth about three inches! Unlike a whale catcher there was very little to do on watch. At full speed of 68 revs per minute the engine would last a thousand years! Provided it didn't drop through the rusted bottom of the ship! The boiler pressure had been dropped from 250psi to 180 psi (pounds per square inch) for safety reasons? The engine would obviously go faster when the boilers had been new. The engine was hand lubricated by a 'Greaser' on each watch. A few drops of oil dripped into the bearing brass cups every ten minutes or so. Engineers didn't do such things on a big ship, they walked around in white boilersuits. They even had a pumpman to start and stop the pumps! In trimming the ship, ballast had to be pumped over from one tank to another, probably in a pump room amidships. The engineer's position must always be near the controls. Records were kept of events in a logbook in a desk. It was interesting to see big ship routines that I had not been aware of until now. Every day at noon exactly, the number of engine revolutions was recorded. The twenty four hour revolutions of the engine were used to calculate the daily distance travelled by multiplying the number of revolutions by the 'pitch' of the propeller, (distance travelled in one revolution). This would be checked against the calculations of the officers on the bridge from sightings with a sextant. The difference allowed, called the 'slip,'

197

was two and a half per cent. This variable could be for sea conditions, currents or head winds. It could even be because of bad steering but I wouldn't dare mention it! The deck officers blamed the engineers and vice versa. All clever stuff!

Captains who knew the many currents in the sea could sometimes gain a couple of knots. I was told that a contra flow north and south existed round the bulge of South America which gave a ship another two knots and ships accepted this economical gift thankfully. The charts used by sailors had a steady collection of information from ancient mariners since the great explorers such as Sir Francis Drake in his ship the Golden Hind, Magellan and other brave characters who distributed their names to various parts of the world. Christopher Columbus didn't circumscribe the world but he thought he had when he discovered America in searching for the East Indies and found the West Indies. His intentions were to reach the East by going round West until he came to the East. It was a good try but the riches of the East failed him. His records invited further exploration though and he received belated credit. Captain James Cook was more precise, his records and maps were constantly consulted and amended as time evolved. He was the first true navigator who knew where he was on the globe with the first accurate method of finding Longitude with a Harrison clock keeping accurate Greenwich time.

Somewhere over the other side of the Atlantic Ocean two days from Aruba we ran into a hurricane! Or did it run into us? It lasted for about three days. Weather forecasts at sea in those days were unreliable. This was my first experience of very bad weather aboard a big ship. The sea appeared to be boiling! There didn't seem to be much pitching, the up and down motion. The ship was so long it was supported by quite a few waves. It rolled a bit and 'yawed' slowly. That effect is when the ship slowly swings the bow port and starboard as she heads into the oncoming sea. The sea was wild. I had seen bigger waves in Antarctic waters but this was the first time I had experienced a sea like this in a big ship. I didn't like it, especially on an old vessel so long well past its sell by date. Was I scared? I suppose I was, all the time when I was at sea, it's being scared that makes you careful. I always went through a mental emergency drill when I went on a different ship noting where the lifeboats were and not fastening my cabin door, putting it on the brass hook provided for this purpose. The door could be jammed fast in a collision or even damage from a heavy sea. Most of the big ship men disappeared in this hurricane and were seasick. A Salvesen Office clerk poor lad, going to the factory to work was very seasick. I think some of it is psychological. I had a friend who came on 'sea trials' with us when I worked in the shipyard. He became seasick the minute the telegraph rang 'stand by' with the ship still tied up to the jetty! White faced he would go to his cabin and only reappeared when we had returned and tied up. Catcher men were immune to any sort of heaving about on an old tub like Polar Chief but this was a bit different ! The Skipper managed to turn the great long vessel head up into the weather. It didn't help much, but I suppose it prevented the seas rushing up the obsolete slipway in the stern. Then Polar Chief developed a roll! And what a roll! A deck cargo of two boilers fastened down onto the deck for use in the factory at Leith harbour Whaling Station made the vessel's 'trim' a bit tender.

The roll developed like the swinging of a giant pendulum first to the port side. It rolled over very slowly, I thought each roll would never stop! When it did stop it hung there! Was it ever going to come back? No! It hung a bit more. After what seemed time to abandon ship, she gave a wriggle and started to come back, slowly oh ever so slowly, and then went all the way over to the starboard side! This went on for two days. I hated it! Give me a small ship that bounced over the sea like a cork any time! We were "cabined up" all this time, rain and hail rattled against the porthole. The "saloon" was comfortable enough, sitting on the settee fixed to the Saloon wall. We sat with a foot pressed against the table to stop sliding off our seat. The view through the portholes was grey and wet. Only a few of us went to the saloon and the meals were not even buffet style! We had to search for the food. Three of us went to the Galley and found a tin of corned beef some bread and a slab of butter. We stood leaning left and right as the ship heeled over to manage the spreading of the butter as another opened the kilo tin of bully beef and proceeded to slice it to make thick doorstep sandwiches. Another guy had made the tea. Ship tea was extra sweet, strong and hot because the condensed milk didn't cool the mug as cow's milk does. With big ship routine the cooks had already baked the bread before the weather turned bad. It was fresh, just like mother made!

The hurricane howled and blew hard outside, we staggered from the galley to the Victoria saloon and tried to ignore the roll and satisfied our hunger! The roll wasn't so bad! It was the hanging bit that created a tinge of anxiety. I didn't fancy getting a boat away with old Polar Chief laid on her side, especially in a sea like that.

One result of this stress on the old girl's corsets, the ships ribs, caused the cast iron main sea water discharge pipe to crack! This pipe carried sea water used to cool the condenser from the ship's side to the condenser and then return to the sea again. Quite a big piece had broken out of the pipe. The sea was now pouring into the engine room! Both bilge pumps were opened up full steam while the situation was brought under control. With the condenser out of commission the main engine had to be slowed just enough to vent the steam to atmosphere and give steerage to the rudder.

The weather had improved a bit by now. We catcher men again were asked to help with engine room routines while the ship's engineers assisted the ship's carpenter to build a wooden box around the twelve inch damaged pipe. Ships carry timber and cement for emergencies such as this and sometimes lengths of timber to shore up a failing bulkhead. The pipe was put together and strapped up. The box was then filled with 'fondue' quick setting cement and in a few hours normal service was resumed! In a couple of more days the weather improved and we plodded on.

Two days later we arrived at Aruba an island off Venezuela at the top of South America. S.S. Polar chief lay at a 'mole', a jetty isolated from the harbour. We were here for a few days, I can't remember how many, maybe four? I dressed in a clean white shirt and my best 'Duke of Windsor' grey plaid suit. It was my first time ashore in a foreign port and I wanted to look my best. A foy boat hired by the Company for the time we were in port, ferried us ashore.

I bought a pair of nylons for Dorothy, they were unobtainable at home. We were able to take an advance allowance of £10:00 from the Chief Steward to go ashore. Hard to believe but Sterling was rationed as well as food. It was very hot especially in the suit. My first time in the tropics, I had been quenching my thirst drinking rum and coca cola, in tall straight glasses. Coke was a soft drink so I was told and it wasn't on sale in the U.K. at this time. Neither did it occur to me that the rum was alcoholic for I had not been a spirit drinker. I thought spirits were always drunk in tot glasses, like the cowboys did in the Wild West! Rum and coke was just a name to me like 'rum and butter' toffees or 'bay rum' hair oil. I didn't even know it came from this side of the Atlantic! I was definitely a small town boy.I was in trouble again! Too many rum and cokes!

I ended the day on a Danish tanker called 'Christian Holm' berthed alongside the harbour. The officers of this tanker had enjoyed my company and were very patient with me until I had passed out! They then put my papers and the nylons into the inside pocket my Mum had made secure with a button and button hole, then buttoned it up and called up Polar Chief.

A remarkable ship that served as a dummy battleship and War Transport in three major conflicts.

After WW2 ferried men and materials to Whaling Stations in South Georgia Island bringing oil and protein to feed a devastated Europe.

## History of S.S.Montcalm 16,000 tons

| | |
|---|---|
| 1897 | May 17, Launched for Elder Dempster Line. |
| 1897 | Sept. 3, Maiden voyage Avonmouth - Montreal |
| 1898 | November, chartered to ATL |
| 1900 | June, Became Boer War transport |
| 1903 | Taken over by Canadian Pacific Line |
| 1914 | August, became British Expeditionary Force transport |
| 1914 | October, rebuilt as dummy battleship, HMS Audacious |
| 1916 | January, bought by British Admiralty |
| 1916 | October, converted to oil tanker for Anglo Saxon Petroleum Company, renamed Crenella |
| 1917 | October, taken over by Shipping Controller |
| 1917 | Nov. 26, torpedoed off the Irish coast. Survived and repaired |
| 1919 | Returned to Anglo Saxon Petroleum Co. |
| 1920 | Purchased by Runciman, London |
| 1923 | Bought by Norwegian owners, converted to a whaling depot ship and renamed Rey Alfonso |
| 1927 | Renamed Anglo Norse |
| 1929 | Renamed Polar Chief for Falkland Whaling Co. |
| 1930 | Laid up for lack of orders. |
| 1941 | Became the Ministry of War Transport Empire Chief |
| 1946 | Renamed Polar Chief for South Georgia Co. |
| 1952 | Scrapped at Dalmuir, Scotland |

Compiled by the Author from Shipping Times and other sources.

*SS Montcalm 16,800 tons Canadian Pacific Liner.*

Before going ashore we had been issued with a card bearing our rank , ship and mooring berth. An Officer getting lost must happen quite often. A message was sent to Polar Chief by morse code with an aldis lamp. The message went something like this "please send two men to return third engineer A Dinsdale, a distressed British seaman, to his ship." Later I was told two Shetland sailors were sent to recover me, they had tossed me into the motor boat hired to ferry the crew from the harbour to the mole and back. Amazingly I had no broken bones! Someone put me into my bunk, I presume they did? Again I asked myself how did it happen? I 'came too' the next morning, still in my best grey plaid tailored suit, now badly stained with fuel oil, no doubt from the Danish Oil Tanker! This wasn't like me, I was becoming a danger to myself! The smart suit had been for my 21st birthday. Mum had taken me to Newhouse's tailoring department .A tailor reeking of stale beer had measured me. A couple of weeks later I had a fitting. The half made waistcoat and jacket had been put on while drunken Charlie had expertly marked the fitting requirements and then a last fit. I was very proud of that suit! Ah well, nothing lasts for ever! Unlike my trouble on the Southern Harvester I managed to recover enough before 'smoko' to appear in the mess but I was on record. The officer of the watch would have recorded the message from M.V Christian Holm in the ship's log. It might still be there to this day. I feel ashamed to have been so careless. Worse was to come. The Chief Engineer of S.S. Polar Chief said I would have to appear before the Captain on a charge! I would be 'logged' (fined) and given a 'poor' discharge paper on my return to the U.K. I was mystified! What had I been drinking? I tried to revive myself with a cup of tea, it tasted of rum and made me feel worse. It was funny, 'rum and coke' didn't taste of rum, it just tasted of coke! Now everything I drank tasted of the damned rum and had a dramatic effect on me for a couple of days. The ship was at the mole another two days taking on supplies for South Georgia. I behaved like a Methodist Minister, fruit juice only and none of the fancy cola!

However before Polar Chief departed the majority of the crew were on record! I watched them coming back aboard staggering up the gangway. The Chief Officer had thoughtfully slung a big rope net underneath the gangway extending three feet each side. It surprised me that no one fell into the net but one or two nearly went through the handrails of the gangway. The ship's doctor was up half the night stitching up wounds from stabs from sabres worn and wielded at the first sign of trouble by the Dutch Police. Aruba was a Dutch colony at this time. Some of the lads tried unsuccessfully to smuggle booze aboard by climbing over the chain link fence. The harbour was a fire hazard are, no booze allowed and strictly applied.

In the last moments before the mooring lines were cast off a small vessel came alongside. Sides of beef were hoisted aboard in a rope net. I took some photographs of this action. Shipping agents did last minute business and hopefully nothing or nobody that should be aboard was left behind. It would be nine months before we passed this way again. I was glad to see the back of the place! Once we got under way the Chief had a word with me and said the Captain was not going to 'log' anyone. When I asked why he said that the Captain had had a party in the saloon and they'd wrecked the place! The carpenter had repaired the damage. As long as we had done no permanent damage to the ship we were okay. "Moi do damage to this old tub?" I was the only thing that got damaged, an innocent abroad!

Passing through the tropics the cabins became hot and humid. The modern foam rubber mattresses had a pool of sweat on them when we got out of our bunks. We took to sleeping on deck. One or two bright lads made scoops from big empty bully beef tins. These were sticking out of the portholes about eighteen inches and deflected air into the cabin. With the ship moving at six knots it was almost forced draught! In a few days the ship had rows of them on each side.

It seemed a miracle to me how a big and slow ship like Polar Chief had escaped being sunk by U boats during the war! The Germans probably didn't think it worth a torpedo or that it would founder before it made port. The bridge was armour plated. It had not been removed in its peacetime role. But it was a lucky ship! And we had a good Skipper. The heart of the ship, the old steam engine was a simple machine only 25% economically efficient but very reliable.

The Captain had arranged for 'Father Neptune' to come aboard. This was a great day and full of fun! A swimming pool was constructed on the fore deck. It was made from wooden planking and lined with a big tarpaulin. Filled with sea water, as fresh water was at a premium only available at set times, the pool had a platform on one side level with the top of the four foot deep pool. All crew 'free watch' were invited to attend the visit of Father and Lady Neptune, accompanied by their retinue which was nine strong in total.

*Ceremony of 'Crossing the Line.'*

All were appropriately dressed in the strangest of costumes, some borrowed from the bridge signal flags, the galley and ships hospital and in one case the toilet! A toilet seat suitably decorated served as a ceremonial collar around 'sparky's' neck (ship's electrician)! Neptune's barber (asdic Able Seaman) with a pirate bandana on his head carried a cut throat razor 12 inches long (made from wood). Other assistants carried a stool for the victims to sit on, a bucket of 'shaving soap' and a 4 inch paint brush! 'Medicine' for the victims was carried by Neptune's Doctor (the ships Bosun). The Captain in full dress tropical whites came down from the bridge to the fore deck with his Chief Officer to receive our visitors. We onlookers sat around each side of the deck, some climbed up and sat on the deck cargo of the two boilers, port and starboard sides of the ship. From the forec'sle, (the very pointy end of the ship, paint store and rope locker) to the sound of a loud trumpet blast, (the ship's steam whistle) emerged the noble figure of Father Neptune carrying a fine trident accompanied by his Lady Neptune and the accompanying rabble! I didn't hear all the dialogue but the Captain greeted his esteemed visitor and enquired the reason we were so honoured. "To initiate all persons not having previously crossed the equator before" was the reply! I was busy with my camera. What a pity film was still in short supply but I captured the afternoon quite well in black and white. The entourage took up their respective positions. Father Neptune hardly recognisable as the cockney Nobby Clark (engine room greaser) dressed in a resplendent wig and costume made from old rope uncoiled into curly strands of "hair" stitched together as only these old sailors can. Lady Neptune similarly dressed but with a silver tiara on her head. The pair of them were seated on a flag covered throne, a plank between two barrels, in front of the starboard deck cargo boiler. Neptune's barber and assistants were on the platform, level with the top of the pool. The stool was now in position awaiting the first customer.

Neptune's doctor administered the medicine to the first initiate. I don't suppose it was anything other than alcoholic, as they all seemed to like it! The initiate then climbed the short companionway and mounted the platform, sat on the stool facing the Bridge and was lathered up with the 4 inch shaving brush! Two sailors in shorts with pirate bandanas, ships signal flags, on their heads waited in the pool to ensure no harm came when our doctor's victim was not so very gently

*Father Neptune,*
*alias Nobby Clark,*
*engine room greaser in charge.*

pushed into the tank to a roar from the spectators! This doctor was making his first trip with Salvesen's to man the small two bed hospital on South Georgia Whaling Station. He was well liked. A good mixer and a proper sport! I believe the Captain's name was Beugh. He was going to be Port Captain of the Leith harbour Whale factory Station 1948-49, both relieving the Captain and Doctor who had over-wintered from the previous year. About ten other first timers followed him. It ended with the pool full of men carrying on like kids! By nightfall all was cleared away. Morale was high, the Captain had done a good job.

What surprised me about the 'Crossing the Line Ceremony' was that I hadn't heard a whisper about it previous to the day !I knew the greasers well enough in my stint in the engine room, Nobby Clark and I often had a chat. It was a well kept secret! A committee must have taken some time to arrange and prepare the costumes even if the trident and razor theatrical props had been in store from other trips. I still have the photographs I took that day when we were so very happy and thankfully sober!

Whilst aboard the whale catcher Sondra I had to visit the factory hospital during a four hour stay for bunkers. I had a cut on the shin which wouldn't heal. Before I left the doctor asked me to go into the two bed hospital ward and have a word with "Sinclair." Being a young catcher sailor man he didn't have many visitors, "cheer him up" he said. Sinclair was a young Scot's sailor on a catcher working with one of the factory ships near the ice cap. He was down below passing a new rope up through the deck. This rope was put on the winch to haul it up, somehow a kink in the rope wrapped around his ankle and he was

*Note the armoured bridge window.*

*Gently does it! A fine pair of heels caught on camera.*

hauled up to the deckhead where the rope went through a hawser to the deck. The Chief stopped hauling when they saw blood and flesh coming through the hawser. Sinclair lost his leg below the knee. He told me the first aid was a tourniquet to stop the bleeding aided by putting the stump in a bag of flour. The analgesic was a bottle of rum to drink as required. He was then transferred to a Buoy Boat, a converted Corvette, and taken at full speed for a couple of days to get him to the Island Hospital. He looked comfortable enough and I sympathised with his misfortune and tried to make light of it. "Wha't will arr de wi' only one leg", was his complaint, "will his girl still want to marry him?" I made some cheerful responses, I thought he wouldn't let it get him down, after all he was a catcher man! My impression was confirmed when years later I had read a book some chap had written on whaling and he mentioned that Sinclair was now a cook on one of Salvesen's vessels. A regular Long John Silver!

Passing through the tropics the Chief Engineer gave us a few jobs to do on deck. Winches to repair, broken teeth in the gear wheels! Dentistry on a large scale! There were no power tools. Holes were drilled with a hand operated ratchet drill and 'stand' clamped to any place available with which to put pressure on the drill bit by means of a screw jack. A screw thread was made in the hole and a bolt tightened into the hole. The bolt was then cut and shaped with a hacksaw, a hammer and chisel to form the tooth. The Chief was quite creative in repair work! We took our time on this benevolent work in the spirit of the request that we occupy our time fruitfully while the weather was fine.

As Polar Chief moved further south it became colder and we were left to our own devices. Sailors are great raconteurs, we spent many happy hours yarning, and listening to funny stories. A gunner travelling down with us to join his ship had generously given me a bottle of whisky after I had cut his hair. Now we were cabin'd up with the colder weather I decided to open it. I had chosen four mates to have a tot with me. The door was locked! It was an unusual brand of Scotch "Red Hackle" no one had heard of. With mugs at the ready, I pulled the cork and poured the golden nectar. Within two minutes there was a knock at the door! It was Neptune's Barber, a Scottish radio operator. He said he could smell whisky a hundred yards away! I asked him in and he joined the company. I reckon one of my mates had put him in the picture, but he was a natural comedian and entertained us. He was very welcome.

With his wonderful repartee we had a pleasant evening listening to his tales of foreign parts and characters. This was the way we passed the time at sea. The uneventful days went by, breakfast, smoko, lunch, dinner at six o' clock. I made friends with men I would not see again. I often wonder how many are still alive today.

Polar Chief in spite of her age and trials came alongside at Leith Harbour, South Georgia. No one seems to say goodbye on these occasions. In dribs and drabs we drifted away to our designated posts. I carried my gear along to the Sondra lying at the short bunker jetty and once again went aboard.

# CHAPTER 16
# WHALING, THE SECOND SIX MONTH'S SEASON.
*Arriving at South Georgia 1948 season.*
*Back aboard Whale Catcher Sondra.*

I was disappointed! There'd been some changes. The Chief Anker Andersen wasn't there. This Chief was a younger man, about forty years old. He was also cynical and made snide remarks about the British during the war. I was astonished at his attitude and didn't feel comfortable with him. What about the Norwegian quislings I thought? Not a good situation to have on a small ship. However I gave him no cause for complaint and he recognised my signals. I decided later that he was not a happy man in himself, well his side lost! I ignored him as much as possible. There was another disappointment too. Malbut was here still with his ulcer and toothless grin, except when his ulcer was playing him up, which was some part of every day! I had to admire his fortitude. He was doing right by his family painful as it was. It meant I had to put up with him coming on watch late at times but it could have been worse. Other changes, no Louie, the excellent cook! Again a younger man, tall and strong, very blond, not very articulate he had a breezy attitude, a typical Norwegian sailor! He did all right as a cook but not as good a cook as Louie. Louie who cooked beyond the call of duty when we'd had a good day. Louie would sit with a dixie full of boiling oil and make enough sugared doughnuts to fill three tins. With the batter and a stick spinning it round and round until the ring was shaped. Then pour more until the batter was all turned into professional dough nuts. They were put in big empty biscuit tins warm with sugar sprinkled over them. These doughnuts had a wonderful texture and lasted us for a week. This was a real treat under our frugal circumstances. No Louie this trip, what a loss! Another treat we used to make was to take a tin of condensed milk and put it in the water boiler for a few minutes. When opened it was toffee! I was pleased Christian Christiansen had returned as Gunner, I felt safe with him in command. The Assistant Engineer and firemen Ghandi and Johansen were still with us, that was good, we worked as a team down below.

The 'Second' Mate told me that during the 'overwinter' radar had been fitted on the bridge; "would I like to see it." We went up onto the bridge, the 'holy of holies' to an engineer. A cupboard had been built at the back of the open bridge to contain the radar tube. The screen was tiny with a three inch tube to represent thirty miles. The Mate switched it on and a thirty mile area of the fjord where we were moored glowed in green as the yellow line swept around the screen.

Down below in the engine room seven tons of ballast had been laid along the bilge keel in the form of 'pigs' of cast iron. These were then set in concrete. I was told that for one ton of material topside seven tons were required on the keel. That sounded about right to me. The more the better!

The routine was just the same, the first weeks were short days and very bad weather. One trip with the engine at half speed the ship was pushing into great seas. Johansen and I were at our posts, me by the steam throttle, Johansen sitting in the fireman's working well, three steps below the engine room deck level in front of the boilers. Both of us were hanging on as Sondra lurched forward at each wave, up and over! Then thump, into the trough and up and over again. To our complete surprise the telegraph gave an emergency double ring 'full ahead!' We glanced at each other for a split second. "Full ahead in this sea… madness?" I opened the throttle full, not knowing what to expect! Sondra leaped forward, the bow rose high, the engine room deck was at a steep angle, at the same time she heeled over to port until I was lying on the side of the engine. Hanging on to the throttle wheel I looked up at the skylight above the engine cylinders, I saw the tops of the waves. We were on our beam end in a trough between two giant waves. The ship reared back, the telegraph rang again,' half ahead.' Thank God! I slowed the engine speed, and we carried on for another hour then the sea calmed. We entered Cumberland Bay fjord. The telegraph now rang for full speed as we raced down the three miles of smooth water to the bunker jetty. This was the usual approach, showing off with a big bow wave to impress the shore gang I got the telegraph "finished with engine" and went up for a mug of tea. Passing the ship's lifeboat on the upper deck I noticed the lifeboat was hanging on the davits. The steel chocks the boat had been sitting on were bent flat to the deck! We had been well over for the sea to do that! I was surprised the men on the open bridge had not been flung into the sea. No one spoke about it. The reason for full speed could have been for more power to push up an extra big wave or to avoid a small house size 'berg concealed behind a wave. We stayed in for the night. The lifeboat chocks were repaired, next day the weather had improved, and it was business as usual.

Returning for bunkers and stores the routine was we came down the fjord at full speed. Approaching the jetty, which projected about fifty feet from the shore of scree (shards of rock), at the end of the fjord, the telegraph rang 'half speed'. As the bow came level with the jetty we then went full astern, the ship's propeller churned up the sea under the stern and the vessel stopped and pulled nicely alongside whilst a sailor then stepped onto the jetty and threw the mooring rope over the bollard. All very 'tiddly' as the ship was 150 feet long. Two thirds were left sticking out from the short jetty. It looked good.

In the engine room it was a different story! The small single cylinder engine that pushed the main engine valve gear over to go astern was only used infrequently and was cold. Water in the steam pipe to this 'reversing engine' had to be drained through a small tap and the little engine warmed up to be ready for use. I'd done this scores of times with no bother. This single cylinder engine had a large handwheel that was pulled around to start it. Without this pull the steam would just push the piston to the top of the cylinder and stay there, it needed the pull to get the wheel spinning and piston to return at each stroke. Usually a single pull would do it! I was on duty and had prepared everything for this manoeuvre. When the telegraph rang down for 'full astern' I couldn't move the handwheel! Steam had condensed in the cylinder which was full of water! The few seconds it took to start it and go astern proved too long. Sondra was still going ahead! She lurched up onto the beach. I was horrified! We were aground! The three inch voice pipe over my head broadcast faint voices on the Bridge aloft giving orders. The telegraph returned to 'stop engine.' My common sense told me not to go astern now in case the hull was damaged! At least we were not going to sink stuck up on the beach. After the longest ten minutes in my life the telegraph rang 'slow astern.' I opened the throttle, the engine turned slowly but nothing happened, we were still stuck! 'Half astern and more steam!' A few minutes, nothing! Stuck fast on this beach of scree. 'Full astern!' I opened her up! The engine at 250 revs! The after end of the ship throbbed. On the bridge they were wagging the rudder! I felt the ship stirring, slipping back from the beach, then she bounced a little, we were afloat What a relief! Now try again 'slow ahead' gently Sondra moved forward and was made fast alongside. I shut down the engine. Thank Heavens an inspection found no damage. An Asdic dome had been fitted, used to locate submarines during the war. We tried to use it now and then, to seek the whales with little success. Fortunately it was safely in its housing. I went topside expecting to have to give an account of my part in the fiasco but not a word was said! Well, it wasn't the Royal Navy. It wasn't any other navy way of coming alongside from half ahead to full astern! The next time we came in the drill was the same! I had done it many times before without incident and I saw to it not to let it happen again, Maybe they gave me a little more time to move the valve gear to go astern? I was certainly on my toes!

I was sorry when Ghandi had to leave the ship. It happened one night in very bad weather. Johansen and I were on watch, at two o clock in the morning Ghandi should have come down to change watch with Johansen. Ten minutes went by and we were worried. Ghandi had to come from the fore deck and in this sea a big wave could have knocked him down or even took him over the side! I told Johansen to go up and see what the problem was. He did not return. I was then on my own for a couple of hours whilst the ship was taking a heavy pounding with the weather. I heard nothing until near the end of my watch when we had gone into the factory fjord for shelter. The Chief came down to handle the boiler burners and assist me with the manoeuvres to come alongside. Then I heard little Ghandi had been flung from his top bunk and was laid behind the cabin door unable to move in the narrow space between bunks and bulkhead. The fall had broken his hip. They had to jemmy the door off to get to him and he was taken ashore to the hospital.

We sailed the next morning at daylight with another fireman, a young Norwegian lad. I didn't have the same rapport with this lad, he worked well but was a bit dour. A few weeks later when we came in for the four hour bunker stop I was delighted to see Ghandi standing on the jetty with his leg in plaster up to his groin on two crutches! He was expecting to return to Norway on the next ship to come in to the factory in a week or so. He had hobbled quite a way to the jetty to say cheerio. My delight was tinged with sadness. It reminded me how transient life is. I wouldn't see his jolly face again. I never did get used to the idea of "ships that pass in the night."

Half way through the season, another Christmas went by, and I accepted the Officer aboard Duty for the evening. The little Phillips radio tuned in to the short wave BBC overseas service. It was only good for the news, which seemed very remote. Neither Malbut nor I were interested in the football scores on a Saturday. At least we knew what day it was but it didn't seem to matter.

I didn't think the work could get any harder until one day, we had been chasing hard for hours with little to show for it. We had caught a Sie whale, the minimum size allowed. While we were stopped to prepare it for towing I saw Johansen peering through the small inspection hole of the boiler furnace. He kept a good watch on the furnace whenever the burners were turned off, as now with the engine stopped. The furnace glowed red with the residual heat. This was the only time it was possible to see the condition of the boiler water tubes. He called me over to have a look. At first glance I didn't know what I was looking for, then my eye adjusted to the faint thread like jets of boiler water that emanated from about half a dozen tubes. The boiler tubes were leaking and at 250 pounds per square inch pressure. How could a pin hole, because that was about the size of it, be made in the wall of a boiler tube? There were a few of them and this was serious. I called the Bridge and asked for the Chief. He came down and had a look. We got under way. I realised how serious it was when he stayed with me as we flashed up the boiler again, and he remained the whole time doing the worrying for all of us. The level of boiler water in the sight glasses was going down. We were losing boiler water quicker than we could put it in. We used all of our fresh water in the tanks and also had the evaporator making fresh water from the sea. Three hours later Sondra came alongside the jetty. There was only an inch of water showing in the sight glasses when 'finished with engine' rang down.

The boiler fires were shut down. Three rows of tubes were going to be removed and new tubes fitted. Boilermakers from the factory ashore came aboard and did the actual changing of the tubes. We removed the manholes from the boiler drums and crawled inside the drums to expand a few of the ends of the new tubes while the boilermakers had a break. The job took three days and nights. Cold ship, no shore steam was available as it would be in a home dockyard. Once the tubes were changed the boilermakers left us to replace the manholes, fill the boiler and raise steam. We slept during the waiting time between jobs. I just laid on the cabin floor in my dirty clothes, sleeping for a couple of hours here, a couple of hours there. Raising steam took about twelve hours. The temperature has to be applied slowly making sure the boiler water is circulating evenly over all the tubes as they expanded with the heat. Initially a burner would be lit for ten minutes or so then off for five gradually warming it through. One of us could take a nap. It was bliss to take my clothes off, turn in and sleep until eleven thirty pm when Jamie called me with a pot of tea. We were ready for sea, it was midnight, my watch! After working on and off for three days I was like a zombie, I hadn't had my clothes off during those three days I went below and performed the necessary actions to steam the ship to sea. Johansen kept an eye on me, without the boiler the firemen had been free of duties for three days. He was very helpful.

The day arrived when the gunner would try out the radar set. We'd been at sea for a few days and finally caught a good sized fin whale. Towing it back to the island as we approached only the tops of the snow covered peaks were visible Thick white fog surrounded the whole coast. I had seen this before I went down for my watch, so it must have been around noon. About half an hour or so later the telegraph rang to reduce speed to slow ahead .I guessed that the boss would make use of the radar to get into the narrow entrance to the fjord. He wanted to drop this fin whale at the factory buoy and get out again to carry on the hunt. There hadn't been much sight of the elusive whales for the past few days. I visualised the scene on the bridge, the Gunner peering into the cupboard at the three inch screen, the dot in the middle being the ship, the sweep hand going around leaving a fluorescent image of the mouth of the Leith harbour entrance. Knowing him he would have a sailor on the gun platform peering into the fog. I reduced the speed until the engine was turning very gently. So gently that at the first impact, should it happen I could stop and it would do no damage. The ship's bow was built extra strong to fend office. We didn't make an impact but I heard and felt the grating sound and bumps as we rubbed along the small outcrop of rocks that guarded the middle of the entrance to the fjord. It was only a bit of paint rubbed off so worth the effort. In a few minutes we had cleared the mouth of the fjord, the telegraph rang for half then full ahead! The fjord was clear of fog and we stopped to drop the fin at the buoy. I was pleased when the boss decided to go on to the bunker jetty and top up our fuel and "lay in" for the night. In the morning a breeze arose and the fog dispersed. It was business as usual. To my knowledge the radar was not used again. I think it was probably an ex RAF job. There's more room to manoeuvre up in the sky but the small scale of the radar made it less suitable for a ship.

To illustrate the need to see ahead in fog this story explains how a sailor can use his senses to do just that. One evening at about eight o'clock after a rough day the Gunner had given the Chief a bottle of gin for the officers. The Chief and about three of us off watch were drinking the gin with a jug of hot sugar water, a hot toddy, very nice! It eased the aching stomach muscles. Sondra was steaming back to the factory with a couple of whales we had caught. It had been a busy day. I would be 'turning in' for a couple of hours sleep before my midnight to four o 'clock in the morning watch. The sea was calm. The ship's speed towing two whales would be about ten knots, twelve miles an hour. Suddenly Sondra heeled hard over! Alarm! The ship continued to turn hard a'port. The Chief led the way aloft. He dashed up the first steep companionway, stairway, for those unfamiliar with nautical terms, then up the second companionway onto the upper deck. Thick fog obscured anything more than a hundred yards from the ship. Now as we stood silent listening, we heard the splashing of the sea against the side of a towering ghostly white iceberg glowing just a say visible in the grey fog. Sondra now was running alongside the 'berg. It was only a few hundred yards further along when the helmsman turned the ship less urgently, now that we were clear, to regain our course for 'home'.

The sailor on the open bridge, at the helm, had sensed a drop in temperature of the fog that surrounded the giant 'berg. Another sense to confirm the 'berg's presence was the sound of the sea breaking against the side of it's icy walls. High up on the bridge the sound of the ship's engine cannot be heard. The sailor was alert to any change in his surroundings. Radar would have registered a 'berg but in the circumstances these men trusted their instinctive senses. If I remember correctly the Japanese bomber planes were seen on that fateful Sunday morning at Pearl Harbour. They were discounted because they "shouldn't have been there". Fortunately we had finished our ration of gin before this bit of a scare. I went below to my bunk and slept peacefully until called for my midnight watch. It was not always easy to sleep so!

The first and only time I had been privileged to see the Atlantic 'rollers' I had wakened to the unusual motion of the ship. The peculiar labouring of the engine was followed by an increase of revolutions as Sondra almost 'freewheeled' sliding down the giant waves. I realised that Sondra must be climbing up these giant waves and sliding down the other side. It caused me to slide in my bunk, first to the top of the bunk, then to the bottom. At the same time there was a rumbling noise coming from the deck above my cabin. Something had come adrift and was rolling about on deck !I chose to ignore it and dozed fitfully hoping someone would do something about it.

I didn't have long to think about it before the Mate opened the cabin door and told me to get up and give him a hand to secure a 40 gallon oil drum which was loose on deck. This had been roped to the handrail around the stern. The unique motion of the ship had freed it and it was now 'a loose cannon' on deck. I quickly dressed and pulled on my sea boots. The Mate led the way onto the upper deck to weigh up the situation. The view amazed me! Sondra was steaming up giant waves, and reaching the top, the little ship lowered her bow and slid down the other side before approaching the next climb.

We waited until Sondra started to climb a wave before we climbed down the steel ladder to the lower deck to secure the rolling oil drum. From there I was able to see clearly from the crest of a wave that each wave was unbroken from one horizon to the other. They were in uniform wave formation from as far as I could see to port and starboard and as far ahead as I could see. The sky was jet black but where was the light coming from? It could only have been from the thousands of bright stars undimmed by the sharp clear air and probably assisted by the swirling phosphorous from the sea. We had to judge the movement of the ship when to move onto the rolling drum and make a temporary lashing until the moving deck assisted us in getting the thing where we could make a proper job of it. I don't know who had roped it up in the first place, my mum could have done a better job. I went back to my bunk and wedged myself in to reduce the sliding effect and slept better knowing that it was a friendly sea for us. As a boy I had heard sailors talk about the Atlantic rollers They were feared by the "big ship" men. The constant stress on the hull at bow and stern then on the crest of the big wave at the centre was thought to break a ship's back? I was happy in a small ship, not too small though! Jamie came with a mug of tea at eleven thirty to call me for my midnight to four am watch.

Christian Christiansen the Captain/Gunner was a proper gentleman. He was very precise in his work. I was only on the Bridge once and saw how he checked with binoculars that the whale was of the permitted size, and not a protected species such as the 'right whale', which had been named by the sailing ship whalers, for obvious reasons, it was not too big to handle and didn't sink when it was dead so they could tow it back to the brig.

One day I went on watch at noon. The Gunner had fired the harpoon and missed twice in the previous eight till twelve watch. This was very unusual. He was always careful to get near enough to make a professional kill, ideally this would be less than sixty yards and would be quickly flagged and floated off so we could pursue other whales in the vicinity. Delay meant the school of whales would get too far away from us to catch up with them again. By the time I had settled in to my watch, the 'double ring' on the telegraph came indicating we were racing to approach a whale. Now we were stalking the selected animal, half speed then full as we had passed the whale as it blew and dived again, this went on for a few minutes then "bang" I rapidly stopped the engine dead! A voice from the bridge came down the copper voice pipe in Norwegian "arr boom" This was the way of saying "a miss" Precious minutes wasted hauling the harpoon and line back in, then 'full ahead' again for another try. At the 'go on' double ring of the telegraph I opened the steam full to the engine,

I was always concerned for the big end bearings as they were knocking a bit, we were treating them roughly! Again the harpoon was fired, again came the voice "arr boom!" In the few minutes we were stopped while the crew recovered the harpoon and rope the Gunner's high pitched voice came down the overhead pipe from the bridge, "Mr Dinsdale."(this was a very rare event, the Gunner to speak to the engineer.) "Aye aye Captain," I replied curious as to this personal conversation. The thin voice came again "try to manoeuvre a bit quicker please, you're too ****ing slow!" I was shocked, I took a pride in my handling of this big brute of a steam engine. The Boss was upset at missing the target! It wouldn't hurt the whale because the target area was very small, just the head. A miss would go over or under the head which does not seem to affect the whale who is generally at slow speed feeding on the plankton that is rich in these waters. As well as adjusting the speed of the ship, the Gunner has to signal from the gun platform to the bridge which direction to steer to be in the correct position when the whale surfaces for the few seconds it takes to 'blow' I replied to his expletive instruction in a contrite voice, "sorry Sir." It was all my fault that he couldn't hit the thing! More manoeuvres took place, finally a bang! This resulted in the call I was glad to hear "arr fast fisk" which isn't difficult to interpret into English. In no more ten minutes the whale was alongside, flagged and floated away and we were off after another one. I had opened the steam control valve as quickly as I could without the impact that would damage the big end bearings but I didn't think that would improve his aim any! Am I being sarcastic? Never mind, by the end of my watch the gunner had a bagged a second whale. This was an average good day, honour was restored, and we had made a professional job of both kills. Also by despatching each of the whales in about ten minutes the animals would have had minimal stress. Sondra with Christian Christiansen's skill would remain top boat.

A few times we went ten days and never saw a whale. A depression took over the whole crew. W.C. Sondra cruised along all the daylight hours, wasting costly fuel. I had considered this lack of bonus along with the risk factor in deciding to work another season. Not a difficult decision, I am not a gambling man but I enjoyed the shipboard life, each day was different, different sea, different sky. We sailed on day after day, it could become a habit? The alternative was the shipyard, not a good prospect. I had heard of work for engineers at a new chemical factory being built along the road to Redcar "Wilton Works" as it came to be known. The reports were mixed. Billingham I.C.I. was a terrible place, smelly fumes and dirty, I would go back to Smith's Dock for the present.

As the season passed I began to look forward to returning home again. Eventually as the weather worsened, short days of heavy weather, sleet, snow and hail I knew that the end was in sight. I didn't volunteer to overwinter. It meant 18 months away from home. I had more to live for, I admired the men who did it, marvelled would be a better word! Perhaps they were desperate men who knew no other life. I was learning that my life was turning out to be not so bad even though I came from a broken home. I know I have been well blessed having a good mother who taught me to behave well, and a lovely girl who became my wife and completed the job of making me a gentleman.

Sondra came in on the last day of the season, it was probably mid April. I took little time to pack my gear. I left the little Phillips radio with a guy who was staying to work over winter. I don't remember the 'trade', we had no money to speak of I was in a benevolent mood, his need was great and I didn't want the bother of getting it home. It may not have survived the journey. As at the end of the previous season, I humped my gear along the shore to the same very old lady who had brought us down here. The S/S Polar Chief would hopefully take us back to Liverpool. Nothing too eventful occurred on this trip.

Polar Chief now over fifty years old only managed a stately six knots with a following sea. In her prime years as a North Pacific Liner built in 1897 with boiler steam pressure of 250 pounds per square inch she would do about twelve knots. She was scrapped in 1952. This may have been her last trip from the South Atlantic. Passing through the tropics we spent many hours on deck. A couple of evenings two of our crew entertained us with a guitar and accordion. One song was "O Maggie Maggie May" A girl from Liverpool who evidently was very friendly, "they have taken you away" I can't remember why! Then there was something about Lime Street which ran down to the Mersey ferry, it was a nostalgic ballad and a bit naughty. All the old sailors seemed to know these songs. There was a Company song too but being on a whale catcher ship with a majority of Norwegians I didn't have the chance to learn it, although I can still remember a nostalgic Norwegian sailor's song.

"Here min sang du klara aften stear/ner du sum funklay heet po himmlen bloe', ta en hilsen med di til en fearner , til en ven Jeg aldi tinker po." - - - In English, "Hear my song you bright evening star as you twinkle high in heaven above, take a message with you on your journey to the one I'm always thinking of." Of course the Norwegians would say I sang it with a Danish accent!

Coming up the middle of the Atlantic we only saw one other ship. This vessel was passing across our bow about a quarter of a mile ahead of us. Even though it was dark it was visible in different shades of grey with the magic light of the stars and places its deck lights failed to illuminate. Merchant Navy courtesies were exchanged in morse code by aldis lamp. "S.S. Polar Chief bound for Liverpool." And the appropriate signal was returned "bound for" and their destination. This was a custom in the days before radio and satellites so that if a ship failed to reach Port or was overdue its last known position would be known and a search could be made.

Thirty days or so after leaving South Georgia we came into the River Mersey and the S.S.Polar Chief moored up in Gladstone Dock. The whaling season had ended and I had returned from nine months in Antarctic waters. This would be my last trip whaling. The Customs men were gentle with us this time, a selective search, "you, you and you!" I went before the ship's agent and was paid off with a 'good discharge paper' to present to another shipping agent when applying for a job. I received my travel warrant and got a taxi straight to Lime Street railway station. Dorothy was staying with Mum at 68 Granville Road I was going home to my beloved wife, family, things familiar and friends.

For two seasons I had endured months at sea living in rough conditions. Unlike the able seaman, I was a skilled engineer and could find work ashore. I would return to the shipyard. Unlike today, an old man of eighty seven, life was very simple then and people were better off for it.

# CHAPTER 17
# HOME AGAIN RETURN TO THE SHIPYARD
*Home sweet Home.*
*Back to my dear wife and ready to settle down.*

I had paid off the ship with another cheque for about £800. With the previous year's earnings safely in the bank we now had the means to put down a deposit and buy a little house. We bought a two bedroom end terrace house behind Middlesbrough's Albert Park and I went back to work in the shipyard. Dorothy furnished the house with a very good second hand, solid light oak dining room suite for which she paid £25. Her mum had given us a lot of her linen and other items which were a help too. For the sitting room we bought an Indian square carpet. Wall to wall carpet was not common in 1949. Our next purchase were two comfortable rocking chairs each with a tall back, wings and side arms. We also bought a large Echo radio which was heavy, but reception was good. With a good coal fire in the grate we were comfortable.

After living in our own house for eighteen months Dorothy's mother had fallen and broken her leg. The hospital had to put a plate in her leg to pin it then put it in plaster up to her thigh. Her second husband Jimmy Davidson wanted Dorothy to go over to Hartlepool and live with them until her mother was able to look after him and keep house again. I already knew what a rotter he had turned out to be and said, "well who's going to look after me?" I told Dorothy that "we'll get your mum over here!" We brought her to our house in Newstead Road and put a bed downstairs for her. This was easier for Dorothy and it was by far the best solution. After many weeks when she had recovered she returned home but wasn't happy living with this gentleman. Dorothy returned home one day after visiting her mum and asked me if her mum could come and live with us. The decision rested with me. Now I had a problem. If I said "no," Dorothy's mother was unhappy, so Dorothy was unhappy, this would make me unhappy - - - Her mum was a very nice person the answer seemed to be to have her come and live with us. So, I said "yes." Now Dorothy would be happy, her mother was happy and I could be happy with two women to look after me. In the shipyard we were working six days a week at the time on poor pay to restore the economy that had not recovered from the war. Having two women in our household turned out very well.

I had two women who cared for me and a built in baby sitter when baby John eventually came along. Dorothy's mother didn't have her state pension for two years until her second husband retired but it didn't matter in fact she earned her keep and was a good help to Dorothy. I treat her as I would my own mother. We had sixteen happy years with never a wrong word. If you want to be happy make someone else happy! I find that philosophy works most of the time if people want to be happy! .There are some poor souls though who don't know how to be happy, it's difficult to do anything for them they must work it out for themselves.

Dorothy had said early in our relationship that if she was happy she felt that something would happen to spoil her happiness and she would have to pay for it. This was perhaps because her father had died when she was fifteen years old. It must have made a big change in their circumstances although Mr Fell probably with his position in the shipyard would have some insurance. After we were married I never heard her say that again. Reading her diary I found that I had made her very happy and that is a great consolation to me now I only have my memories of those happy days. Many years later after her mother had died if Dorothy was a bit cross with me, and I probably deserved it coming into the house with muddy shoes or some such thing, I'd say, "you wouldn't dare speak to me like that if your mother was here, she wouldn't let you!" Then we would laugh and the love we had for each other grew stronger.

I went back to Smith's Dock shipyard, the same job as before. It was hard physical work fitting engines into the ship's hulls. It was always difficult to see a ship sail away and me not on it. The sea can be an attractive lazy life if you are content to live it. Your meals are provided, and on big ships you have a steward to make your bed, not far to travel to work, routines in the engine room, sea views all round on deck. There were some very difficult times at sea too, breakdowns! All hands in the engine room! Break watches and work round the clock until the job was finished. But you forget those times! We only remember the good times, I was afraid that sea going could become a habit.

I had been away from Smith's Docks for two years whilst I was in the Antarctic. The orders for whale catchers had eased off. A few specialist ships of 10,000 tons were built like the S.S. Lovland a cargo steamer built for A/S Sunde, Farsund, Norway. Another was the S.S.Arakaka, a cargo and passenger steamer built for a Liverpool Company. This was before the days of the long distance aircraft passenger planes. I wasn't interested in that type of ship. Another was the motor vessel The M.V. Borealis a fruit and passenger carrier, an investment by Fred Olsen & Co. of Oslo. Now in 1949 there were a few orders for small oil tankers, and still one or two catchers. "Smiths" had built a couple of small oil tankers fitted with their own design of steam engines but only about two thousand horsepower, the world demand for oil required faster and bigger oil tankers.

Two Greek entrepreneurs, Onassis and Livanos, had foreseen the expanding market for oil. The era of the horse which had served man for a thousand years and more was nearly over. We still had coal delivered for a year or two with a horse and cart. The milk man and his horse disappeared after the war with the advent of the electric float which rattled along the streets in the early hours. They returned to base in the early afternoon crawling along with their batteries needing recharging. The motor car was now affordable not only for the doctor but his patients too!

The days of the Marine steam reciprocating engine was also over. To raise steam with fuel then use the steam to move the engine was only

25% to 30% efficient. The boiler fuel was the residue from the crude oil after the higher octane's such as petrol were extracted. The W. C. Sondra had been very wasteful with fuel especially when towing whales back to the factory. At night the flames from the boiler were visible above the top of the funnel. This poor economy was tolerated because of other advantages. One it was a quiet engine, simplicity and reliability were most important consideration. Diesel engines were reliable up to a point but noisy. The whale catchers built after the war had twin boilers of a more efficient type made by 'Foster Wheeler & Co.' The design of the diesel engine where the fuel was injected direct into the cylinder was more economical than the steam engine. I had experienced a ship with a multi cylinder four stroke diesel engine and the noise of the overhead valve gear in the engine room was painful to the ears. Smith's Docks got an order for an oil tanker with a 'Doxford' diesel engine. The engine had to be 'bought in' from a Sunderland firm, 'Hawthorn Leslie & Co.'

The launch of the biggest vessel yet built by Smith's, was the 28,000 ton oil tanker named 'Atlantic Duke', the Doxford engine to be installed had to be delivered in sections.

The all steel fabricated bedplate was enormous in comparison to the smaller cast iron steam engine bedplates I was familiar with. I worked with the squad that erected this engine in the ship's hull. When the engine was fully built in the engine room it stood about forty feet high and the same length. There were no valves to clatter noisily in this engine as it was a 'two stroke' The pistons themselves acted as valves to exhaust the waste gases into the exhaust chamber surrounding the cylinders. What was unusual about this engine was that each cylinder had two opposed pistons. The bottom piston was connected to the crankshaft in the usual way with a connecting rod. The opposed piston rod sticking out of the top of the engine had a bar across it with two rods fastened at each end passing down through the exhaust box which surrounded the cylinders into the crankcase where they were connected to crankpins opposed to the crank of the bottom piston. It sounds a bit complicated but if there is any advantage in such an arrangement it is because the power stroke is driving two pistons with one ignition. In the conventional arrangement the fuel gases pushed against one piston and the cylinder head. This meant the five cylinder Doxford engine had fifteen connecting rods. That's a lot of moving parts in an engine where the crankshaft weighed sixty tons. The 700 degree exhaust gases from the engine when running at sea passed through a bulkhead to deliver the waste heat from the engine to furnaces of one of three 40 ton fire tube boilers maintaining steam for the ships auxiliaries, and steam electric generators. When steam was required in port it was necessary to light oil burners in the boiler furnaces to drive the auxiliaries. If the ship had to discharge the cargo of oil itself when there were no facilities ashore to do it, steam would be required for the 10,000 horse power cargo pumps. The ships electricity was generated by one of three steam engine generators running at 500 revs per minute. When manoeuvring the main diesel engine, compressed air was required to start the engine each time a change from ahead to astern was made. This compressed air was admitted from the two giant compressed air bottles each about five feet in diameter and twenty feet high that stood upright in the engine room. Coming into port stopping and starting the main diesel engine the compressors also needed smaller steam engines to maintain the pressure. Coming in or out of port, engine manoeuvres required two or three engineers on watch, one engineer at the controls, another to switch over the compressed air bottles used to start the engine and recharge the empty one. A junior engineer's job was to log all the telegraph signals from the bridge. No moving parts were visible at the control platform on the lower deck of the engine room. The engine was as quiet as a mouse, it was necessary to look at the revolution indicator to make sure it had started. The only moving parts visible were high up at the top of the engine. The upper piston connecting rods moved up and down through the engine casing driving the sixty ton crankshaft round. The engine speed at full ahead was 130 revs per minute, driving the ship along at 17 knots (about twenty miles per hour). Two of the three boilers were maintained on "stand by." If the cargo was crude oil and very thick when cold, it was necessary to fire up a boiler to supply steam to coils in the oil cargo tanks. The cargo was heated before coming to port to warm and thin the oil to enable the pumps to discharge it ashore. Two large 10,000 horse power reciprocating steam pumps capable of pumping the cargo ashore within fourteen hours occupied a pumping chamber amidships the width of the ship.

When the ship was empty the bows stuck up almost out of the water due to the weight of the engine and after superstructure. To trim the ship sea water was pumped into the cargo tanks to ballast and level the vessel. Experiments were made at sea by the Chief Officer to trim the ship slightly nose down one day and another day up, to see if it improved the propeller efficiency and speed. I never heard the result. It was a Friday morning, the 28,000 ton Atlantic Duke was lying at the fitting out jetty, newly painted with a fancy modern shaped funnel. The shipyard platers had found this difficult to fabricate. Funnels for whalers were generally round, straight and no problem for the platers. She was all ready fuelled up to leave immediately after the sea trials along the coast off Blyth. The ship would then proceed to New York on the Sunday.

At about eleven o'clock on the Friday morning. I was looking forward to having Saturday off. The shipyard manager called me over, and informed me that "the Superintendent of Atlantic Duke would like to have a word with you. Will you go and have lunch with him," he said. My natural curiosity and a free lunch persuaded me to go.

The Superintendent in a strong Greek accent and demanding voice told me he was not satisfied with the Greek engineer's knowledge of the ship. "Please, we want you to sail with Atlantic Duke and we give you American rate of pay," he told me. He had caught me at a weak moment, talking about money! Without asking my dear Dorothy I replied "yes!"

My dutiful wife took the news without question. I couldn't tell her much, how long was I going to be away? I didn't know. Where were we going to, America? That's a big place It stretches from Novas Scotia to the bottom of South America. On Saturday morning

I had to go shopping for a few things for the trip such as khaki shorts. Dorothy came with me and we went into a workwear supply shop and asked the girl assistant if they had any khaki shorts. "Yes," the poor girl said, "what size neck?" Dorothy and I both laughed, the girl thought I was speaking Geordie. The Geordies of Tyneside pronounce shirt as short. The Girl thought I was a Geordie'!

# CHAPTER 18
## 1952-53. M/V ATLANTIC DUKE
*28,000 ton Oil Tanker, not a very good idea but an experience.*

*MV Atlantic Duke, 28,000tons, at Atlantic City, USA 1952.*

It was fortunate that Dorothy's mother was living with us, I had not expected to be away long. I wouldn't have accepted the job otherwise. I thought when the Atlantic Duke made a trip to Europe I would be able to sign off and then return home. However, Atlantic Duke didn't return to Europe and I was away for ten months! We made many regular return ten day trips with oil from Venezuela up the Delaware River to Marcus Hook, 15 miles from Philadelphia.

For the first few trips I was unable to go ashore in America because I had not had time to obtain a U.K. passport and my merchant navy passport had had to be returned to some merchant navy office when I paid off in Liverpool. I'm not sure why this was, but it meant that it was impossible to sign on a ship without first informing the office and it being returned by post. This frustrating procedure was possibly thought up to keep some official in a job; it is a common feature in British Government circles. After two or three trips retuning to Marcus Hook, the Livanos Company engineering superintendent took me by car to the British Consul in Philadelphia. There I was fingerprinted, photographed, and my age, date of birth and other identification details were then entered onto a temporary passport. It would have been nice to have had time to see a bit of Philadelphia where much of America's history was made with the Liberty Bell and early buildings but I was not a tourist. We went straight back to the ship.

At least I was now able to go ashore when we came into port, providing there wasn't some job to do on the main engine. I went for a walk to the main street of Marcus Hook and did a bit of shopping. I had made an arrangement before we sailed for a sum of money to be sent to Dorothy regularly from the Atlantic Oil Transport, Livanos Company office in London.

It was to be hard work, a new ship with all the teething troubles usually associated with new devices. Because of losses of ships and men during the war and the increase in trade there was a shortage of marine engineers. A young English man from Hartlepool, Peter Richards had been signed on as an assistant engineer. He was put on my 12:00 to 4:00 'watch.' Peter was aged about twenty one or two, quiet and well behaved but I thought not very interested in the engine room. He didn't ask any questions, always a bad sign.

The food was excellent. The Greek Captain was a gourmet! Wherever we called on the American coast he filled the freezers with the speciality of the region. We had salmon from Canada, large green melons from the Deep South, beef from Texas, sweet peppers and eggplants, some people call them aubergines. I particularly enjoyed the food, 'meljanis,'which is a Greek recipe, aubergines cut in half, stuffed with mince and onion then baked in the oven, delicious! I had now been introduced to the wonderful flavour of garlic which was not well known then outside the Mediterranean. The Norwegians hadn't used garlic when I was with them, it was a Latin thing.

Peter my assistant engineer was not a dedicated 'Company' man. After a few trips he went to the Captain and 'paid off' the ship! In America too! I was astounded when I heard the news. In retrospect he may have had relatives in the States to give him some support. Peter was ready with immigration papers to become a citizen of the U.S.A. He'd never mentioned a word of his intentions to me, but he'd had his passport and worked his passage very well! It was unusual for people to have a passport in 1950 so it had been premeditated. Clever man! Many years later I learnt from a friend in Hartlepool that Peter had joined the American Air force and had achieved the rank of Colonel.

Later in the seventies when air travel made it possible, he had visited Hartlepool to see his family. We didn't get to know each other but I often wondered how he could leave his family in England and settle in America. He never spoke about his people but was friendly enough. When I was working and unable to go ashore he would ask me if I wanted anything and do a bit of shopping for me.

One trip Atlantic Duke made was to deliver our cargo of oil to a refinery in Texas City on the far west of the Gulf of Mexico. For some reason we couldn't off load our cargo immediately and we lay alongside for four days. This was a good opportunity to spend some time ashore. I was given permission for Peter and myself to have the afternoon off watch. We went ashore and soon found that even just walking about the high humidity was a bit of a problem. Perspiration soaked our shirts and the waistband of our trousers. We went into a bar for a soft drink and found relief in the air conditioning .The barman recognised we were 'Limeys' and engaged us in conversation. "Where are you from?" "Middlesbrough,"I replied. "Never heard of it!" Then he told us of the 'blast' of 16th April 1947, he called it the recent blast! It blew up Texas City and set fire to homes and caused great damage. The story was that of a ship loaded with nitrate fertiliser which in certain conditions becomes explosive. The hundreds of tons of nitrate caught fire and the captain ordered the crew to abandon ship. The barman said that an attempt was made to tow the ship out of the harbour but the inevitable happened and the ship blew up. It must have been bad for people to be still talking about it four years later. There was a small church, which looked very English, with a clock tower and a tall pointed spire. On the hour a peal of bells played, ringing out the tune we use to accompany our National Anthem. This music is a hymn in the USA.

We went ashore the next day and took our bathing costumes and towels to go to the beach in Galveston. This was a twenty minute local bus ride from Texas City. It seemed a popular trip because the bus was just about full. Again our English accents created a frisson of interest amongst the passengers. It wouldn't happen like this on an English bus. Americans are not afraid to engage in conversation and we had to respond to their questions and information of local gossip for the whole journey. My neck ached from turning to the couple behind us and it was with relief we came to Galveston and dismounted at the bus stop on the sea front. We went onto the beach and changed into our swimming trunks. There was a party of three young couples, probably on holiday, lounging on the beach. The three wives were friends and had towels, flasks of coffee and snacks with them. They were spending a few hours in the sun. The humidity didn't seem so bad near the sea. We asked the couples if we could leave our clothes and gear with them while we went for a swim. Again we had the exclamations of "oh, you are English?" They made a few jokes about things being bigger and better in Texas! Then one said about his friend, "but he's not from Texas, he's from Idaho!" Well I didn't know exactly how far away Idaho was but I knew he was a long way from home because Texas is a very big State. We went down to the sea and had a swim for a while but the sea was eighty eight degrees fahrenheit and we were glad to come out to cool down!

The American people have a very different outlook to us which was an education to me. I didn't know at that time that Peter was planning to join them. I like meeting people and would have liked to have spent more time learning more of the American way of life but fate had deemed that was not to be.

I had been fortunate to have seen the things I had seen. Many people are born to live and die without seeing much outside their immediate surroundings. It must be very dull to just exist. Most young men need some interesting activity or they get into mischief. This seems to be the problem with some of them today. Kids say, I'm bored, they expect the local Council or someone to find something for them to do. They should be told to do some voluntary work but they expect to be paid for any little job they do! Health and Safety forbids anyone to ask anyone to do any voluntary work, they might be sued damages for instance. Parents must take some responsibility for this. My son John and his pals joined the cub scouts and eventually he got his Chief Scout award. His mum and I took part in fundraising garden parties I took on the Scout Group Secretary's job, it needed a lot of tact dealing with old committee members who could always tell you why your suggestion to a problem would fail. My answer to that was, well what do you suggest? They had nothing to say so my suggestion was carried and I made it work! With young Scout leaders who had suggestions for everything I found it best to let them get on with it and if it went pear shape help them out with a bit of my past experience. I remained Group secretary for twenty one years before I found another dad to take it over. I can say without contradiction I left it better than I had found it.

Now back to Texas City. With the cargo of oil eventually discharged, Atlantic Duke sailed south to Venezuela on the north coast of South America for another cargo of crude oil, then back north to Marcus Hook in the Delaware. There was never an opportunity to go ashore at Venezuela, the ship was loaded in quick time and the area was under high security.

Some of the young Greek engineers had little experience of big ship marine engines, some of them probably had worked on fishing boats. They were intelligent young men though, who only needed showing the routines once. On the job training is the best way of learning routine work and experience is acquired over many years. Murphy's Law requires a lot of study too, as "what can go wrong will go wrong at the most inappropriate moment." A good engineer anticipates Murphy by paying regular attention to maintenance.

For the first six weeks, the Greek Chief Engineer Michael Loupis and I worked six hours on watch and six hours off until these lads could handle a four hour watch. This was routine stuff checking temperatures and flows of cooling water etc. The following pages you may find a bit technical but it includes a few funny stories of things that can go wrong with a new ship and crew, so ignore the technical bits and get the overall picture.

The first of the 'teething troubles' we had experienced was a loss of main engine lubricating oil. It was stored in a five hundred gallon tank mounted at the top of the spacious engine room. This 'lube' oil was gravity fed to the engine crankshaft and bearings then pumped back up to the tank to be circulated continually. A clever design, the height of the lube oil tank would give a pressure of about ten pounds per square inch to the engine, enough to lubricate every bearing in the crankcase. A 'sight glass tube' down the side of the tank indicated the level of oil. During the first few days on the maiden voyage the level was slowly going down indicating a loss of oil? The Chief Engineer was berthed amidships below the bridge. I phoned his cabin and informed him of the loss of the lubricating oil. He thought this could be caused by oil lying in cavities in the bedplate of the new engine not draining down to the sump where the pump suction pipe returned the oil to the tank. "Okay not to worry, top the tank up", he said. A couple of hundred gallons of oil restored the level but in a day or so the loss continued. A junior engineer was detailed to search under the engine room deck plates for a suspected leak. The return pipe was checked, no leaks were found. There was never this problem with a steam engine. With the primitive steam engine, oil dripped into the bearings via small copper tubes from oil boxes with a battery of tiny pumps operated by a thin steel rod connected to the engine. When the engine moved, the pumps pumped the little amount of oil used to lubricate the engine which then leaked from the bearings and ran into the bilges. This was then pumped away with the bilge water. At high speed some of the oil was thrown out into the engine room, not a lot, but the engineer got his share. Everything was visible in the open steam engine. I enjoyed seeing the steel connecting rods flashing in the yellow light given off by the oily lamp bulbs as they went up and down, speeding around to the hiss and puff of the steam whispers escaping from the piston rod glands.

The diesel engine was sheeted in with thin steel plates. Small port holes allowed the engineer to see little of the moving parts working in a spray of oil. In the cathedral like engine room of M.V. Atlantic Duke the Chief Engineer Michael Loupis, came down to the engine room and looked into the six inch diameter glass windows in the manhole covers of the enclosed engine. The glass on the inside was smeared with oil and the lamps inside the engine revealed nothing. It was almost possible to see Loupis' brain working with his facial expressions, and after a minute or two his eyebrows shot up! One hand was raised with a finger pointing skywards, his mouth opened in a teeth showing grin. He'd got it! "We must ask the Captain for permission to stop" he said. He left the engine room went up to the bridge and returned a few minutes later. "Okay, stop the engine." This would have to be logged and the reason for the stop recorded. I went to the control module and took hold of the big steel handle with its ratchet lever that lifted the "dog" which engaged in the teeth of the fuel control quadrant, bringing the lever to zero. The engine revolutions of 120 revolutions per minute shown by the pointer on the indicator came to rest. A junior engineer removed the engine casing centre manhole cover. It was made of cast aluminium, not heavy, about three feet diameter. There, in the sump of the engine bedplate was five hundred gallons of our missing engine oil. The pump filter, a metal 'top hat' cylindrical shape with holes in it, was here this pool of oil. The junior went inside the engine and fished around for the filter. A shout of glee, surprise, and wonder arose. It was all Greek to me, literally! The young Greek junior pulled out on to the engine room deck plates an oil soaked dark brown floppy object? My thoughts were "what the hell! How did that get in there?" It looked like a dead dog! This brown short haired bundle lay on the steel deck plates, and as the oil drained away what appeared to be a dog's leg gradually took the shape of a jacket sleeve. It was an old brown jacket! Now I could place it! The Doxford Diesel Engine was built at Sunderland and sent in pieces to Smith's Dock. It probably weighed 150 tons give or take a few tons. Whilst we were erecting the engine in the ship's hull, a job that lasted a few weeks. Smith's Dock employed a canny old chap to go around with a long handled paint brush and a gallon tin of oil. With the long handled paint brush he brushed oil on all the shiny steel parts of the engine to prevent them from rusting whilst they were exposed to the weather. I was too amused to be embarrassed, thankful it was nothing worse. It had not stopped the flow of oil to the pump thank goodness. The oil was recovered and the engine started up again. I had noticed the old chap at times take his coat off on a warm day and hang it on one of the connecting rods of the engine. He must have wondered where his jacket had got to! In any case the engine had not been carefully inspected before it was closed up for the sea trial. Livanos Co. were impatient to get the ship into service. These things happen, sometimes with serious results. We were lucky this time.

The diesel oil was almost like paraffin. Equipment had been installed in the engine room to run this Doxford engine on "boiler oil", the lowest grade of oil from the refinery. At the time boiler oil costing three pounds a ton. Diesel oil cost eight pounds a ton.

In the engine room, high up in the for'rard bulkhead five tanks each of which could hold twenty five tons of fuel were built. One was filled to supply the engine with twenty tons of diesel fuel, the daily requirement at sea. Another would be filled with the next days supply to settle and allow any ingress of water or grit to be removed with separators. Before the black, thick as treacle, boiler oil could be used to fuel the engine it had to be heated to thin it and put through these separators. These machines, Laval oil separators, driven by an electric motor running at 1500 revs a minute, had a spindle with conical discs spinning around in a chamber. This flung any water, sand and grit out to drain while the oil separated to a pump to be returned to the clean tank. When the main engine propelling the ship was switched from diesel to this hot boiler oil the engine continued to run but the speed dropped from 120 revolutions to no more than 100 revs. After a few hours running at this speed, reducing the ship's speed pro rata the

232

Captain ordered us to revert back to diesel fuel in order to maintain the ship's schedule. No doubt Livanos Head Office based in Wall Street, New York were monitoring the experiment. It was a disappointment.

When we arrived at our port of delivery up the Gulf of Delaware to the Sun Oil Co. at Marcus Hook 15 miles from Philadelphia on the Delaware River it would take about fourteen hours to discharge our cargo of crude oil. This didn't give much time to spend ashore but we often walked along the road from the Sun Oil quay then turned left to Main Street. We would call this the High Street. It was very wide by English standards, about forty feet with single story shops on each side. A little wooden white painted church had a spire and the place had a village feel to it. Most of the houses were built of wood with large open porches with chairs or benches where the occupiers could sit and chat with passers-by at times.

We usually took fuel for the next trip here at Sun Oil. The Captain only allowed us to take enough fuel for the trip with a bit to cover any bad weather in order to carry maximum cargo. It was my duty to liaise with the shore office and open up the fuel line valves to accept delivery and check the tank levels. I was in the engine room checking the fuel situation when the Chief telephoned from his cabin on the bridge and told me to take bunkers of two hundred tons of diesel fuel and six hundred tons of boiler oil. This was unusual we normally used more diesel than boiler oil. I realized he was going to run the engine all the way on the rough fuel! I reminded him of the result of our experiment. "Don't worry" he said kindly, "I have made an account." We departed from Marcus Hook in ballast with diesel oil fuel to the engine supplied from number one tank. The pilot left the ship at the mouth of the Delaware Gulf, there were no more movements on the telegraph for engine manoeuvres "full ahead" was signalled, steady going. Chief Engineer Loupis now came down to the engine room, and told me of his 'account.' "We will make a mixture" he said. His account was to put seven tons of diesel to fourteen tons of boiler oil, enough for a daily run and run the engine on that. There was no means of stirring the mixture in the tank but I put the boiler oil first to be thinned by heating it, then to the separator to clean it. Now the seven tons of diesel was pumped into the thinner boiler oil. We had twenty one tons of fuel for a daily run. This mixture was then switched to the engine. The engine revolutions remained steady at 130 revs per minute. We went up on deck and looked at the exhaust from the funnel, there was no smoke, there was complete combustion! It was a success! This saved Livanos Co. £8 per ton (diesel) minus £3 per ton (boiler oil) £5 x 20 tons per day at sea, seventy pounds sterling per day, £490 per week. Months later Michael Loupis was promoted to Superintendent Engineer of the Company. His remit was to go around Livanos' fleet of tankers and repeat this saving. He asked me if I would go with him but I declined and I wasn't keen to remain on the ship with some other Chief Engineer. I got on well with Michael Loupis but before he left for his promotion I had decided I had had enough. I had hoped we might do a trip over to Europe where I could make an easy journey home but the possibility was remote.

One of my routines was every Sunday morning to change over our auxiliary machinery. Atlantic Duke had two of everything, but three steam driven electric generators in fact! Only one was required for power, with one on "stand by" and the other to work on if any work was required.

A fifth emergency diesel generator was mounted in the 'after' steering flat, level with the main deck Things would be desperate if this was required such as no steam or flooded engine room! I started it up and ran it for a few minutes each week. This was to charge up the 12 volt batteries that turned over the diesel engine and to make sure it was ready for use if needed.

My cabin door was opposite the engine room door. When an alarm went off I would go down to be sure the engineer on watch could cope. Gradually I was able to leave them to it. However things occurred from time to time that were 'not in the book.'

At about eight pm one evening, the number one generator running to supply electricity to the ship failed. The light in my cabin grew very bright then went low until only the filament glowed red. Then it went off altogether, the ship was sailing at seventeen knots in total darkness. I lay in my bunk waiting for the engineer on watch to start up the number two generator. Several minutes passed. In dismay I heard the sound of spanners and a hammer. They were going to repair it! It was obvious a spring had broken in the governor which regulated the steam engine's 500 revs per minute speed. The ship was travelling at seventeen knots, at night without navigation lights or instruments. I heard the hammer being used on the generator cover nuts. I swung out of my bunk grabbed my torch and went down to find three of them around the machine. They were going to change the broken spring.

"Avrio" (tomorrow in Greek) I said, and proceeded to start up the number two machine. The cylinders on this engine were cold, I opened the steam valve slightly, the steam was very wet, water knocked in the cylinders. I opened the steam valve a bit more, gave the generator engine a few minutes to warm up at low revs then as the rev counter rose to near four hundred revs. I went to the Main Electric switchboard 'breaker' (a big two pole switch) on the number two panel, pushed it in and light was restored. Soon the generator was up to full speed. I returned to my cabin and rested until my watch at midnight.

Another of these extraneous duties was when I heard muffled voices from the engine room and thought I'd better have a look. I stepped across the passage to the engine room door and looked down. The place was full of steam. As I went below I could hear live steam issuing from somewhere but it was impossible to see anything. On the engine room deck below, Nico the Greek "second engineer" was shouting into the ear of the Greek "third engineer" (the noise of the steam made normal conversation impossible). Another junior engineer was standing there looking lost. I put my head close to Nico who spoke enough English and told him, "we must shut the main steam valve off and then find the problem later." He thought that was a good idea and disappeared into the steam. I went up on deck to the emergency valve wheels. These were on long spindles to isolate the steam from the top of the boiler just below the ship's upper deck. As I approached I saw the valve wheel turn. The bold Nico was on the boiler tops closing the steam valve. With the main steam shut off the problem was soon resolved. The auxiliaries, generators etc, were on another steam main and not affected. The Chief Officer had been using main steam at 250 p.s.i. in one of the big 10,000 horse power cargo pumps to move ballast and clean tanks. After the steam passed through the pump it was returning to the condenser at 160 pounds per square inch, This would need more cooling sea water than that for the light running of the generator and other services. It was good engine room economic practice to reduce the cooling sea water to the condenser so that the condensed water returning to the boiler was warm. Now with the reduced cooling water the steam remained at a pressure high enough to blow the water out of the condenser and the water holding tank that was open to atmosphere where it was pumped back to the boiler. The Chief Officer should have informed the engine room of his intentions to use the amount of steam involved and the engineer on watch if he knew his job should have increased the speed of the sea water circulating pump cooling the condenser to cope with the extra volume of steam. This is why I had been asked to sail with the ship but I couldn't be on duty 24 hours a day! Even an experienced crew needs time to settle down on a new ship but with these Greeks it was difficult beyond the call of duty. Unknown to us, this malfunction of overheating had damaged the condenser brass tubes that carried the sea cooling water.

While we lay at the unloading jetty and the cargo was being discharged the pump man drew my attention to the level of boiler water. The boiler water sight glasses were near full and excess boiler water was overflowing the condensed water tank where it was to be pumped back to the boiler. I tested it for salt thinking the condenser may be leaking the cooling sea water, but it was fresh water! Where was all the water coming from? I telephoned the Chief and he suggested I test the river water, I was surprised to find it was fresh water. Atlantic Duke a 28,000ton vessel was 100 miles up river from the sea. America has some mighty rivers, I was not aware of the possibilities. The condenser was leaking and it had to be repaired before we went back to sea .Salt does serious damage to a high pressure boiler. All hands turned too and we spent twenty hours down in the engine room making repairs to three condenser tubes split with the excessive hot steam. These jobs were becoming beyond the call of duty. It was bad enough on an old ship, this new ship was a hard ship! After ten months often working two watches seven days a week my health was beginning to suffer.

I was treated well and given a gratuity each month on pay day when I went up to the Captain's office to be paid in U.S. dollars. This would help Britain's economic crisis; it certainly helped mine! As I have already said the food was excellent, but I was 'worn out.' It was all work seven days a week living on the job. I took a watch in the engine room four hours on and eight off. noon until four pm and midnight until four am.

The Chief Engineer expected me to give him a hand with problems of the freezer chambers where the ship's food was stored. The young Greek engineers on day work could have done this and improved their knowledge. Perhaps the Chief was grooming me for a Chief's job! I found out later the boss Livanos had designs that way for me.

Chief Loupis asked me to assist him to take 'indicator cards' and 'tune' the engine. This was done by fitting an instrument to the engine cylinders one at a time. A chart clipped to a drum on the instrument indicated the pressure against the stroke as the engine was running. This was a check on the horse power of the cylinder. Fuel was then adjusted to each cylinder to balance the engine. It was a hot but not uninteresting operation. We came on deck to have a break from this job working on the hot engine cylinders. The Chief noticed the sun was not on our port side, "Aaaah! The sun, it's over there! It should be on this side !" he exclaimed. "Come!" As he ran along the gangway to the bridge. I dutifully followed. "Now what?"I thought. The Officer on watch was busy on deck, whilst the two sailors on watch were repainting the deck with roller brushes on poles and trays of paint. This was 1951, it was the first time I had seen a roller paint brush. There was no one on duty on the bridge. The helm (steering the ship) was on automatic pilot from the bridge. This controlled a two cylinder steam engine in the stern steering "flat" which moved the rudder when the hydraulic oil pressure through two small gauge copper pipes was varied from the bridge by the automatic control gear. This was set at the compass bearing to keep the ship on the required course. A two gallon copper tank under the "binnacle" (the steering wheel mounting which also contained a compass) held a reservoir of hydraulic oil. The Chief lifted out the dipstick, the tank was empty. Atlantic Duke had been going around in big circles all morning! We called the Officer of the 'watch.' It was the Chief Officer again! He filled the tank and reset the ship 'on course'. For a Chief Officer he obviously had no idea of delegating the simple task of checking the oil level to the men on watch. Come to think of it, it should have been checked by the shipyard's men before the ship put to sea. Being on the maiden voyage and only a few days out there was a reason for the oil to disappear and we found the leak and repaired our loss. A daily check on the tank level would have revealed the problem before the tank became empty. Old man Georgio Livanos would have been hysterical if he'd known his new ship had been going around in big circles for hours! The figures for the daily distance travelled, calculated for each day were adjusted for the next days until the error 'disappeared' - fiddled is the word I was looking for! I was learning a lot of things you don't learn in higher education!

Being one Englishman among a crew of Greeks some of whom spoke little English and others who spoke better English than me I learnt the Greek alphabet and soon picked up some important words on an oil tanker. Such words as "Fire!" This word I learnt one night when the engine room phone rang and the Third Officer shouted from the bridge "fotya!" "fotya!" I asked one of my engine room workers to interpret for me, he said fire! was the interpretation! I asked him "Where is the fire?" "From the top of the funnel," he replied. I was relieved to hear that! The boiler room on the mezzanine floor aft of the engine room bulkhead occupied the width of the ship. I climbed the steel ladder to the boiler room door, and inspected the boiler furnaces through the peep holes. One of the three 40 ton boilers was "working" heated from the engine exhaust. The other two boilers were "banked up" they had been working, oil fired when steam was required to steam out cargo tanks. I found what I was looking for, a furnace with a low 'wall' of 'clinker', (ash like residue left over after the boiler oil had been burnt, the result of bad combustion). This was glowing red hot, bits were flaking off and obviously going "up the chimney" to frighten the deck officer on watch! I took one of the fire irons a 12 foot long steel bar with an end like a garden hoe and broke up the clinker and raked it from the furnace. The Sudanese fireman watched me and I asked him to be sure to tell the other guys not to let the clinker get like that again. We had about a dozen of these Sudanese firemen. It could have been any one of them who had neglected to keep the furnace clean.

I often found the firemen on watch in the boiler room with a prayer mat saying prayers to Mecca. We needed all the prayers we could get. I didn't mind as long as the furnaces were clean of clinker and there were no sparks from the funnel. This was a ship loaded with highly volatile crude oil that gassed off in the open air. When taking the crude oil on board canvas 'chutes' are put in the tanks and fastened high above the superstructure to allow the gases from the oil to escape as the tanks are filled. Some gas escaping from the open hatches contacting the paintwork of the ship caused the paint to melt and strip off from the ship's side. This is what the 'yanks' called a 'hot-ship!'

One trip to the Delaware River after unloading we went round to Chesapeake Bay up to Baltimore. Here Loupis told me we were going into dry dock. I thought I would have some rest from being on watch. Loupis and I prepared the engine room for dry dock. This required the exhaust steam from the electricity generator and other auxiliaries normally condensed, to be vented to atmosphere, there would be no

238

cooling sea water for the condenser. I could have fallen out with him when he insisted that a certain steam valve had to be shut, I told him "No" but he insisted and I let him get on with it. As the valve closed, the lights in the engine room darkened as the steam generator slowed down with exhaust steam unable to escape. He swiftly opened the valve again. "Humph!" was all he said but he never challenged me after that. It wasn't a dry dock in fact but a 'floating dock'. The ship moored up over the big sunken pontoon and this was then pumped out to float and lift the 28,000 ton ship out of the water. The Ship's hull was going to be painted. I thought this would take all night at least from my experience with Smith's Docks. First men on ladders scraped the hull clean of barnacles, then they painted the hull with brushes on long bamboo poles. With a number of men it took many hours. I had only been in my bunk for one hour when the Chief called me. "Come on they are floating the ship" he said. Imagine my dismay! I crawled reluctantly from my bunk and went on deck to see how our allies during the war had painted a ship's bottom in little more than an hour. We didn't need scraping probably because of the new anti fouling paints that were introduced about this time. A 'gantry' with nozzles and hoses had moved along the ship on rails and sprayed red lead paint over the hull. Round the stern where it was not able to reach, men with hoses completed the spraying. This would not be as good a job as the old way. Old loose paint was scraped off and brushes were used to rub the paint well into the often rough surface.

There was a lot of unemployment in Greece for the Greek lads at this time. One young sailor chap told me he was sending his money home to keep his whole family, Mum, Dad, brothers and a sister's dowry. Some of these young men were five years at sea, the ship never going near Greece. They probably dare not ask for leave in case they didn't get their job back. The ship owners were multi millionaires! We need entrepreneurs, but I wondered if they were aware of the conditions these lads worked under when they were multi-millionaires, when is enough, enough? The underling managers who set the rates needed to be more generous, it was not my problem.

I had had enough, and although the food on ship was very good I had lost weight, In fact I was skinny. An opportunity arose for me to get off this ship. This part of my life with some of the crazy things that went wrong would take a long time to tell.

After we had loaded crude at one port a British pilot, as he was leaving the ship, told me we were overloaded and that the Captain would not discharge cargo to the permitted plimsoll level. The pilot said there was a danger that the crude oil cargo pressing on the deck could split the welded seams and advised me to leave the ship when possible. I had once witnessed myself when the ship was being loaded, crude oil coming over the tank tops on deck. The smell of the gas was intoxicating and dangerous with a static spark. I didn't think there was great danger with the overloading. Our chaps had built the ship it was strong but the British were not sailing her. When we got to sea it was apparent we were low in the water and the ships speed was reduced. With a heavy sea running, waves broke over the long deck. I decided I had had enough.

We had a regular run to the Sun Oil Co. and this lovely small town of Marcus Hook, fifteen miles from Philadelphia. A doctor made a visit to the ship. I went to him and showed him my tongue which was a bit black. He diagnosed stomach trouble and reported that I was run down and needed a check up ashore. This was where I took the opportunity to leave "M.V. Atlantic Duke". I went ashore with the Livanos Company Scottish Superintendent. We stood on the jetty for a while as Atlantic Duke moved away from the jetty. A telephone rang at a box near to us; the 'Super' picked it up. It was Georgio Livanos asking what was Atlantic Duke doing. The Super said "she is just going astern." Georgio then said "why is she going astern, she should be going forwards!" The Super told me this as we got in his car and laughed as we left the dock area. I marvelled as he drove over elevated roads, flyovers, common now in England.

We arrived in New York and he booked me into a hotel on 47th Street, off Times Square, for ten days. I paid a visit to the Livanos Offices in Wall Street. They made an appointment for me to have a medical examination with a doctor in a consulting room that overlooked Central Park. He said I was okay, probably run down.

The hotel did not do meals. I had to go out to a diner for my breakfast and I took the opportunity to see a bit of this famous city. There was a subway entrance only a few yards from the hotel on the corner of 47th and Times Square. I used it to go down to the Battery Gardens looking onto the river and saw the great Cunard Liner Queen Mary coming in. She sounded her ship's horn. It was a strong low pitched sound that vibrated pleasantly in one's ears just long enough to announce her presence without being a nuisance. I felt proud and amused to see people as they walked past turn to each other and mouth the words, "Queen Mary." I decided to seek a passage home and went to the Cunard Shipping offices to price a passage to the U.K.. For me the lowest tariff would cost £60. I could just afford it if necessary.

I visited Livanos Company office again and had a chat with the big man himself Georgio Livanos. He asked me to stay with the company "you will become Chief Engineer" he said. I thanked him and said I would like to go home. I was sick I told him, but I was actually sick of working with 'nice but hectic people,' however I didn't tell Georgio that!

A passage home was arranged on a Livanos, USA built, "Liberty Ship" leaving in a day or so from Newport News, Virginia. Livanos Company were prepared to give me a passage home which was kind of them They wanted me to fly to Newport News to join this vessel going to Europe. I said I had heavy luggage. I'd never flown before and preferred to go by a 'Greyhound' coach from the impressive New York Central Station. The bus wheels were five feet high, the engine mounted underneath. It was a twelve hour journey, with limited stops, doing ninety miles an hour on the turnpikes

It was dusk by the time we called at Washington DC for a comfort stop and exchange of passengers. Now on the open road we passed mile after mile of flat fields, some brown soil others with what looked like corn maize. I was surprised how flat the whole country was all the way. This was where the American Civil War had been fought and over a hundred thousand men killed. We arrived at Newport News, Virginia, on a cold grey morning near some miserable docks. It was just breaking daylight, too early to look for the ship.

I sat in the comfortable bus station waiting room until about nine a.m. until the place gradually woke up. A black lady came and sat down beside me. I was getting some funny looks but thought no more about it. Twice on this journey I had made a spectacle of myself by sitting in the part of the waiting area reserved for black folk. The back of the bus was also taboo. I always preferred the back at home. This was 1952 in America. Gradually it dawned on me I was in the black section of the seating area again! I stayed where I was as a matter of principle but the folks must have thought me of me as being strange!

I found the ship ready to sail. I don't remember the ship's name, it was a wartime built USA Liberty ship. They had been expecting me and had waited a while. The Chief Steward showed me to a comfortable cabin and I ate with the Captain and his Family. He had a wife and a little girl about four years old with him. She was puzzled at first because I spoke in English with my limited Greek, then she got the idea and tried to help me.

We sailed from Newport News Virginia on this Livanos ex-American Liberty ship carrying a cargo of iron ore. This is a dreadful cargo that can shift and give trouble in a heavy sea. When the cargohold was opened up by the Chief Officer for an inspection I had a look down into the hold. The heavy iron ore appeared to be a small heap in the bottom of the hold. In a bit of a swell as the ship rose to the top of the wave the bow and stern sagged and vice versa. I don't like big ships even this one, only about ten thousand tons! It was an uneventful trip wallowing across the Atlantic at ten knots with the wind in the right direction.

After about ten or twelve days, which seemed like months, we entered the Kiel Canal at night and moored up. German Customs Officials came on board. I heard their voices as they passed along the accommodation corridor. They were in jovial mood and one said sotto voce "Heil Hitler" to muted laughter. It was very early morning, still dark, I dressed and went to the galley and had a pot of tea and a rough breakfast. The Captain saw me and said he had arranged for me to leave the ship with the shipping agent. An agent would arrive at about nine o clock to see me off.

I went to see what was going on in the saloon. Four or five German Officials were already there, they had arranged their interrogation interviews in the ships Saloon. They checked everything! The ships' cook, poor chap, was going through his manifest (list) of goods in stock with a very formal Customs official in green uniform, Long green overcoat with black edges to the collar, shiny black belt, peaked cap with gold braid, jack boots and fancy badges. The interview was conducted in English but the cook spoke very little English. With the bit of Greek that I had I was able to assist as interpreter in this assessment of the cook's stores. How many bags of sugar, raisins, potatoes, flour etc. What a load of useless information! Why did they need to know? The German Customs Officer thought I was Greek! He congratulated me on my command of English. "Thank you I said , but I am English!" This caused a bit of a flutter among the German officials who sat around the ships saloon. They looked at one another and returned to their duties in what seemed a more respectful manner.

I imagine they were wondering what an Englishman was doing coming from America on a Greek "tramp steamer" and leaving the ship in Germany. A spy comes to mind! In the Yorkshire vernacular "I said nowt!"

I left the ship; my pockets stuffed with "Camel" cigarettes and Havana cigars bought in New York. I was told by the Captain that even seven years after the war no one was allowed ashore with foreign currency. I put a twenty dollar bill and a few smaller notes in my sock. I had been messed about by Germans a lot in my short life and they were not going to give me any more trouble. Foreign currency and cigarettes were verboten (forbidden) in Germany even seven years after the war because of 'black market' problems. It probably wasn't then necessary so long after the war but Germans love having regulations. All contraband should be handed to the Customs officials to be locked away until the ship departed. I had bought Dorothy some nylon stockings,as well! They were not going to be locked away as I was departing before the ship. The Germans had not thought of that possibility! A shipping agent arrived, a tall good looking blond haired young German fellow in his early twenties, wearing a brown trilby hat and a long grey herring bone overcoat. He spoke better English than I did, he put me into a taxi to the railway station at Kiel. He gave me my rail ticket. I was very surprised to see it said from Kiel to Middlesbrough with instructions to change at Nieumunster. This seems strange but I do not remember buying any other ticket on the journey. Finally he gave me a ten deutschmark note from Livanos Co. to see me home on the route. I still felt uneasy being in 'enemy' territory. I personally hadn't signed any agreement of their surrender. It occurred to me that if we had capitulated in 1940 he might have been in England giving me a hard time. His honest face with pale blue eyes softened my angst. He could have kept the ten deutschmarks for himself, I wouldn't have known. The 'Heil Hitler' in the passage was probably a big joke to the Germans now! It had been a joke to us English always, especially since Charlie Chaplin's film "The Great Dictator."

I decided to be magnanimous and took a beautiful Havana cigar, plentiful and cheap in the USA at this time, from my inside pocket and gave it to him. His surprised face and pause changed to a beaming smile which gave me so much pleasure. I thought for a second he might have had me arrested for disobeying the Customs orders. It may have helped him to come to terms with our past history a bit. The enemy syndrome that bothered me was purged. Even now the stupid war still leaves a sense of sorrow, what misery a few men caused to millions of people. Why!

After the short local train journey from Kiel to Neumunster during which a burly passenger realised I was English and proceeded to tell me of the "bombbing" as he pronounced it, of Hamburg. The British and Americans had totally flattened the port. Churchill had decided that the German people would not want war to happen again in twenty five years time. With arm movements to illustrate the bombs falling he interspersed his story with German sounds of explosions, Booomb! Booomb! Booomb! People sitting near were taking an interest in this bit of theatre and I felt a bit threatened "yes" I replied, "we had the same, my house was damaged " This seemed to pass the responsibility for who bombed who over to them and the atmosphere calmed down. They started this bombing of civilians, did they expect me to apologise?

A silence existed until we came to Neumunster and I dismounted with my luggage on to a cold empty undamaged old railway station. A shop window had the usual items for travellers but I was only interested in something to eat. There wasn't much to choose from and decide to wait until I got on the train. I hadn't long to wait for the North Express train to come steaming into the station. I looked for a porter. A heavily built porter in a dark grey shirt, black trousers and a soft black cap with a shiny black peak came forward to carry my three cases to a carriage of the North Express, which was coming from Sweden to go to the Hook of Holland. He put a leather strap through the handles of the heavy cases and humping them onto his shoulder walked to the opposite platform and stowed the cases into my carriage. I only had the ten deutschmark note to give him for a 'tip' I gave it to him not expecting any change; I would soon be out of Germany and wouldn't need it. I had twenty dollars in my sock. He very honestly gave me nine marks and some coins back. I returned the loose coins to him to make the tip a mark and said "dankescheun", one of the few words I knew at that time. I wondered what life would have been like without the war? The depression may have continued, there's a thought! Money can always be found for wars it certainly makes the money go round!

It was a corridor train, warm and comfortable, I settled down for the long journey. Funny me noting that, In England we still had the old fashioned carriages generally unheated designed from the stage coach each with it's own door and seats on each side. .We trundled across Germany. I had nothing to read and dozed most of the time. It was now dark and I looked out at the lights of this country we had struggled against for five long wasted years and brooded on where we were going now. I got into conversation with an English gentleman in my carriage. He spoke with a cultured intelligent voice and said he was with the British diplomatic service. He asked me where I had been, I told him of my trip with Livanos Tanker Company and my wish now to get home. He suggested we go along to the dining car for dinner. He didn't say he would pay, but then I wasn't a "distressed British seaman."

I surreptitiously took the twenty dollar bill from my sock. I decided to have a succulent steak, meat was still rationed in the UK and I had had nothing to eat since my rough breakfast early that morning before leaving the ship and the ships cook still asleep. I sensed an air of servility from the waiter in the dining car. I probably used the last of the German marks, I would have given him a tip, there would be some German marks change, I was tired and didn't care. The diplomat asked me what I proposed to do now I was returning home. We discussed the options open to me and he recommended if I had no commitments to the contrary, to emigrate to British Columbia in Canada. He said the climate was very good. It was just north of California and there were excellent opportunities for young engineers. It was something I would have done if I had been single and free. The problem was I had commitments, a wife and mother in law and my own mother living on her own, I was all she had, and she would one day need me. I have no regrets.

The train stopped late in the evening as we came to the German border, police in uniforms reminiscent of the 1939 war thriller films came down the corridor stopping at each carriage to check passports and papers. I produced my temporary passport. I was a bit worried they would find some technical fault with it. I had sailed without an official passport. I had been annoyed that the first few trips into the USA I couldn't go ashore! The train waited at the German border, The German Police inspecting our papers with serious faces finally alighted, they were probably disappointed at being unable to discover some paper irregularity. I had been worried my Philadelphia British Consul Passport would give the Germans a problem, however it didn't seem to bother them. The inspection over the train moved slowly on a few hundred yards through 'no man's land' and stopped again. This was Holland. I hadn't a clue where I was. Dutch police, in light brown uniforms this time, more serious faces looking at the same papers. This was late 1952, the early years of the 'Cold War.' Everyone was looking for Russian Spies! England had quite a few upper class misguided fools who despised their own country for the ideology of a very dubious regime. They should have concentrated on putting their ideas to improving their own country but they were weak treacherous idiots incapable of improving anything. Finally the train pulled into some port of the Hook of Holland. There I boarded the ferry to cross the English Channel and home. I had felt strange in Germany which had been enemy territory a few years before. We crossed the English Channel in a cold but dry, fairly calm night to Harwich. I stood on the after deck of this pre-war channel ferry. It had probably gone to Dunkirk in 1940 to help bring back our army who had been so hopelessly overrun by the German panzers. What kind of Government and generals had been in charge of defending old England or Britain as we now are? My old granny could have done better. Churchill had been warning them for years but he was despised and called a war monger until the weak foolish ministers had to concede. Pity we ever had a parliament. A benevolent dictator like Cromwell is what's required. Or a strong King like Henry VIII. This was the mood I was in as I stood on deck all the way over from Holland. I was thinking this would probably be the last time I would be at sea.

The lights of England blinked up ahead; then we came ashore. I was pleased there was no great problem with Customs men. I was tired having travelled from Kiel to Neumunster somewhere near Hamburg, across Germany and Holland. The train north was there at Harwich to take me to Darlington. There I walked along the platform with a porter to the train for Middlesbrough. I promised myself this would be my last trip to sea. I would seriously consider the new I.C.I. Wilton chemical factory near Redcar. It would be a change from ships and engines. I would put up with the smells!

I returned to our little house in Newstead Road. It was December. I was reluctant to find a job immediately. I thought I would sign on as unemployed, as indeed I was! There was no holiday pay. I had paid national insurance all my working life. Time I got some back. I went into Middlesbrough Unemployment Exchange as it was called then.

I sat in a chair next to a tall Jamaican chap. We waited patiently, he was called to the person behind the little window and after some confidential conversation he came back and sat next to me. "They asked me if I can dig" he said with a Jamaican accent "I can't dig, can you dig?" "No I can't dig!" I said. I would learn to dig if I was desperate I thought. It was then my turn to speak to the face at the window and put my case, a British seaman home from the sea and unemployed. "No unemployment benefit for a British sailor" I was told. I was not even asked if I could dig or anything, just told to "get another ship and get to sea again!" The official attitude to the British seaman seemed to be 'out of sight, out of mind!'


# CHAPTER 19
## DEC. HOME, JOIN I.C.I. TO AVOID THE SEA

*Arriving home in December 1952. No more to go a'roaming.*
*Starting work at I.C.I. Wilton Works, Redcar. 4th January 1953.*

I settled in at home then after applying for a job at I.C.I. Wilton I was directed to present myself for work on the fourth of January 1953. New starters had to attend the Medical Centre for a comprehensive medical.

I was allocated a locker, and provided with a boiler suit and a pair of boots. It wasn't what I'd been used to in the family like shipyard, nor as an engineer officer in the Merchant Navy. It was very much like the Home Guard Army and took a lot of getting used to, mainly the type of people that had been recruited as foremen and assistant foremen. Probably they'd been blacksmiths, millrights or motor mechanics from their method of working. The mechanical fitters were of uncertain vintage too. Workers had been drafted from ICI works all over the country and houses provided for them. It seemed to me they were given priority in promotion. There is a Chinese saying, to people they wish to curse, "May you live in interesting times." It was very interesting work but I was only a number. I accepted the humility of being told how to do a job by supervisors who had much less experience than me. It amused me when their instructions went pear shape.

Imperial Chemical Industries, Wilton Works had been a green field site in 1947. Now after six years I.C.I. had built a power station and a polythene plant with a first class canteen, medical centre and workers amenities. I was put to work on to Polythene 2 construction. Polythene was then a recent plastic derived from crude oil. It was made by compressing the ethylene gas from the crude oil to approximately 30,000 pounds per square inch pressure. I was given instructions as to how to fit the strong steel pipes and connect them up to various parts of the plant. The compressors to compress the gas to this enormous pressure were made in Germany. They were driven by a shaft passing through the wall of the building by a seventeen foot multi-vee belt pulley system driven by large electric motors in this adjacent building. This design was to isolate any escape of the highly inflammable gas which could cause an explosion. We also installed the bases for these electric motors.

After about two years on construction work I was asked or delegated, I'm not sure which, to another new plant Thallic Anhydrite. I will not attempt to write about this plant's history. It was to make a form of artificial resin from naphtha, already made on a batch process, but now on a more profitable constant feed process. After spending a few years and millions of £'s on this plant and unable to operate it for more than a couple of days it was written off. Alexander Fleck the Chairman of the Main Board after an interview with each one of the various managers had given the management team an extra £1 million to make further modifications but the plant still failed to achieve the design expectations. My humble opinion of the plant from an engineer's point of view was I wouldn't have even contemplated such a design. A good hands-on engineer knows if a design looks right it'll work right and this plant didn't look right, it was a very expensive Heath Robinson design! The thallic resin when molten had fumes I became allergic too. I developed bronchitis and was off work for two months. When I returned I reported to the Works doctor and asked to be transferred to the Nylon Works that had been built on Wilton Works for a few years now. He agreed but was emphatic that it was not the thallic fumes which had caused my bronchitis. I agreed to satisfy him and moved my gear to the Nylon amenities block. This enabled me to continue working for I.C.I. and I began to consider myself an I.C.I. Company man.

For a couple of years I worked in a team on the mechanical side of the works. Overhauling pumps and maintaining steam jacketed steel pipes carrying molten products. Other pipe lines ran in trenches and

248

over roads on steel framed bridges transferring liquids and gases to other parts of the works. It was menial work to that of a marine engineer. There were no engines to speak of but pumps and small machines all driven by electric motors. The pay was good and the conditions were as good as the Company could make them. Dorothy and I would often go to dances at the I.C.I. recreation club. Holidays with pay was something we enjoyed too after the poor working conditions in shipping.

I was offered a transfer to instrumentation, a new occupation that had arisen over the post war years with I.C.I's excellent innovative outlook. This was due to the automation control of the five plants that made up Nylon Works. Each plant had a large control room with scores of instruments some controlling and recording, others indicating tank levels, flow of materials and so on. I was given a six weeks courses on electronics and other disciplines involved with automatic control valves that operated on low pressure compressed air. After a couple of years on general Instrument work I was asked to maintain the instrumentation of a plant control room. This was very satisfying and I enjoyed my job until my retirement from I.C.I.

First Aid training was available and I thought it was something that would be useful. It was very good training. Doctors acting for St John's Ambulance Service examined us for certificate awards. A team of 'injured' actors wore make up to show various injuries and from our investigations we diagnosed their injuries and provided first aid treatment. It had to satisfy the doctors of our proficiency. When the real thing happened, there was not always time for the official treatment.

One day a leak of sodium gas ignited and blew the roof off a section of the Thallic Plant. Two or three men were burnt about the face, not seriously, but suffered shock. I treat them as 'walking wounded' with blankets to keep them warm until the works ambulance arrived. The nursing sister arrived with the ambulance and wanted the men as stretcher cases with the blankets just so! Fires were still blazing on the plant and there was danger of further explosions so I told the ambulance man it was not necessary to stretcher the casualties, they were walking wounded, remove them as quickly as possible and be ready to return for more. When the firemen arrived there was a problem of using water to put out the fires because sealed drums of sodium blocks in oil may have been open to the air. Sodium is a grey putty like substance, it produces hydrogen gas when immersed in water and the hydrogen gas explodes readily.

I.C.I. was a good Company to work for. One or two of its lower managers, who came from all kinds of backgrounds, resented a man who knew the answers to some of the engineering problems. Others wanted your expertise to deal with a problem but also wanted to take the credit for it. This attitude damaged the Company when they promoted less able men who would not expose their own weaknesses and suppressed men who were more experienced. I became tolerant towards the system; I didn't want to be exposed to the rivalry that pervaded the foremen class. The pay was good and the demand for the product seemed certain for many years.

Dorothy and I decided to move to a larger house. We looked at new houses being built in the village of Marton six miles south of Middlesbrough. We saw a nice three bedroom semi-detached house with a biggish rear garden. The price was £1900. We had to put a deposit on it and then sell our house in Newstead Rd. I had no problem finding a buyer for our Middlesbrough house but I made the mistake of accepting the buyer's advice to use his solicitor, He said it would save time and money. Only for him it did! His solicitor's search found that a "Max Lock" Town planning scheme involved our road being extended to form a cross town route. Our house number 34 was to be demolished. The buyer wanted us to drop our price. I took advice from another solicitor who put the words in my mouth "you're not going to drop it are you?" We didn't drop the price, but property was going up at the time and with solicitors fees we made nothing on the sale. We were resigned to take the loss and move to a better location and house.

Marton was the village where the great navigator and seaman Captain James Cook was born in 1728. We attended Saint Cuthbert's Church where he was baptized. He only lived here for a few childhood years then moved six miles to Great Ayton where he went to school. He later worked for a Mr. Walker of Whitby. Eventually he acted as an agent for Mr Walker, meeting ships coming up the coast from Dover and doing business with cargo at various ports en route before moving on to his years of exploring the seas to discover New Zealand and Australia

When we first came to look at the house in Gypsy Lane, the walls were only built up to the first floor. The road already had some houses built before the war. The original lane that remained was narrow with

250

eight foot high hedges on either side. Fields opposite the house ran through half a mile of country to Marton village. The back of the house had fields that went a mile or more to Nunthorpe village. There was no street lighting. A butchers shop 'Bruntons' was next to the village pub called 'The Rudds Arms', both.half a mile away down the narrow country road which ran into the village. On that first visit to see the house Dorothy had looked around at the rather wild area and said, "I don't want to be buried in the country." I replied "don't worry, the town will come out to meet us!" I never imagined that in time we would have wide roads with so many traffic lights, and be surrounded by estates of hundreds of houses as we have been. It was all for the good, within fifteen years we had good new schools for our son and shops nearby too.

Mr Cresswell, the builder, didn't want to put in any extras such as additional power sockets. Only one was allocated to each room. We had to go to town to choose the fireplaces. There was no such thing as central heating. Things were still rationed to a certain extent, this was October 1954 and building materials were in short supply because there was a lot of building going on.

People take for granted the schools, shops and street lighting which were lacking in the early years. In those early days one of the indigenous locals, Mr Bartram, set up a travelling shop. A butcher from Great Ayton came around every Friday evening. The newcomer housewives who gathered around the vans to do their weekly shopping became good friends and helped each other with baby sitting and other social acts of kindness.

On New Year's Day 1955, the 'North Yorkshire Hunt' came down Gypsy Lane. It was a colourful sight, the huntsmen in their red coats on fine horses, the dogs milling around. The horn sounded and they were off over the fields and away. I don't envy them as I'm more of a beachcomber myself. Why do good socialists dislike the people who can afford these activities. It's colourful and does no great harm. The same people who can afford it generally support and volunteer to manage and help many other unpaid activities that local governments find they are unable to undertake for some reason or other.

There was much to do in a new house. The walls were painted with emulsion and the floors were bare boards. We moved in in October. Our Indian carpet from the Newstead Rd house went into the front room and I stained the bare floorboards around it. The kitchen with it's

251

concrete floor had only a sink in a corner with a wooden draining board, a gas heated hand operated washer with a manual wringer, and a gas oven. An old chest of drawers cut down, made a work top. The breakfast room where we ate was heated with a paraffin oil heater. This produced a lot of condensation and the walls ran with moisture.

The first alarm came after heavy rain. Flood water ran down the fields at the back of the house and the rain water unable to soak readily into the heavy clay land formed pools, the level slowly rising. I was at home and kept looking at the situation hoping it would not become any worse. The water eventually reached the drive of the house. Dorothy had had a dark blue Wilton carpet fitted in the hall and up the stairs. It was very expensive and had been hand sewn around the edges to fit the area. They didn't fasten carpet down in those days. I prepared for the worst and lifted the carpet and was thinking what I could do to save the furniture. Luckily the flood water ran across the road and didn't get any higher. The builder of the houses put in bigger surface water drains and this episode was not repeated. Marton is a hundred feet above sea level; I had not expected floods at this level.

Dorothy and I now considered the time was right to start a family, I had a steady job where the future looked bright, the economy of the country was improving and we were happy and contented.

It was in autumn 1957, that Dorothy told me I was going to be a daddy. She had known earlier but wanted to be sure. Her mum was delighted and said she hoped it would be a boy because she had wanted a boy when she had brought Dorothy into the world. I'm not too keen in writing of my personal life but continuity requires the telling of it. On the 16th April at nine o clock in the evening I took Dorothy to the maternity hospital in Middlesbrough. At five thirty next morning the phone in the hall rang, I jumped out of bed and practically fell downstairs grabbing the phone to be told by a nurse that Dorothy had given me a son.

John grew up to be a boy we could both be proud of. From the local comprehensive school he went to Newcastle University for five years to become a Dental Surgeon and became an associate of a local dental practice. When the Principal retired, John with another associate bought the business and now have a busy practice. My granddaughter is now in her third year at Leeds University reading medicine.

With my loving wife and a happy marriage I have avoided the trials and tribulations that coming from a broken home may have given me.

It is a lesson for any person interested in sociology. Have I been lucky? "Yes!" I believe people have to make their own luck, no expert can tell people how to achieve it. Just keep your nose to the grindstone as my mum used to say and you'll get on, but only if the opportunity arises, and we have to be ready to grasp it when it does.

In the nineteen eighties I.C.I. was having problems with their business costs and were offering early retirement to certain categories of people. At fifty eight years of age I qualified for this move and I gave it some thought as to the consequences. I had thirty years of service with I.C.I.. I would get the company pension and a lump sum. I talked it over with Dorothy and we agreed to accept the change for the good of my health as much as anything. I was too old to seek a job anywhere else, I thought!

During a rare visit to my doctor to see if he had any solution to a bit of sinus trouble which came from the many years of ammonia fumes often present on the Nylon plant I was attached to, he checked my blood pressure. He said it was very high. He put me on a beta blocker. This controlled my blood pressure and had little side effects except to slow my pulse down. I wasn't the type to lose my temper, it didn't achieve anything and in my job I needed to keep a cool head to solve the problems that arose in the control room and on the plant.

Marton village was now a suburban sprawl. Two adjacent district councils can't agree about diverting the road leading south from Middlesbrough to create a bypass that would relieve the amount of traffic flow. The traffic had increased steadily from 1955 until later years the result at peak times is the 'Marton Crawl'. Vehicles back up at every junction on the six miles from town, then crawl along to the next junction. The area is saturated; it can only get worse.

When we first set up house in Marton in 1954 Dorothy had joined St. Cuthbert's Parish Church and made many friends. I joined her in the Church activities. It could be hard work with jumble sales and garden parties but it was a lot of fun too.

One of my axioms when I was working in difficult conditions is that, nothing lasts forever. It had helped me get through many difficult periods in my life. In 1963 for example, my mum who had had an operation for cancer was unable to continue running her own home and had gone into Council sheltered accommodation. In 1966 after a few weeks in Hemlington Hospital, very near to our house in Marton, I was visiting her every evening. On my last visit I found her asleep and after sitting there for some time I left her a little note of something not important but just to let her know I had visited. Next morning the phone rang, it was the Hospital to say she had died early that morning. I had to go and collect her clothes. I left her new slippers and dressing gown with the ward. The nurses were always pleased to have decent stuff for old ladies in need. Mum's funeral was just a couple of weeks before her seventieth birthday on the 29th January. It upset me very much. We had been through such a lot of difficult times together. She had been a very happy person always willing to help anyone in need and well able to get them over their troubles. It pleased me that Mrs Scrafton's little Spiritual Church was well represented at the funeral service at Middlesbrough Crematorium. I was too upset to respond to people's kindness. It took me four years to shake off my disappointment for that's what it was. I had forgotten that nothing lasts forever, best to enjoy what you have and I had a loving wife and Dorothy's family still to enjoy.

*Our last holiday in Mallorca 2003. Dorothy was a good sailor when all around her were feeling sick.*

*My Dad Fred Dinsdale and my son John, at the Rover Stand, Stewarts'*
*Park 1966*

I was there when Dorothy needed me. Her sweet and lovely Mum
took ill one night after washing up the supper pots. Dorothy had put
John to bed and I was on night shift, ten pm 'til six am. I had left to go
to work about 9.30pm. When I arrived on the Nylon plant the boss
came out of his office and said, "you've got to go straight back home."
No reason was given. I went back to the car and when I arrived home
they were putting Dorothy's mum into the ambulance. Dorothy went
with her in the ambulance. Our GP, Dr Boyes was in the house waiting
for my return, to look after John. We went to the hospital next day to
see Dorothy's Mum, however she was in a coma. Within a few minutes
as we stood by the bed, she passed away as if she had been waiting for
us to arrive before she departed. Years later if ever Dorothy was cross
with me, I would say, "you wouldn't be allowed to speak to me like that
if your mother was here," and we'd have a laugh. I had been the son she
had always wanted and I was pleased to play the part.

After my mother had died one of my brothers, who had been
brought up by my father's family, invited me to attend the 1966
Cleveland Show in Marton's Stewart's Park. I was invited to call at the

Rover Car stand where my father, who had the Rover franchise for South Durham and North Yorkshire, would be holding Court. New model cars were on display in the area around the Rover Company caravan, there to take orders and entertain past customers as guests. I took John aged eight with me. I was told that my father was inside and to go in. He was sat in a comfortable carver chair with a cigarette in one hand. He looked an old but distinguished gentleman elegantly dressed in a light tweed suit and dogtooth overcoat. His grey bowler hat was on his knee and he had a tall glass half full of light amber fluid nearby. His whisky and water I presumed. We had little to say. I introduced him to his grandson John. "A good family name," he said, which quite surprised me! Many years later doing some family research I found that his great-grandfather was a John Dinsdale. An acquaintance of my father's came in to see him and he introduced me as his son and said about me, "he has just lost his mother." This sounded very strange coming from my father, for my mother had also been his wife! I left saying I would visit him at the business where he lived in his office, a large back room which looked out onto the upmarket car showroom.

*Captain John Loupis and the author aboard M/V Mary P, 1964* *(see page 259)*

I did go to see my Dad now every week often during the day when I was on shift work. I did tell him that Mum had told me he played the cello while she played the piano. "She didn't play very well," he said! You should have given her a few more years to practice I thought, but he had mellowed a lot and I didn't want to rock the boat. He had had a housekeeper but she probably got fed up with him. He had always been a hard man to deal with and she left him. I often wonder if he ever wished he had been a good husband to Jessie his very capable wife who would have really cared for him. He threw it all away because he would not set a home up for her when he could well afford it.

I was told by a nephew who worked in the business that two men in white coats came one day and dragged poor old Fred out of his office chair yelling for help and took him to a Nursing Home at Middleton St George. I went to visit him every week. The male nurse would unlock his door and let me in. At first he had his whisky sent in, always 'Ballantines,' and we would have a drink. There was only one glass so we shared it. It was like a communion cup. I became sorry for him having to spend his last days in this narrow bedroom.

He asked me to go and see his solicitor Jack Trotter, to get him out of the place. I made an appointment and passed the message on. "Oh yes," said Mr Trotter, "I will go and see him" was the reply. He had been my dad's solicitor for many years. He had probably arranged my father's business to become a limited company of 10,000 shares, 5,001 in my father's name and the 4,999 shares divided between my two brothers and his live in secretary cum dogsbody who had worked in his office from being a girl. Mr Trotter as the Company solicitor was probably involved in my father being sectioned and spirited away. There is some doubt about the fact that he was sectioned, as he was lucid when he wanted to be. The result of my father's request to see Mr Trotter was that his medication was adjusted. A few weeks later my father 'conveniently' died before any more action might have intervened, not that I was tempted to go any further but I met the male nurse and he told me my father's medication had been discontinued.

Earlier when my father was in one of his lucid moments I told him he had been a hard man. He cried, tears ran down his face. It was difficult to forgive him for all the damage and suffering he had inflicted on us all, his own family! He suffered self-inflicted misery. I doubt if he had ever been really happy for all the posing in his red coat riding to the hunt, racing outboard speedboats and sailing his forty eight ton yacht out of Whitby harbour to France. Always at the back of his mind did he not think that nothing lasts forever and what will the future be? Perhaps he didn't!

I attended his funeral. Jack Trotter the solicitor was there. He was a burly florid faced man and gave me an anxious guilty look. He died three months later. I had obtained a copy of my father's Will from Somerset House and was able to see how the estate had been left. I had been left two hundred and fifty pounds in the Will, the same amount as the six grandchildren, but excluding John. A codicil to the Will had for some reason later cancelled my interest. A solicitor friend of mine later called at my house and asked me if I wanted to contest the Will. I had not asked him to come to discuss it, I hadn't thought of it in fact. He said I had a good right to something but I declined the offer. I had no interest in the business which eventually went into liquidation. I thought my two brothers were entitled to all they could get from it. I didn't need any of it. What I had wanted was what I had been deprived of, a good family. They had experienced a dysfunctional family. I had experienced being deprived of many things money could buy but was more fortunate with having a sensible mother.

My going to sea with the Greek Oil tanker M/V Atlantic Duke now brought an interesting period into our lives. The Chief Engineer Michael Loupis had often written to me in his best calligraphy, as he was so proud to call it, from various ports of call. He would have liked me to join the Livanos Company again but I was now settled in I.C.I. for a long run with a pension at the end of it. I had no need of the lonely life of a sailor.

Arising from my encounter with the Loupis family Dorothy and I had had our first holiday abroad in August 1978. This was following an invitation from John Loupis, the son of Chief Engineer Michael Loupis. I had formed a good friendship with Michael in the months we worked together sailing on the oil tanker Atlantic Duke. On one of the 1951 ports of call he had introduced me to eighteen year old John, then a third officer studying to become a Captain. Michael had kept in touch for ten years before we were to meet again. This was in 1963 when he came to supervise work on one of Livanos' ships M/V Atlantic Lord in dry dock at Smith's Dock for a few weeks refit.

We invited Michael, the Captain and a few of the ship's officers to our house and we had a bit of a party. Michael spent some time with us. He was staying in a hotel near our house and I invited him to have an evening meal with us a few times. Dorothy's mother made a fuss of him giving him English specialities of sea food he so enjoyed like crab and kippers. The Greek sailors often spent five years away from home in those days. Jobs were scarce in Greece and there were many men ready to step in if a vacancy occurred. He came to say goodbye before they sailed away and that was the last time I saw him. He was a very good friend and a gentleman. His son John phoned a few years later to say that his father had died at the age of seventy two years. A life spent mainly at sea. He had retired but only lived for a year or two to enjoy the wonderful detached home he had had built in the best part of Athens. Heavy smoking would probably account for his early death.

When in port if the harbour held any fish he would drop a hand-line over the ship's stern. On one occasion when he had caught a small flat fish he phoned me to come up to his cabin after my watch for a can of beer and to eat the fish which he had salted and put in his fridge. We ate it raw, fish doesn't need much cooking. I remember the humorous stories he liked to tell especially of Mr Crook a Superintendent of the Company who he said was an Alopix, in Greek 'a sly fox', with his accompanied gentle rumbling laughter.

In 1964 his son Yanni, John in English, who was now a Captain phoned me. He had brought his ship carrying gas from Algiers into Hartlepool. He said he would take a taxi to come and visit us. He came with his Chief Engineer and spent the evening with us. Captain John invited Dorothy and I with John, now aged six, to visit his ship the M/V Mary P. (MV is Motor Vessel). We had an excellent Greek dinner on board. The steward waited on table and the cook was delighted to have visitors aboard to cater for. Each dish was produced with enthusiasm and we made appropriate acclaim of praise for their efforts.

Early in 1975 a surprise phone call came from London. It was John Loupis again. He had taken his eldest son, Michael, named after his father, to a London eye specialist. A gust of wind had slammed a window shut in their apartment; the glass had broken and a small piece of glass had cut young Michael's eye. During this time we arranged for young Michael to stay with us, at a later date, for a month in August to improve his English skills.

Michael, fourteen years old, flew into Heathrow, travelled to Kings Cross and caught the train to Darlington where I met him for the first time. It wasn't difficult to pick him out. He was the only young person not accompanied by an adult. I was very impressed by his maturity. A Greek, only fourteen years old, travelling alone through London. His character was equally impressive, polite but with a strong sense of purpose beyond his years. We rented a cottage in Kames on the Kyle's of Bute for two weeks holiday. I had built a Mirror sailing dingy which we towed behind the car. We stopped at the Scottish Border for a sandwich and a flask of coffee which Dorothy had prepared. A car pulled up nearby and a Norwegian gentleman got out to take a break. He engaged us in conversation and satisfied with the interlude drove off. When he had gone Michael made a remarkable observation saying, "what a thin voice that man had!" The word thin was most appropriate and more expressive than funny or high as one might expect from a young teenager but coming from a Greek youth speaking English impressed me very much. The cottage looked onto the beach where we were able to keep the boat. The weather was very poor, for the first few days. We went to the local shop and bought a bag of coal. Michael hadn't seen coal before and I showed him how we lit a fire with paper and sticks. He was fascinated by it and called it carbon. He took a piece of coal home to show his family. He complained that Greece had no minerals but limestone and marble.

We sailed the dingy up and down the two or more miles of the Bute passage used it to go fishing from time to time. The Scottish seas were full of fish then. We were catching mackerel four at a time. Dorothy cooked the fish but we were asked not to repeat it. The conditions improved and one afternoon I rowed all of us over to the Isle of Bute just to have the view from the other side.

Young Michael spoke better English than I did. One day he was laughing at me and I asked him what he was laughing at. He replied "you because you are going around saying where's me glasses?". You should say "where are my glasses?" But I surprised him too at times with some Greek phrases. We did exchange some of our idiomatic sayings for example, "it's raining stair-rods, or cats and dogs." They say in Greek "it's raining chair legs", "Eina vreki Kareklas" in Greek. Another translation problem was with the English question, "what's the matter?" Michael couldn't understand its meaning. I explained it meant "what is happening?" Michael told me in Greek it was, "Ti trekki etho," or "what is running here?" The English alphabet doesn't help the translation. As I write this Michael is now almost fifty years old. We still keep in touch though I'm sure we will none of us ever forget our Greek / English family ties. In 1978 Captain John Loupis kindly invited us to arrange to visit them at their home in Athens for a couple of weeks in August.

I thought that Dorothy would be alarmed at going abroad. People like us didn't do that sort of thing then. I told Captain John of Dorothy's possible reservations and he replied, "let me speak to her" he said in a

Captain's commanding voice. I passed the phone over to Dorothy and watched her face as he spoke for a few minutes. A serious looking Dorothy affirmed what he said and that was that. We were going to Greece!

The flights were booked and we arrived at the airport to a Loupis family greeting. We were whisked off to their apartment in central Athens. August was extremely hot but we did some sightseeing taken by car to the nearby Acropolis and walked up to the ancient Parthenon. John told me of the Greek soldier who the Germans had told to take down the Greek flag. Reluctantly he did so then wrapping himself in the flag, he threw himself off the edge of the Acropolis and killed himself. That is the kind of proud people the Greeks are. I was very moved at the sublime beauty of the Parthanon in solid marble. How do such civilisations fall into decay? But as I say, "nothing lasts forever, more's the pity." Captain John was at home for a few months due to oil tanker ships being laid up which was convenient for our visit. We only stayed a couple of nights in Athens and then went by car to the family's summer house between Oropus and Kalamos, eighty miles from Athens, on the north coast facing the Isle of Evvia.

The summer house was about a couple of hundred feet from the beach, two stories high clinging to the side of a dry ravine which ran down to the sea. It had a wide veranda all around the building with a marble composite floor. On the kitchen side of the house we ate at a table on the veranda. We practically lived al fresco and slept on single beds on the open veranda. With a sea breeze it was comfortably cool in the shade. We went en family to the beach after a lazy breakfast. John's wife Anthi had prepared a meal in a big commercial square stainless steel baking utensil and handed it in to the beach taverna to be cooked for us at one o clock. After swimming, not very well on my part but Michael was like a bronze fish in the water and dived to bring us sea urchins from the sandy sea bed. They cut them open and ate them raw, I tried one but it did not have much taste to me. As one o clock neared Dorothy John and I with seventeen year old Michael, and his younger brother Kostas trailed back to the house. John and his wife Anthi brought the cooked meal back to the house in the car. After a satisfying meal with a couple of glasses of the local retsina wine we would have a siesta from two o clock until about five. This was the routine for all the residents in their summer houses scattered over both sides of the bowl shaped ravine. The sun directly overhead beat every living thing

261

into a torpor of silent stillness. Not a bird squeaked!

At five o clock life would slowly recover. Strong Greek coffee made with a brikee, a small teacup size steel pan boiled enough water to make each cup of strong coffee. This was loaded with three teaspoonfuls of sugar and sipped with appreciation leaving a layer of thick coffee grounds in the bottom of the cup. The men would establish their macho image by not shaving for several days. It seemed their way of rebelling against the discipline of their formal business life. The Greek character seemed very positive to me. There was no understatement as we would have in Britain. All was black or white!

One evening Captain John put a black polythene bag of household rubbish out by the side of the narrow road. We were sat talking and taxes came into the conversation, I asked John what rates he paid on the summerhouse property? "What are rates," he said. "It is the local tax we pay," I replied. John raised his voice an octave or two, "I pay my taxes, why to have a local tax, that is enough," he replied. "Well who pays to take the garbage away?" I said. "I don't know, maybe when I pay the electric bill they take so much," he replied. I decided to be satisfied with that, it was something he didn't like to talk about! Next morning a lorry with about six men came along the narrow roads collecting the rubbish. Democracy was at work in the cradle of the democratic system. Bureaucrats must have a hard time in Greece.

John's next door neighbours were Eleftheria, freedom in Greek and her husband Demitreous, Jimmy in English. They had a boy Kosta nine years old and daughter Effie eleven. Kostas was nicknamed Bouloukos in Greek because he he they said he was fat! Poor kid. I would say he wasn't fat but chubby, a very happy boy always with a smile on his rosy face.

John and Jimmy decided to take us by car to show us the Greek countryside as far as Volos and the Meteora. Dorothy and our son John went with Effie in the Loupis family car, I went with Jimmy and Eleftheria's in their car. I sat in the front with Jimmy who was not very confident with his English but I had some Greek and Kosta Loupis with his pal Bouloukos Kostas, fat Kostas, both spoke good English and like Michael they had very sweet gentle accents. They enjoyed helping me with interpreting the word I was looking for in Greek. Greek is a big language with three forms, the Ancient Greek, the more formal Katharavaser Greek and the Demotic people's Greek.

It has evolved in written form for a couple of millennia. It has many word distinctions to apply to a case where we have only one or two in English. It makes interpretation of the Greek sentence to an English person difficult if they choose a word unfamiliar to him.

It took a few hours drive to reach Volos stopping on the way once or twice for a comfort stop. We passed a lake or reservoir I was told which served Athens. The whole plain of Attica seemed to be occupied by the city of Athens at that time.

Volos was very much like any other Greek harbour. It had a wide frontage with a few fishing boats and ferries alongside as far as I can remember. I do remember the small bronze model of the ancient vessel commemorating Jason's trip with the Argonauts to find the golden fleece. We booked into a very nice hotel and went out for a typical Greek meal. Plates of different things on the table to partake of and plates filled again where necessary. We never saw any smashing of plates in the tavernas by the way! That's only for tourists. Next day we toured around the Meteora, There were very few cars on these roads. We passed through one or two white washed villages that had not seen any changes for many years. Old men some fat others very thin sat on the ubiquitous kitchen chairs outside the white washed cottages, all with a few days growth of white whiskers on sunken cheeks, sitting in little groups. Some of them played backgammon or other board games on small square tables.

We came to one small town where Jimmy called into a shop for a few minutes where he had some business to attend to. I never found out what his business was but he was a happy man and whatever it was he had no worries about it. However a few years later I was sad to hear that Jimmy had some financial difficulties and the family disappeared from the radar. Jimmy's wife Eleftheria was a lovely lady and was very upset when they had to give up their lifestyle. Anthi consoled her but I never heard any more about them.

We came to this area with many strange 'sugarloaf' mountains standing a few hundred yards from each other. These were the Meteora, and many of them had a monastery perched on the top. Access was by a winch and basket arrangement. One of these monasteries was accessible from the road so we were able to go in part of the building but the women had to have covered arms and shoulders and Captain John was angry because he was not allowed in wearing his shorts. "What is the matter with them," he said, "do my bare legs excite the monks. Bah!" There was nothing much to see, a few small icons and we could light a candle for a few drachmas. How did this life in a monastery arise from Christianity I asked myself?

Michael and his cousin Michael Komianos, both eighteen years old, came to stay with us for a month in August 1981 before they went to Athens University. We took them to see much of the Yorkshire countryside. They were fascinated by York Minster. "Why so big?" said Komianos gazing up at the high columns. The Yorkshire moors were a lesson for them as a cold wind blew through their thin jackets. They said, "if it's like this in August then what is it like in winter?"

In Whitby, sheltered from the wind, it was more amenable and they were interested in the walk along the piers out into the North Sea. The old lifeboat was inspected as were the fishing boats lying along the quayside. I'm sure we had fish and chips sat by the bandstand because it's what we always did when in Whitby! It was pleasing to have been able to entertain them and give them the experience of British life.

John took them to the local pub one night. When they arrived back home he told Dorothy and I that Komianos had flirted with the young barmaid and had nearly dragged her over the bar! It amused him and we found it had been taken in good part by the locals. They then left us to fly back to Athens.

Unexpectedly a day or so later, Michael telephoned to inform me that his father Captain John had been very ill when they got back home and he had subsequently died. Michael said it was a very painful death. He was not yet fifty years old. It was a shock to us, he was so young and we had lost a very good friend. He had complained of back ache when we were visiting in 1978. I understand he had lung cancer and like his father he was a heavy smoker. I was surprised the doctors could not give him pain relief. Michael was crying as he told me. I wished I could have held him and comforted him but there was little I could do. I wrote to express my sorrow to Anthi and said they must think of John as being away at sea until we all come into our final harbour and they are together again.

Michael Loupis kept in touch while he was at Athens University and wrote to say he was coming with a friend to do a postgraduate. course at Bradford University, something to do with Computer design. This would be in 1984. I wrote back and said they must come and stay with us for a few weeks before they started at Bradford. An older Michael, now twenty one years old, came with his friend Gregori doing the same course. The Greeks still had primogeniture. Michael was now the head of the family. The family was in good hands. They arrived the day Dorothy and I were going on holiday. Dorothy had filled the freezer and fridge with food and they would have to fend for themselves for two weeks. When we returned the house was in good order and we got to know his friend Gregori Gealouse. He was a very cheerful and polite young man. His family had a farm in Greece but Gregori was disappointed in the farm being too far north to grow cotton which was a profitable crop. We took them to Whitby and across the Transporter Bridge to Hartlepool but our ancient buildings were nothing compared to the Acropolis.

After a few weeks to acclimatise them to our summer climate and British lifestyle I took them down to Bradford along with their luggage and they rented a house and moved in. Several weeks later they rolled up in a little old banger of a car Gregori had bought. It was tiny but I had to admire the nerve of the pair to drive it up from Bradford to Teesside. It could have gone so wrong if the little monster had broken down but this is the Greek brave temperament.

Gregori had a reasonably good knowledge of engineering and was interested in seeing a second hand tractor while he was here. They were very expensive in Greece and probably partly because of the cost of transporting the machine back home, not a good purchase from England. It would be more feasible coming from Germany or somewhere nearer Greece.

When their three month course ended they flew back home to start a career in computer communications. A year or two later Dorothy and I were invited by Anthi and Michael to come to Greece and stay with them for a couple of weeks. Michael's Uncle Niko Komianos divorced from his wife Maria (nee Loupis), also hosted our stay. It was his son who had stayed with us in 1981. Niko Komianos imported white goods into Greece and was an expert at entertaining Japanese businessmen I was told.

Anthi's birthday was celebrated at a country house restaurant with a vocalist who sang one song after the other so that conversation was deemed not polite. Figs were growing up the open side of the dining area and although the food was good Dorothy and I were like fish out of water. It was nice to see Anthi given a happy birthday and she radiated us with her appreciation. The next outing Niko arranged for us was a dinner at the Limani, the Little harbour where all the magnificent big yachts were berthed. They were tied stern up to the quay. Crew members in white slacks and shirts were on duty as one or two expensive cars would pull up alongside and more expensive females and partners would alight in evening gowns and suits to go aboard for dinner presumably. What else at ten o clock in the evening in Athens. The Greeks do eat very late in the kalo kari, translated it means, "good time", and is used as we use the dubious word summer. It's not a good time for all Greeks. I felt sorry for the waiters and people who had to work during this hot time.

Before we returned to England, Niko took Dorothy and I to a 'James Bond type of hotel', the Hotel Athenaum Intercontinental, 89 - 93 Syngrou Avenue, Athens. The floors were open mezzanines leaving the high and enormous centre space open from floor to ceiling to act as an instrument to show the rotation of the earth by a golden ball about fifteen feet in diameter. The ball, suspended and swinging from the ceiling by a long wire, had a pointer affixed which very slowly described a circle of several feet diameter marked out on the floor responding to the earth's axis. We sat for some time at a table with a drink, at the side of one of the floors, which were painted in shades of cream and gold colours. We gazed around at the upper class of high flyers visible on each floor. The room windows were all facing out row on row a very clever design. Niko obviously knew the staff here very well and spoke to one of the many managers for a while. I came away with a box of matches from the Kava cocktail lounge! Maybe that was the floor we had been on? It was quite an experience for a couple of poor Brits from Teesside!

The following day Michael saw us safely to the airport and we had a good flight home. We were coming back to our very different lifestyle of British weather with no exotic karpousi, the large green water melons we had been eating every day from Anthi's fridge. They were not introduced into Britain at that time and even now are not as big or often in demand. So our friendship with the Loupis family rested for a few years. Their sincere hospitality had been greatly appreciated. Life went

# CHAPTER 20
# RETIRED AFTER THIRTY YEARS
# WITH WILTON I.C.I.

*Retirement and the later years. A Night Porter's Job.*
*1998 Our holiday to celebrate our*
*Golden Wedding Anniversary in Rome and Sorrento.*

I had retired from I.C.I. on the 28th January 1983 after thirty years of old fashioned loyal service. It then to rained for six months! Not very kalokeri as they say in Greece. Do you remember the Greek words for good time? Not very conducive to doing jobs outside. Being retired I wanted to start replacing window frames at the back of the house. I passed some time reading in the local branch Library and did a few indoor jobs around the house. I now started going to church with Dorothy and enjoying the company at the church socials. At one social in the Marton Hotel, we sat at a table with the Vicar and his wife. I was surprised when he had supped three pints of beer in the time I only had managed one! It showed he was human and I took to him. He didn't drive so I offered to take him on his parish visits to the housebound. He was down to earth, a nice chap and we remained friends for many years until he died. .

Having completed work on the house a job advertised in the newsagent's shop window interested me. We were managing to live on my Company pension and an annuity I had invested for ten years but I had six years to wait before my State pension was due and I found myself at a loose end, bored in fact. A job would give me an interest and what I might earn give us both a better lifestyle. The vacancy was for a night porter's post in a local hotel. I didn't want too stressful a job and thought this would be interesting. I discussed it with Dorothy who had been used to me being on shift work and working nights too. Our son John was married now and she would be on her own at night but she agreed for me to apply. I phoned and the current manageress Janet Smith answered. In a broad Manchester accent she asked, "how old are you?" Oh, I thought, this would bar me but I told her the truth, I was sixty three. "That's all right as we don't want anyone too young" she said. An interview was arranged and the hotel was conveniently near. When I arrived the place looked as if a bomb had hit it. Floorboards were up, fittings were ripped out, plaster and dust was everywhere. She took me into a tiny back office and gave me the job description. The hotel belonged to the Bernie Inns chain. The hours were ten thirty at night until eight thirty in the morning. The night porter who was leaving did not want to change from the ledger system to the computer system which was being introduced. "Would I be able to manage a computer," she asked? I replied "yes," because in I.C.I., I had some experience of programming and early computers. It was a commercial hotel with twenty three rooms. I was given a green jacket to wear and would be behind reception. I had a chat with the other night porter they had interviewed, who said he had no occupational pension and would like to work four nights. I would be satisfied with three and we mutually agreed that I would work three nights, Sunday, Monday and Tuesday. He would work the other four nights. The hotel refurbishment took another few weeks to complete.

After working several nights I discovered the job description would be more accurately described as night manager. The boss's accommodation was attached to the hotel. After cashing up the bars and restaurant and doing what they called their actuals and voided meals on the computer they were sent off by email to head office in Northampton. The manager then went off to their abode leaving me to get the bars customers away and see the staff off home. There was always one or two residents to check in, arriving late. Part of the job was to run the lounge bar for one or two of the residents who often entertained guests until after midnight. The boss would tell me if we had any entertainers coming in late who were out performing at some venue. On one occasion a troupe of Irish musicians came in at about one a.m. with their instruments and sat winding down until nearly four in the morning. They were very well behaved and I enjoyed their company for a while at the bar but I was glad when they decided to retire for the night. It was the best job I could have chosen. I seemed to have the right temperament for it. Two lady cleaners came in at six thirty in the morning for a couple of hours hovering and dusting. There was a busy turnover of residents, often staying for only one night. Exceptions were teams of young men on special missions who would come down with surveillance equipment at six in the morning. They returned from their surveillance before I came on duty next night and repeated the early morning exists for a week or more. The residents who were leaving had breakfast and left before my shift ended. I had a float of thirty pounds and checked residents out who were leaving and then entered the transaction in the computer. When a late customer came in for a room I had to put that let into the accommodation frame of the computer. The Restaurant and bar frames of the computer were closed during the transmission to Head Office. The night porter was the only person who handled cash so I was very careful with the hotel's business. One night stand arrivals, gentleman would expect me to give a discount after midnight but generally I weighed the customer up and charged accordingly. Gentleman and his lady... with posh car... no luggage...and his excuse I'm tired driving it's a rotten night, we'll break our journey? Yes sir, but I'm sorry I'm unable to give a discount during the week. We always had a good occupation of our rooms. But it was nice to let the last one or two rooms if possible.

Weekends were different because the hotel was nearly empty. I found it easy to judge the genuine cases, and I would get what I could for the room. A complicated one was when a mini-bus pulled in late one night and a dozen Ghurkha soldiers piled out. The young officer in charge asked me if I could take them in. I said, "but you'll need three or four rooms and the full rate would be more than they could afford." I wanted to help these lads because I knew of the loyal service they had given to our country and they only wanted a comfort stop. I eventually let them have one room for £25. That was well below the going rate for a double room. They would be able to use the bathroom and doss down for a few hours but first I would make them coffee and sandwiches on the house. He seemed pleased with the offer and I showed them into the lounge bar and sat them down at the round tables while I went into the kitchen and made two big stainless steel jugs of coffee and a pile of ham sandwiches. I left them to get on with it while I went into reception to put my unconventional let into the log book. They couldn't have afforded more but I had made a sale and the company was £25 better off. They finished off the food and all trouped up to the room. I left reception and went over to the bar to clear up the coffee cups and things but those lads had done it for me, the tables were clean and everything moved back into the kitchen. The young Ghurkha officer told me they were on their way from Catterick camp to somewhere in Newcastle and thanked me for the comfort stop. They left early at about six a.m. I though I'd better check the room and on going up was very impressed to find it in pristine condition. No other group of residents would have behaved as impeccably. They must have dossed down on the floor. I felt very humbled and pleased at their kind response to the risk I had taken. I could have been in a bit of bother if they had upset the room.

I did contravene company rules one night when the boss told me a ships pilot was expected to come in late. I was to give him a room and whatever he wanted. He was a Dutch Pilot and had brought a Super tanker over from Rotterdam. These multi-million pound ships draw forty foot of water and the North Sea is not deep enough in places. The hotel had an account with the Shipping Company's Agents. He arrived and looked a bit stressed. He asked for a pint of lager and a sandwich, I gave him the pint and went into the kitchen and made him a beef sandwich. He then went to his room with instructions to call him at six a.m. with a taxi to the airport in order to fly back to Rotterdam. When I went to the computer to print his bill he said he had no English money for the taxi would I give him ten pounds and put it on the bill? The hotel rules said that no money was to be ever passed over the reception desk. In I.C.I. we had been told rules are for the 'guidance of wise men and the obedience of fools.' These pilots were very responsible and powerful men. If I refused this reasonable request the hotel could lose the account. The money was going on the bill, he would sign for it, what was there to be negative about? I too had been in a similar situation when ashore in a foreign port. I gave him ten pounds in change, put it on the bill and he signed it. When I came in the next night the boss who knew nothing of the circumstances started reading me the rule book. He couldn't understand why they needed a pilot to cross the North Sea and so on. I explained the how and why of the hotel's obligation to seamen in a major shipping port. He was an ex-chef who had talked his way to becoming a manager but he had a lot to learn. However he accepted my reason for breaking the rules and I had no more bother with him.

There were roughly sixty part time staff employed in the hotel, comprising barmaids, room maids, cleaners, etc. All were working sixteen hours a week to comply with their state benefits except for a few chefs and full time staff. I worked thirty hours a week but when it came to holidays if Alan, the other night porter, was on holiday I worked seventeen nights in a row! Alan likewise would do a long run of nightshifts when Dorothy and I went on holiday. It was a good time, Dorothy managed the house on my wage and we had my I.C.I. pension to fall back on if required.

Another manager and his wife took over. I was now a few weeks short of being sixty five. I mentioned to the boss that I should be retiring soon. "Oh, leave it until I settle in," he said. The time to retire never arrived. The managers were moved regularly every couple of years, my retirement was never brought up. The Hotel was taken over by other companies four times in the seven years I worked there. I must have made myself indispensible!

Breakfast was served at seven thirty a.m. prompt. Some residents wanting to be away early came down before seven thirty. One morning the chef hadn't arrived by five past seven. I went into the kitchen and turned on the grills and started grilling the bacon and tomatoes. I asked one of the cleaners to come into the kitchen to make the scrambled egg, orange juice and toast. At seven thirty I was able to serve breakfast and check out a couple of early leavers. The chef came in at nine o'clock. I later heard that there was some confusion as to who was on early turn.

Now Dorothy was able to save both our pensions. Dorothy's pension was for the years she worked as secretary at the local school. These were good times, I was semi-retired, and we were both young enough to enjoy life and had enough time to enjoy it.

We had our first real holiday abroad in March 1985 at the Hotel Sabinal in Roquetas de Mar in Almeria, Spain. This was a couple of years before I had taken the job at the hotel. The cost of a holiday in Spain was £300 for 28 nights. Who could resist this in the month of March. Four or five of our retired friends had encouraged us to take the same holiday and we enjoyed it very much. I had swotted up some of the Spanish language, just enough to ask a simple question. It's a hobby of mine I find crossword puzzles very difficult but I can take an interest in languages especially if it may come in useful. We could take a stroll into the town and back again. After the evening meal it was nice to stroll along the promenade with just a cardigan to be comfortably warm. It was very good for Dorothy who was not in the best of health now but you wouldn't have known it. She was very happy and never complained of anything much; had a nice character and was easy to live with but I didn't recognise it at the time. We changed the venue to Fuengirola a few times and once went by coach to Rimini in Italy.

Coach travel was a good way to see places like Switzerland. We passed close to Mont Blanc and it was a very interesting trip. We enjoyed sightseeing. A holiday at Ostend was a base to see the three capitals, Paris, Amsterdam and Brussels.

For our Golden Wedding Anniversary in 1998 we had four nights in

Rome and ten days in Sorrento. That was a wonderful time. We stood with the Romans and saw the Pope slowly pass quite close-by in his 'Popemobile.' This was the Corpus Christi service and after the service a procession of Cardinals and all the lesser orders assembled and slowly moved on to the Basilica di Santa Maria Maggiore. The people followed and we walked with them through the streets. Above us were open windows, decked with banners hanging out over the sills, with the occupants looking out onto the crowds below. A choir singing at the Pope's old palace was relayed along the whole route for a half mile or so until we came to the road where our hotel was situated. The walking had tired us both and we decided to call it a day. We were moving on the next day by coach to Sorrento. We returned to our room and packed our cases.

The following morning, leaving the hotel with our luggage in the coach, we left Roma and travelled feeling rather subdued after all that we had seen in Rome. We stopped on the route south and called at the Monte Cassino war graves. We spent a few minutes in the beautifully kept cemetry, British, Polish, Canadian and other soldiers from various countries lay row on row, each marked with a white headstone in tidy green enclosures. One headstone which I read was a British teenager only seventeen years old. I stood for a few minutes in respectful prayer for these young men who had been deprived of a reasonable life and thought of their mothers who had also made a great sacrifice to save humanity from an evil ambitious people. We got back into the coach in a subdued silence for the long drive to Sorrento.

We arrived at the Hotel Conca Park. They had cheerful Italian staff to greet us. Our room was quite pleasant but was close to and looked onto a cliff face which was covered in green vegetation. Initially Dorothy thought she might prefer moving to the other side of the hotel but there the rooms looked onto the road and swimming pool. We found the cliff face very interesting with pretty birds which sang and flitted about the shrubs. They were fairly tame and would come to our balcony to eat a few crumbs we put out for them. In the dining room we sat at a large round table with two other couples for dinner. We all had an anniversary of some sort to celebrate and they were surprised to hear we were celebrating fifty years of a happy marriage.

Dorothy and I explored the narrow streets of Sorrento avoiding the young people driving around on their motor scooters. We spent some time in the Old Port by what was once a fishing harbour. It was a climb

272

back up to the main town but we had no difficulty and went there quite a few times.

A visit to Pompeii proved a bit more difficult. We went by train from Sorrento Station. Tickets have to be bought at a Tabac shop in Italy for buses or trains. The journey took about twenty minutes stopping at several small stations. We got off at Pompeii and a short walk took us to the admission gate. When I went to pay the girl she said, "have you identification, you are pensioners?" "Yes," I said, and produced my National Pensioners card. "Then you are admitted for free," she said. So they recognised some of the E.U. rules! We wandered about the streets of old Pompeii for half an hour or so. I was having trouble with a weak spinal disc pressing on a nerve and getting up and down the high pavements to road level was becoming painful. We agreed we had been there, seen enough and made our way back to the train. It was a good service and didn't have long to wait for a return train. After many stops we came to a station that said Piano Sorrento. I was a bit doubtful about it but we got up to leave. I stepped out on to the platform when the doors suddenly closed behind me and Dorothy was still on board! She had the tickets so I thought I would be unable to get on the next train to follow her. There were no staff about to ask. I decided to walk to the hotel from here, it couldn't be far. I walked a few hundred yards but there wasn't a soul about, then I saw a woman scurrying along ahead of me I asked her in Italian, "where is Sorrento?" Not a very precise question but all I could manage. She probably thought I was a mad Englishman and pointed ahead and said "Si! Si!" I carried on for a mile or so. I came to a square with a few shops where lots of youngsters on motor scooters were stood chatting. School's out I thought and spoke to a handsome dark curly haired young man. "Can you give me a lift to the Hotel Conca please," I said. He had finished talking to his friend and replied in perfect English, "sure, get on," indicating the back seat of his scooter. We zoomed off and I realised I would have had another couple of miles to walk if young handsome here hadn't been so obliging. He was not going into what I now call big Sorrento, we were going down to old Sorrento. I must have looked a strange sight an old man with my straw hat jammed on my head sitting on the back of this buzzing little scooter with an engine not much bigger than a garden grass mower. Handsome demonstrated his skill in racing around corners with me hanging on with my face tight with the force of the passing air. Finally we arrived at the hotel. I had asked my scooter chauffer his name, "Como se chiamo," how are you called, in Italian, a useful phrase to have. "Roberto!" he replied. I invited him into the hotel and he had a word with the receptionist, he probably told her how he had rescued me from my senility. I took him up to the room to check if Dorothy had returned. I should have asked the receptionist. We had a drink of fruit juice and went down again to wait for Dorothy where we had a chat and he told me he was only fifteen years old, he was already six feet two inches tall! His height had surprised me when he got off the scooter. He said he played in the Sorrento Juniors basketball team. His parents had a greengrocery business in Piano Sorrento. I often wonder how he developed as he got older and wish him well. I paid him for his petrol and trouble with a few hundred Pesetas. He went away delighted. A disappointed Dorothy appeared. She had waited at the Sorrento station for me following on. With my luck I could have missed her and been arrested for not having a rail ticket. We saw an example of this in Rome, inspectors came on the bus we were on where you have to buy your tickets at the tabac shop and punch it when you get on the bus. This young woman didn't have a ticket, it was not a good thing to do, from what I could understand they would prosecute her. This train incident of ours could have spoilt our holiday but the whole hotel had been told of the mad Englishman coming in on a motor scooter. I had received some strange looks from some of the residents. I was embarrassed but glad of the fun I had unwittingly caused at seventy four years old.

On the anniversary of our wedding day, the 16th of June we took the ferry from Sorrento to the Isle of Capri. I enjoyed the ferry ride but wasn't too impressed with Capri. It was very hilly but green and had a cool sea breeze. I preferred Fuengirola with its five miles of beautiful promenade and beaches we used to plodge along at the waters edge. From Sorrento we bought a beautiful wooden musical box inlaid with a Sorrento scene. When the lid is opened the music it plays is, "Come back to Sorrento." Oh, if only we could! It was a happy way to celebrate our Golden Wedding Anniversary. We had many good memories of those nice people we met in Sorrento. I was sad to leave the place. The North of England is not the best place to live it seems but our commitments keep us tied to the place.

We travelled to Naples Airport to fly home. At the time it was totally inadequate for the amount of flights going through there. Passengers for an Israeli flight were already waiting for their plane. There was a heavy presence of armed police with sub machine guns who patrolled around in twos often conferring with an officer which was a bit disturbing, as though they were expecting a terrorist assault any minute. There were not enough vacant seats for some of us Brits flying to Manchester. Frank who had been at our table in the Sorrento hotel gave his seat to Dorothy and went to get us a cup of tea but the small refreshment kiosk had closed at 10 am, regardless of the business that could have been made with two plane loads of passengers as potential customers. The Israeli's moved out to board their plane and now there were seats for everyone. We didn't have long to wait before we were boarded. I decided not to use Naples Airport again. I had arranged an Airport Connections car to pick us up at Manchester and after an uneventful flight during the early hours of the morning we landed on time. Our driver was waiting for us as we came out of arrivals and in just under two hours we were home.

# CHAPTER 21
## ALONE AFTER 59 HAPPY YEARS OF MARRIAGE.
*An Invitation to a Greek Wedding in Athens.*
*Our last holiday in Mallorca 2003.*
*Four years to say goodbye.*

In the year 2000 a wedding invitation came from Athens. It was from Michael Loupis. His brother Kostas was, at thirty something, at last getting married in July and would we come? It would be the hottest time of the year, 30 plus degrees centigrade. Dorothy said it would be too much for her and that I should go by myself. I replied that if she couldn't go then I wouldn't go. The invitation lay for a few days and Dorothy still insisted that I went. She felt sorry she was unable to go but I knew she would be very uncomfortable and may indeed be ill if she did go. Eventually John said he would take good care of her while I was away and that she would be happier if I went. We had been married fifty two years and it was a difficult decision to make. In the end I thought it would be kinder for both of us if I accepted the invitation and phoned Michael to tell him I would be coming alone and to arrange a flight. Michael replied he used a flight to the U.K. via Brussels to Newcastle and would have his agent book one for me. It was more convenient for the North of England. John took me to Newcastle Airport and saw me into the departure lounge. I felt unhappy being on my own after last coming home alone from America in 1952. The thoughts of seeing my Greek friends compensated a little. There's not a lot of pleasure travelling by air, I had a difficult transfer in Brussels. The arrival concourse is very long with moving walkways in places which helps. I was carrying my hand luggage on a strap over my shoulder and my disc was aching with every step. I had twenty minutes to catch my connection; I passed through the centre Concourse of the airport with its glittering stock in its shops and was making for gate number ten when a flight girl told me the gate had been changed to number one. I walked back to number one and finally got on the plane. It was a small rather old plane but that pleased me, it would have a good history, new planes may develop faults. We landed in Athens an hour late at one o clock in the morning. Michael and his wife Vassou had waited to meet me. My suitcase was not on the carousel, in fact half the passengers cases were not on the plane. I had to queue to get a claim form, complete it and hand it back. Michael was very patient. His job involves flying all over Europe for the E.U. He said that Brussels airport is notorious for failures. It was the first time I had met his wife, her name is the feminine of Basil. Basilia but the Greek alphabet hasn't the letter pronounced Ba. It is made by saying B with the lips slightly open, the teeth close together and making the sound Ve. The sound comes out between B and V therefore Vassou short for Vasilia is easier for an English pronunciation.

Michael's mother Anthi a widow for some years had married again and Michael and Vassou had moved into his mother's apartment. It had been stripped out and tastefully modernised. Vassou was very kind to me. Their children, a boy, Yannis, John and girl Dimetria, feminine of James in English. They were staying with Vassou's parents at their family home in the village of Palumba in Arkadia.

As the day of Kostas' wedding approached we made the four hour drive west from Athens over the congested, very busy dual carriageway to the Corinth Canal. Here the road became isolated as we drove into the high wild Peloponnese countryside stopping for half an hour at a first class Motorway comfort stop. Unusual I thought out in the wilds but it seemed to do a steady bit of business. We carried on for another hour or so to the Bistemi family home in the very impressive village of Palumba.

I met Michael and Vassou's children, her mother and father and was shown to a cottage style bedroom where I would sleep that night. Mr Bistemi was a councillor for the district and I was conducted around the village to meet some of his friends. Michael, Mr Bistemi and I ate a couple of times at the taverna for meals except for a simple breakfast. We did eat as a family the first evening. Next day Vassou and her mother ate with the children. On one occasion as we sat at a table in the shade of a tree in the sweet air of the Peloponnese, a car rolled up and the local doctor along with the priest got out. They came across to greet Mr Bistemi and we were introduced and they sat with us for some time. Very little English was spoken, it was just a courtesy call. I joined in the conversation at certain points speaking Greek, so much so the doctor enquired what part of Greece I came from! It seemed a wonderful lifestyle that the people there lived with their large detached houses, in well-spaced out plots of land. I think most of them had apartments in Athens too. But I just had to wonder at the great climate and space they seemed to have. I did envy them somewhat but am cautious of the grass being greener on the other side, never wish for something you might regret having later.

We returned to Athens and next day I gave Yanni, John in English, then five years old, a model car. I had taken eight year old Demitria a couple of real looking puppy dogs, they had lovely identical soft fur, white bodies with black patches. Demitria, loved them and carried them about with her all the time I was there.

The day of the wedding we got changed into our best clothes. The ceremony itself was held at St George's church in one of the suburbs of Athens. The church was surrounded by trees with a forecourt of white marble chippings under foot in front of the church edifice, where the ceremony would take place. A small table with a white cloth stood near the small church entrance. Round tables to seat ten people were placed at each side of a path designated by waist high standard floral arrangements of exotic flowers laid around short two inch candles every ten feet at each side of the path. The area filled up with some of the best people of Athens, not celebrities but well respected people. Michael's mother Anthi was there in a beautiful black dress with a coral pashmina over her shoulders. She was with her husband Stellios and Michael's children, who were suitably dressed for the occasion. The bridegroom Kostas was mixing with the guests and was carrying a bouquet of white roses which he was to present to his bride Angelica. She was sun tanned and very petite with large brown eyes, her hair pulled back framing her oval face. She was in a white slim dress with multi short skirts from the waist to the long bottom hem, that's the only way I can describe it! Angelica arrived in a white Mercedes car with a large bouquet on the bonnet, the horn sounding repeatedly as it rolled to a stop. Kostas moved forward and opened the car door for his Bride to step out. He gave her a kiss and presented the bouquet of white roses to her. He had been carrying these roses for a good half hour probably, so he didn't forget them. The ceremony was conducted by the priest in a long black gown. He removed his stove-pipe hat. The bride and groom with their respective families lined up in front of the small table with its white cloth, the congregation moved around this area and the ceremony began. It seemed much more complicated than a Church of England affair. This was of course The Greek Orthodox Church, the priest recited a phrase and a layman standing behind him intoned a response. This was repeated a couple of times. An older priest then appeared. I hadn't noticed where he came from, probably the church door that was immediately behind where the ceremony was taking place. He looked older but had a full head of white wavy hair which covered his ears and a short white beard. He was probably a bishop or other, and was an impressive figure in a magnificent long silver embroidered cope. He took over the ceremony for a while, reading from a small book, again I surmised it was about the state of marriage. Then he said a bit more and again disappeared. I was standing at the side of the proceedings looking at the whole picture that made me miss this disappearance trick. It seemed a bit odd in any case. Now the other priest took over. He took a large thin book with a precious metal cover from the small table and held it over each of the couple's heads intoning some appropriate words. Then he offered the book to each of them who kissed it. Angelica's Bridesmaid produced two white headbands connected by a few feet of white ribbon. The priest took these and held them over the couple's heads, reciting some words for a minute then crossing his arms to exchange the rings over their heads. After more reciting the priest took hold of the Bridegroom's hand and led the couple three times around the table followed by the bridesmaid and best man. They then returned to their places with their respective families. The Bride and Bridegroom placed rings on each other's fingers, and after the whole assembly recited the Lord's Prayer, they kissed each other and the ceremony was over.

The happy couple Mr and Mrs Konstantinos Loupis to give him his full title cut the cake and champagne was opened. The congregation moved around for some time greeting each other then settled down to sit at their family tables. During this time Michael's two children Demitria and Yanni moved around the guests with small white cotton bags of sugared almonds to dispense to the guests. Anthi, Michael's mother, very thoughtfully gave me some to take home for Dorothy. I was pleased she had not been forgotten. A sumptuous buffet was then served and the friends and family relations sat at the big round tables with the white tablecloths decked with flowers, bottles of wine and plates of excellent fare. Anthi's ninety year old mother Rosa held court at her table then later moved around exchanging greetings with friends and relations not seen for a while It was an enchanting ceremony the couple will never forget. Music for the younger set was now playing and couples were dancing, albeit with some difficulty on the small marble chippings. There was a very romantic atmosphere and it was about half-past midnight when we decided to leave. Michael had a professional video made of the event and Dorothy was able to see what words would be difficult to convey. He would send the videos to some of the relations who were unable to attend. Many would have probably travelled from some of the islands to Athens for this special occasion. Weddings are very good for family reunions; it's nice when they are as well laid on as this one was but a simple service and the opportunity to have a get together brings happiness to the old folk and is worth the trouble. I had been away for ten days. I had phoned Dorothy once on my mobile, she had been so kind to insist I go. She was going to need me a few years later and I was prepared to give her all the love I owed her.

In 2003 we had our last holiday in Spain, Cala Millor, Mallorca in a very convenient apartment with a separate bedroom. We had been in large hotels before but Dorothy needed meals little and often. Neither of us bothered with breakfast very much. She had agreed to try an apartment where we could please ourselves when and what we ate. It suited our more casual lifestyle and proved much better. We decided to visit a place we had been told was very nice a few miles away. A local bus was available. We got to the near bus stop, there was only another couple waiting there. Then five Germans came to get on the bus, when it arrived the Germans used elbow and shoulders to push their way into the bus. One chap about thirty years old smirked as he managed to push me away. It was my first experience of their habits. We were the last ones to get on! We had to stand in the bus but I would rather stand or not get on a bus than be as rude as those Germans. It was only a half hour ride to Porto Christi. It was a very nice place, even if you didn't own a yacht. We strolled around, sat a bit and watched the world go by. We went in for afternoon tea somewhere then when thinking of returning to Cala Millor. Dorothy had noticed the twin hulled Ferry Boats that called in to the resorts and suggested we go back by boat. I went to the booking office and booked us both onto the next ferry going our way. We only waited about half an hour and went up onto the top deck and sat comfortably without any pushy Germans. The sea was not what a sailor would call moderate. It was rough with a bit of a swell, the deck rolled from side to side and the bow came up and veered from port to starboard as the sea pushed us about. The next resort hove in sight and we got into calmer waters. There was no jetty to come alongside The Captain came gently bow up close to the rocky shore where a path had been made with rough concrete. A narrow gangway was extended from the bow of the ferry and as the captain kept the vessel hovering steady a few feet from the rocks people were able to get on or off the ship. As an ex sailor I marvelled at this manoeuvre I guessed the ship was propelled not by a propeller but by pumping water in a jet from the stern. A passenger stepped lively along the narrow gangway to the pathway over the rocks and the ferry pulled away, a deck hand pulling the gangway back as we turned to continue our journey. It was still a rough sea but Dorothy and I were both good sailors and enjoyed the experience. Another two approaches with similar action embarking and disembarking passengers the same way, then we arrived at Calla Millor. There was a concrete jetty here but the ferry didn't come alongside, the gangway was slid out and landed on the jetty for us to go ashore. It was the highlight of our holiday! It delighted me to see Dorothy so happy.

We had known in January that this would be our last holiday. A medical examination of Dorothy found that she had polyps in the alimentary tract. They had been removed but had recurred again. We had another four years together. Dorothy never complained. I couldn't complain as we had had a long and happy life together, but it would have been nice to have had a few more years.

The little girl I fell in love with when I was five years old as she presented the bouquet to the lady opening the bazaar, died on 25th June 2007. We had been happily married for fifty nine years. We had three years to say goodbye. Dorothy was always serene, she never complained. A few weeks before she died after many weeks in Teesside Hospice and three weeks in a local Nursing Home I noticed a change in her condition. I pulled a chair up to the bed and we sat holding hands. She comforted me! When I sat back she said, "Arthur, will you get married again?" She was gently teasing me as she often did. "What!" I joked, "after all the trouble I've had with you, I couldn't go through this again!" We both laughed. She died peacefully in her sleep at six o clock on Monday morning the 25th June. The previous Saturday I had realised she had difficulty finding the bell push to call the nurse and she needed one to one care. When at about five o'clock my son John arrived, I told him I would stay all night. He said he would go home and return at nine o clock to sit with me. Dorothy was heavily sedated, resting quietly when he returned. She opened her eyes and seeing us both there said, "I'm not going tonight you know." We realised she knew she was near to leaving us but it was a strange thing to say. Sure enough, next morning she was still there. The carer came in to ask what she wanted for breakfast, "just a cup of tea thank you," she said. She had a couple of sips that's all. The carer made sandwiches for John and I. At 12:30 I realised we were in for another nights vigil. I phoned Bette, Dorothy's friend since they were in grammar school, and asked Bette to get a taxi and come to stay with Dorothy for a few hours while John and I went home to freshen up. Bette had visited Dorothy every day for the last two weeks. Dorothy's room was a haven of care and love. At six o clock on the Monday morning John called me, I had dozed off. I awoke to hear Dorothy's last breath.

I arranged with the undertaker to have Dorothy brought home for the last couple of days. The Vicar came to see her home. She was in pink taffeta and lay in the front room where we had often entertained so many family and friends. It was good she would leave for her last journey from the home she had been so happy in for over fifty years. John called on his way home from work. We went into the room to see her and he was pleased we had her home. He spoke of the arrangements for the following day, I left everything to him.

That night I went to bed at my usual time and was content. I could do no more. I was soon in a deep sleep. I woke with a start! Dorothy was calling me, "Arthur! Arthur!" I looked at the clock. I had been asleep for two hours. I sat up in bed astounded, I thought for a few seconds was it possible? I decided it was her voice without a doubt and not my imagination. I decided to speak to her, "It's all right Dorothy my love, I'm all right," I said, then silence. I thought of Mrs Scrafton's ability to receive messages from the spirits of people long gone. The evidence was strong, but I have no ambition to be a medium even if I had such a gift. I lay back and went to sleep again. I woke just after six o clock the next morning. I'm dozy at this time and take a good half hour to get moving. I was thinking of the arrangements John had made for the next day and a bit fed up. Dorothy's voice suddenly came into my head, "Arthur, I've got to eighty one years old it's not a bad old age, now just get on with it!" It was Dorothy's voice, I could not have imagined it, I wasn't even thinking of her at that moment. I was amused, it was so like her to say something like, get on with it! It brightened me up to face the day. I got out of bed and in my dressing gown went down to make the morning cup of tea as I had done for us both every day of our married life. I mentioned this phenomena to the Vicar a few weeks later, he said it would be from my subconscious mind and to be careful of things like that. I was very sure it wasn't from my subconscious mind. Engineers don't have subconscious minds

An old retired priest, Malcolm Spencley came to our church a few Sunday evenings before Dorothy had died and had conducted a Faith Healing Service. The petitioners who wanted his healing prayers went up into the chancel and sat on a chair a server had placed there. I stood in a queue of five people. When it was my turn, Malcolm asked me what my prayers were for, I told him. "My dear wife who is dying from bowel cancer." He placed a hand gently on my head and found the comforting words that Jesus had used. I came away in tears but with the comfort that I could do no more for the love of my life. The ultimate healing takes place when a person dies. Dorothy found that peaceful healing two weeks later.

At a later Sunday morning Service that Malcolm often attended I mentioned to him the experience I had had of Dorothy speaking to me from beyond. Old Malcolm said gently, "don't be surprised Arthur, the Bible is full of people who have had such experiences." I had another experience of Dorothy being near me when I was feeling a bit down one day. I heard her sweet and gentle voice call my name "Arthur,

Arthur," as if to reassure me that I was not alone. I'm not what you would call over the top with religion. To my mind the church evolved from the philosophy of the Rabbi Jesus. But my Jesus was a friend of fishermen and didn't spend much time in the temple. The stories that he healed the sick are credible for there are too many instances from different sources for it not to be true. Claims of Faith healing are still made today. Some of the things he is reported to have said like, "turn the other cheek" require clarification of when to turn the other cheek. Many people would be much more content if they followed his philosophy and teaching. I try not to pray for myself, as what will be, will be.

A few minutes after Dorothy drew her last breath I asked the carer to remove the small five stone diamond ring from her finger, as she had requested, to pass to Emily our granddaughter. This ring had originally been Dorothy's mother's. An impulse made me remove the wedding ring we had bought sixty years ago that I had placed on her finger when we were married. She treasured that war time thin gold ring and would have no other to replace it. Now I removed it to continue the bond it had been between us. I had it expanded a little to fit and wear on my left little finger. Some things are eternal, I know our love will be. I believe the Spirit World is a Great Mystery that one day will be revealed to me. However I am content to wait for that day when all will be revealed.

The funeral was in our little village church where Captain James Cook was baptised. The morning of the funeral the family gathered at the home Dorothy had made for so many happy gatherings in the past. There was no weeping now. I was proud of the respect people had shown for her and grateful for the life we had had together. It was only a short run to the church, past the school where Dorothy had been secretary for some years. She was well known and liked by many of the mums and children, now grown up with families of their own in the village. The church was full. Dorothy had written down her favourite hymns and the psalm she wanted reading. They were the same ones we had used at her mother's service and probably her father's too. I had asked for St Paul's letter to the Corinthians Chapter one, verse thirteen to be read, Faith Hope and Charity and the greatest of these is Charity. That is the King James Bible version. The Church of England changed it to Faith Hope and Love.

I told the Vicar I didn't think it appropriate to love everybody. Love is a sacred state and has to be earned. I would give charity to an objectionable person but not love. The word charity is from the Greek but Greek for love is agapo. The tinkering with words in the Bible by the Church indicates the problems of two thousand years of translation from Greek. Mistakes may have been made in reporting of what Jesus said. If the priests could correct these anomalies more people especially school teachers many of whom these days profess to be atheists or agnostics may find the philosophy more acceptable and pass it on to our children. Was Jesus a Rabbi? I find there are some confusing problems with the early Christian church years and the church history right through the ages. I believe the stories that are credible and consider the incredible ones with an open mind except for suggestions that could endanger our wellbeing, giving everything away to give to the poor for example. It's not sensible to make us all poor as some politicians would have us be, imposing heavy taxes and encouraging families to live on benefits. I don't think Jesus ever meant that! Even so religion serves to give some structure to the community and a chance to sing a rousing hymn is good for the lungs!

After the Church Service with close friends we had the committal service at the crematorium and returned to join others at the local hotel for lunch. The funeral took place on my eighty third birthday. It was nice to see relations who had travelled some distance to pay their respect for Dorothy. We chatted in the home Dorothy had made and it was enlivened again for the last time. It developed into a surprise family party. My daughter in law Gill kindly produced a fancy birthday cake suitably iced for me to cut. Dorothy would have approved, she loved people and entertaining! Coming from a broken home and not having had a family I had enjoyed Dorothy's loving family. Sadly all have now gone except for Dorothy's niece and a couple of cousins. Still it's better to have loved and lost than never have loved at all I suppose. It could have been worse! If Dorothy had not fancied having a dance with me that Saturday night in May 1943, my life would have been very different. I would not have dared to ask her for a dance but she must have seen something in the poor boy that appealed to her, maybe my big brown eyes? She was never bossy but she would gently 'wish' something was done and I would put it at the top of my list.

It was never my intention to write a book. My son John and his dental partner were relocating their practice from a rented council unit to a suitable building they had bought. A builder was contracted to build walls for the surgeries, and waiting room. John said it would be better for them both if I was able to manage the more technical plumbing for the surgeries as they were still working in the rented unit. There was to be four surgeries, two handbasins in each with compressed air for the drills and a laboratory. I was seventy six years old but quite fit and worked three weeks to complete the job as well as helping a fitter with the dental furniture and worktops. I refused to take payment for the work. However John rewarded me in many ways as I got older but giving me his old Windows 95 computer was the best thing he could have done. With the expertise I had gained working on Instrumentation at I.C.I. I was able to master the beast! It was necessary to remember the steps to click to bring up the screen for storing and retrieving information, but what to use it for? I decided it would be useful for the family to write my memoirs.

John had spent five years at Newcastle University and there was never a good time to tell of my happy early years brought up in the Ancient Borough of Hartlepool and of my war time apprenticeship and sea going exploits. I opened a file in the computer and called it 'The Early Years.' When I had revised and edited the thirty or so pages of that section I closed and opened another entitled 'My War Time Apprenticeship.' I carried a pen and old envelope in my top pocket so that any recall of some past incident was recorded to type into the computer the next time I was in the writing mood. Nine years later in 2004 I had seven sections with two hundred and eight pages of A4 text. In 2005 an old friend in Hartlepool telephoned me to say the Hartlepool History Group were having a Gala Day in the Borough Hall and would I come over. I agreed. It was strange to find people regarded our war time days as history. Eddie and I moved around the various stalls and their exhibits. A lady came up to us and introduced herself as Dorothy Geen the secretary of the History Group and could we write an article of our memories for their magazine? I sent her eight pages of My Early Years with permission to select any pieces for the magazine. The Group didn't get Heritage funding until 2006 and then supplied the magazine to every household in the Headland area. Dorothy Geen sent me a copy. It contained all my eight pages of Hartlepool memoirs with a photograph of the shoe shop my Mum had set up in 1924 in an empty shop in Middlegate. I had already had a section of My War Time Apprenticeship published in a Middlesbrough Library History magazine and feedback from readers of both had been very encouraging.

I had never considered myself a writer but before we had wireless and TV we read a lot and told each other stories. This was very much appreciated on long voyages at sea, for following the evening meal we learned to listen and entertain each other with our stories of foreign places and different cultures. The thought occurred to me that if my memoirs could be made into a book it could be sold to provide funding for the Teesside Hospice. This Hospice is only funded 42% by the NHS, 58% has to be found by The Charity Foundation. This amounted to nearly £5, 000 a day in 2011. I hope this story will interest people enough to create some funding for my charities.

These memoirs may help young people of future years to learn how we lived in our day because the same problems keep reoccurring. Nothing changes as the people who govern our lives make the same mistakes as have been made since ancient Rome and beyond as far as human knowledge takes us. Foolish men ignore history, reject wise council and parliaments fail to stop those making obvious mistakes.

I leave my story now to the people following my generation in the hope they will take an interest in our 20th Century history and deny the elitist politicians some of whom have failed the English people by ignoring the common sense wishes of the pragmatic majority for too long. They can't save the world by neglecting England. I apologise for any typing errors or mistakes in this book. I have not had the formal education that is available today and now at eighty eight years old in a few weeks with failing eyesight I have done my best.

Finally I wish to thank my family, John, his wife Gill and my dear granddaughter Emily who have given me encouragement and help in editing the manuscript. I pass the copyright on to Emily knowing she will be generous in supporting Teesside Hospice with some of any profit my work makes.

.

*The author by the M/V Mary P, Hartlepool, 1964*